Preface

This small book contains essential information about academic writing, the writing process, usage, grammar, punctuation, research writing, and source citation—all in a convenient, accessible format. With its cross-curricular outlook, easy-to-use format, and assumption of little or no experience with writing or handbooks, *The Little, Brown Essential Handbook* helps students with varying interests and skills, in or out of school.

The following description highlights as **New** the most significant additions and changes to this edition of *The Little, Brown Essential Handbook*.

A guide to academic writing

The handbook introduces the goals and requirements of academic writing, emphasizing the writing situation, thesis and organization, revision, evidence, synthesis, and use of sources.

- **New** Genre joins subject, purpose, and audience as a key element in every writing situation.
- **New** Expanded coverage of revising stresses whole-essay concerns.
- **New** Academic integrity, including responsible use of sources, is presented as a feature of general academic writing as well as research writing.
- **New** A revised chapter on presenting writing provides information on how to format print and electronic documents.

A guide to research writing and documentation

The handbook helps students find sources; manage information; evaluate, synthesize, and cite sources; and avoid plagiarism.

- **New** A new chapter on tracking sources emphasizes accurate record keeping and offers practical tips for handling sources responsibly.
- **New** Updated advice on using the library's Web portal covers research guides and centralized search engines and also updates the material on databases.
- **New** Expanded discussions of finding and evaluating Web sources—websites, social-networking sites, blogs, wikis, and multimedia—help students discern purposes and distinguish reliable from unreliable sources.
- **New** The revised chapter on avoiding plagiarism gives more examples of deliberate and careless plagiarism, new examples of material that must be cited, and updated advice about avoiding plagiarism with online sources.

- **New** A new chapter on documenting sources discusses principles of documentation as well as bibliography software.
- **New** Updated, annotated samples of key source types show students how to find the bibliographical information to cite each type.
- **New** Updated and extensive chapters cover documentation in MLA, APA, Chicago, and CSE styles, with new models for how to cite social-networking posts, tweets, and electronic books.

A uniquely accessible reference handbook

The book includes numerous features designed to help students find what they need and then use what they find.

- **New** "Essential" learning objectives opening each of parts one to six give students an overview of key content.
- Explanations use minimal grammar terminology: needless terms are omitted, and essential terms, marked°, are defined in the glossary "Grammar Terms" (pp. 272–83).
- Examples use colour annotations and underlining or highlighting to connect instruction and application.
- Highlighting on documentation models makes authors, titles, dates, and other citation elements easy to grasp.
- Material especially for writers using English as a second language, integrated throughout the handbook, is marked ESL and indexed at the back of the book (pp. 310–11).
- Dictionary-style headers in the index make it easy to find entries.

MLA update to the sixth Canadian edition

This new updated version of the sixth Canadian edition incorporates changes to MLA documentation style. Chapter 42, MLA Documentation and Format, and the text as a whole have been thoroughly updated to reflect the new eighth edition of the *MLA Handbook for Writers of Research Papers*, published in 2016.

MLA 8/e style attempts to simplify documentation by giving a single model for all sources, with fewer rules to follow and greater focus on guiding principles. In particular, it speaks of categories (e.g., a "source [that] is part of a larger work") before it refers to specific types of sources (a short story, a journal article)—and thus it focuses on the relationships among the parts of an entry instead of following a list of models.

This updated edition of *The Little, Brown Essential Handbook* outlines this new approach while retaining many specific models of how different sources can be documented.

Finding What You Need

The handbook provides many ways to reach its information:

Use a table of contents

Inside the front cover, a brief contents gives an overview of the handbook. Inside the back cover, a detailed outline lists all the book's topics.

Use the index

At the end of the book (p. 287), this alphabetical list includes all topics, terms, and problem words and expressions.

Use the glossaries

"Commonly Misused Words" (p. 261) clarifies words and expressions that are often misused or confused. "Grammar Terms" (p. 272) defines grammatical terms, including all terms marked ° in the text.

Use a list

"ESL Guide" (pp. 310–11) pulls together the book's material for students using English as a second language. "Editing Symbols" inside the back cover explains abbreviations often used to mark papers.

Use the elements of the page

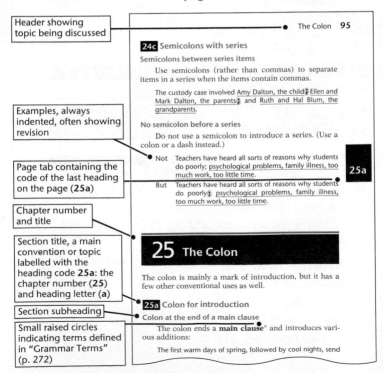

Header showing topic being discussed

The Colon **95**

24c Semicolons with series

Semicolons between series items

Use semicolons (rather than commas) to separate items in a series when the items contain commas.

> The custody case involved <u>Amy Dalton, the child</u>; <u>Ellen and Mark Dalton, the parents</u>; and <u>Ruth and Hal Blum, the grandparents</u>.

No semicolon before a series

Do not use a semicolon to introduce a series. (Use a colon or a dash instead.)

> Not Teachers have heard all sorts of reasons why students do poorly; <u>psychological problems, family illness, too much work, too little time.</u>
>
> But Teachers have heard all sorts of reasons why students do poorly: <u>psychological problems, family illness, too much work, too little time.</u>

25a

25 The Colon

The colon is mainly a mark of introduction, but it has a few other conventional uses as well.

25a Colon for introduction

Colon at the end of a main clause

The colon ends a **main clause**° and introduces various additions:

> The first warm days of spring, followed by cool nights, send

Examples, always indented, often showing revision

Page tab containing the code of the last heading on the page (**25a**)

Chapter number and title

Section title, a main convention or topic labelled with the heading code **25a**: the chapter number (**25**) and heading letter (**a**)

Section subheading

Small raised circles indicating terms defined in "Grammar Terms" (p. 272)

JANE E. AARON ✤ ELAINE BANDER

THE LITTLE, BROWN ESSENTIAL HANDBOOK

6TH CANADIAN EDITION

MLA UPDATE

Ⓟ Pearson

Editorial Director: Claudine O'Donnell
Acquisitions Editor: Matthew Christian
Marketing Manager: Euan White
Program Manager: Kamilah Reid-Burrell
Project Manager: Colleen Wormald
Manager of Content Development: Suzanne Schaan

Media Developer: Olga Avdyeyeva
Production Services: Söğüt Y. Güleç, Cenveo Publisher Services
Permissions Project Manager: Shruti Jamadagni
Text Permissions Research: iEnergizer Aptara®, Ltd.
Cover Designer: Anthony Leung
Vice-President, Cross Media and Publishing Services: Gary Bennett

Pearson Canada Inc., 26 Prince Andrew Place, Don Mills, Ontario M3C 2T8.

ISBN 978-0-13-468178-8

1   17

Library and Archives Canada Cataloguing in Publication
Aaron, Jane E.
[Little, Brown essential handbook for writers]
     The Little, Brown essential handbook/Jane E. Aaron, Elaine Bander.
—Sixth Canadian edition, MLA update.

Includes index.
Revision of: The Little, Brown essential handbook for writers/Jane E. Aaron, Elaine Bander.—1st Canadian ed.—Don Mills, Ont.: Addison-Wesley, ©1999.

ISBN 978-0-13-468178-8 (spiral bound)

     1. English language—Grammar—Handbooks, manuals, etc.
2. English language—Rhetoric—Handbooks, manuals, etc. 3. Report writing—Handbooks, manuals, etc. I. Bander, Elaine, 1946–, author II. Title. III. Title: Little, Brown essential handbook for writers

PE1112.A27 2017   808'.042   C2017-900263-5

Pearson

Pearson Canada would like to thank Cy Strom, editor and writer, for his careful work in documenting what's new in the eighth edition of *MLA Handbook* and for incorporating that information into *The Little, Brown Essential Handbook*.

MyWritingLab

MyWritingLab is a state-of-the-art interactive and instructive solution designed to help students meet the challenges of their writing courses and to assist them in all their future writing. MyWritingLab enables students to use a wealth of resources, all geared to meet their learning needs. For more information, visit *mywritinglab.com*.

Learning Solutions Managers

Pearson's Learning Solutions Managers work with faculty and campus course designers to ensure that Pearson technology products, assessment tools, and online course materials are tailored to meet your specific needs. This highly qualified team is dedicated to helping schools take full advantage of a wide range of educational resources, by assisting in the integration of a variety of instructional materials and media formats. Your local Pearson Canada sales representative can provide you with more details on this service program.

PART 1

Writing

Essential
Writing

Academic writing

- Analyze the writing situation: subject, purpose, audience, and genre. (See opposite.)
- Develop a thesis statement and organize your writing. (See p. 5.)
- Determine the evidence needed to support your thesis. (See p. 8.)
- Synthesize your own and others' ideas. (See p. 9.)
- Use sources responsibly. (See p. 10.)
- Use academic language. (See p. 11.)
- Revise your writing. (See p. 13.)
- Edit and proofread your writing. (See p. 14.)

Writing arguments

- Use the elements of argument: subject, claims, evidence, and assumptions. (See p. 15.)
- Make appeals and acknowledge opposing views. (See p. 17.)
- Organize effectively. (See p. 18.)

Writing in the disciplines

- Learn about writing assignments in literature and other humanities. (See pp. 21, 22.)
- Learn about writing assignments in the social sciences. (See p. 23.)
- Learn about writing assignments in the natural and applied sciences. (See p. 23.)

Presenting writing

- Follow the format of the discipline you are writing in. (See pp. 24, 25.)
- Use visuals and other media appropriately. (See p. 27.)
- Consider design when using *PowerPoint* or *Prezi* presentation software. (See p. 31.)
- Consider the needs of readers with vision loss. (See p. 32.)

1 Academic Writing

Writing is both a way of discovering, recording, refining, and organizing your thoughts—a process—and a tool for communicating those thoughts in a way that others can read and assimilate—a product. Whether you are writing a letter of application, a case report, a market assessment, a family memoir, a research essay, or even an oral presentation (see Chapter 47), you engage in a similar process in order to produce a finished work that fulfills its purpose. Thus, by mastering the features of academic writing, you master the ability to communicate effectively in many other situations.

When you write in college and university, however, you work within a community of teachers and students who have specific aims and expectations. The basic aim of this community—whether in English, psychology, biology, or some other discipline—is to contribute to and build knowledge through questioning, research, thinking, and communication. The academic disciplines do differ in their conventions for writing (see Chapter 3, p. 22), but many academic papers share the features discussed in this chapter.

1a The writing situation

Any writing you do for others occurs in a writing situation that both limits and clarifies your choices. You will most likely have an assignment, and to fulfill it you will communicate something about a subject for a specific reason to a particular audience of readers.

Assignment

When you receive a writing assignment, study its wording and requirements:

- **What does your writing assignment tell you to do?** Words such as *discuss, report, describe,* and *analyze* ask you to explain something about your subject. Words such as *argue* and *evaluate* ask you to make a case for your opinion.
- **What kind of research is required?** An assignment may specify the kinds of sources you are expected to consult and how you are expected to document them.

- **What other requirements do you have to meet?** When is the assignment due? How long should your writing be? What format does the assignment require—a printed paper? a digital project? an oral presentation?

Subject

Most writing assignments give at least some latitude for choice of subject. Consider the following questions to find your approach:

- **What subject do you want to know more about?** A good subject is one that you care about or want to learn about.
- **Is your subject limited enough?** Choose a subject that you can cover in the space and time you have, or narrow a broad subject by breaking it into as many specific subjects as you can think of.
- **Is your subject suitable for the assignment?** Review the assignment to ensure that the subject fulfills the requirements.

Purpose

For most academic writing, your general purpose will be either **explanatory** or, more usually, **argumentative**: you will aim to clarify your subject so that readers understand it as you do, or you will aim to gain readers' agreement with a debatable idea about the subject. The following questions can help you think about your purpose:

- **What aim does your assignment specify?** For instance, does it ask you to explain something or to argue a point?
- **Why are you writing?** How do you want your readers to respond?
- **How can you best achieve your purpose?**

Audience

You should adapt each piece of writing to its intended audience. A business report, for example, may circulate among several readers, each of whom has a different level of knowledge and engagement with the subject, while a political or religious pamphlet may encounter readers who do not share your unstated assumptions. Awareness of your audience will help you to tailor your message effectively.

Most academic writing assignments specify or assume an audience of educated readers or even experts in your subject. In academic writing, you are participating in a conversation about your subject with a community of informed scholars, some of whom wrote generations ago and some of whom (like you) have only recently joined the discussion. Use the questions below to adapt your writing to the needs and expectations of your readers:

- **Who will read your writing?** What can you assume your readers already know and think about your subject? How can your assumptions guide your writing so that you tell readers neither too little nor too much?
- **What are readers' expectations?** For the discipline in which you're writing, what claims and evidence, organization, language, and format will readers look for?
- **What is your relationship to your readers?** How formal or informal should your writing be?
- **What do you want readers to do or think after they read your writing?**

Genre

Writers express their ideas in familiar **genres**, or types of writing—for instance, essays or letters to the editor. In academic writing, the genre conventions of each discipline help to further the discipline's aims. Be sure you understand any requirements relating to genre:

- **Is a particular genre assigned?** An assignment that asks you to write an analysis, an argument, or a report has specified the genre.
- **What are the conventions of the genre?** Your instructor and/or your textbook will probably outline the requirements for you.
- **What flexibility do you have?** Within their conventions, most genres still allow plenty of room for your own approach and voice.

1b Thesis and organization

Much academic writing is organized to develop a main idea or thesis.

Thesis

The **thesis** is the central idea or claim in a piece of writing: the entire work develops and supports that idea. Often, a thesis starts out as a question that guides a writer's research and drafting. In the final paper, the thesis usually appears in a **thesis statement**.

Here are pairs of questions and answering thesis statements from various disciplines:

Literature question	What makes the ending of Kate Chopin's "The Story of an Hour" believable?
Thesis statement	The ironic ending of "The Story of an Hour" is believable because it is consistent with the story's other ironies.
History question	What were the long-term effects of the deportations of the Acadians in 1755?
Thesis statement	Despite the catastrophic deportations of 1755, many Acadians eventually returned to, and thrived in, their traditional homelands.
Psychology question	How common is violence between partners in dating relationships?
Thesis statement	The survey showed that violence may have occurred in a fifth of dating relationships among students at this college.
Biology question	Does the same physical exertion have the same or different effects on the blood pressure of men and women?
Thesis statement	After the same physical exertion, the average blood pressure of female participants increased significantly more than the average blood pressure of male participants.

Most of the thesis statements you write in college and university papers will be either argumentative or explanatory. The first two examples above are argumentative: the writers mainly want to convince readers of something. The last two examples are explanatory: the writers mainly want to explain something to readers. In both cases, however, the writers are trying to *persuade* readers that the thesis is valid.

ESL   In some cultures it is considered unnecessary or impolite for a writer to express an opinion or to state his or her main idea outright. In Canadian academic writing, you can assume that your readers expect you to say what you think.

Organization

An effective paper has a recognizable shape—an arrangement of parts that guides readers, helping them see how ideas and details relate to each other and contribute to the thesis. Academic writing, like most written and spoken communication, is usually divided into an **introduction**, a **body**, and a **conclusion**.

The body is the heart of academic writing, with each paragraph providing accurate evidence, logical arguments, and pertinent examples to support the thesis. Each **body paragraph** has a single topic usually expressed in a **topic sentence**. The topic sentence often begins the paragraph, but it may also occur as a second or even concluding sentence. The topic sentence may even be implied rather than stated. The rest of the paragraph explains, supports, and develops the stated or implied topic sentence. Nothing should go into a body paragraph that does not support the paragraph's topic.

Body paragraphs are developed using different **patterns of organization**. These may include narration (telling a story), description (using vivid detail to help your reader to see, hear, smell, taste, and touch whatever you are describing), process (providing a step-by-step account of how to do something), definition and classification (explaining logically what something is and isn't), comparison (identifying similar elements in two or more items), contrast (identifying significantly different elements in two or more items that belong to a similar category), examples and illustrations, cause and effect, and problem to solution. Most body paragraphs use some combination of these organizational patterns, providing details and arguments to support the topic sentence.

Many writers only write the introduction and conclusion after they have written the body of their essay. If you begin by writing your introduction, be prepared to revise it after completing the rest of your essay. (No matter how carefully you plan, you will discover new insights as you write.)

Introductions and conclusions have special jobs to do and therefore take special forms.

The **introduction** establishes the subject of the essay, motivates the reader to continue reading, and presents the thesis statement, usually at the end of the paragraph. Your introduction may begin with an interesting, relevant statement about your subject that will orient readers to your discussion, but you should avoid sweeping generalizations that go beyond the scope of your specific subject. Then quickly narrow to your thesis statement. Save your detailed evidence and arguments for the body paragraphs that follow.

The **conclusion** ties together the parts of the body, usually by inverting the structure of the introduction. Begin by briefly reinforcing your thesis, reminding readers how you have substantiated your claims. Then you may open your arguments to larger concerns or implications, or suggest further developments, possibly alluding to material in your introduction to provide a sense of closure.

1c

Beyond this basic scheme, organization in academic writing varies widely depending on the discipline and the task. In the experimental sciences and social sciences, for example, writing will often include special sections on methodology and results. **Oral communication** requires more explicit explanations of your organizational structure in order to help your audience follow the development of your thoughts (see Chapter 47). Whatever organizational framework you use, develop your ideas as simply and directly as your purpose and content allow, and clearly relate your sentences, paragraphs, and sections, using **transitional expressions**° so that your readers always know where they are in the paper's development.

1c Evidence and research

The thesis statement of your paper will be based on your analysis of evidence, drawn sometimes from your own experience or logic but more usually from research. Ask these questions to determine the kind of research you may have to do:

- **What kinds of evidence will best suit your writing and support your thesis?** Depending on the discipline you're writing in and the type of paper you're working on, you'll use a mix of facts, examples, and expert opinions to develop and support your ideas. See page 16 for more on evidence in argument papers and pages 21–24 for more on evidence in the disciplines.
- **Does your assignment require research?** Will you need to consult sources or conduct interviews, surveys, or experiments? If so, does your college or university have ethical guidelines for conducting interviews and experiments?
- **Even if research is not required, what information do you need to develop your subject?** How will you obtain it?
- **What documentation style should you use to cite your sources?** See pages 164–65 on source documentation in the academic disciplines.

ESL Research serves different purposes in some other cultures than it does in Canada. For instance, students in some cultures may be expected to consult only well-known sources and to adhere closely to the sources' ideas. In Canadian colleges and universities, students are expected to look for relevant and reliable sources, whether well known or not, and to evaluate and cite those sources in constructing their own arguments.

°See "Grammar Terms," page 272.

1d Synthesis

Academic writing often requires you to read, analyze, and expand on the work of others. Using **synthesis**, you select and respond to others' ideas and information in order to develop your own conclusions. The paragraph below follows a pattern common in academic writing: it opens with the writer's claim, derived from research, analysis, and interpretation of evidence; it supports that claim by citing and interpreting selected evidence using logical argumentation; and it ends with the writer's conclusion, reinforcing the original claim. Throughout the paragraph, **transitional expressions°** (underlined) show the logical connections between sentences.

The students' case for tuition-free education is based on two arguments: that university tuition fees constitute a barrier to accessibility and that student debt is increasing to unacceptable levels. Neither of these claims, <u>however</u>, stands up to scrutiny. <u>For example</u>, Quebec, with the lowest tuition fees in Canada by a large margin, has only a 30.5% university graduation rate, well behind Nova Scotia (48.9%), Ontario (41%), and four other provinces with higher fees (Desjardins 16). <u>Clearly</u> lower tuition by itself does not enable more students to graduate. <u>Furthermore</u>, Frenette shows that only 12% of the differential in university attendance between upper-income and lower-income students is attributable to financial barriers (117). Since tuition fees account for only a small portion of the real costs of being a full-time student, other factors would seem to be more significant for increasing university accessibility. <u>Finally</u>, tuition fees represent a much smaller percentage of per capita income today than they did a generation ago (Desjardins 19). Students will probably continue to clamour for reduced tuition in the name of accessibility, but a student victory will not necessarily lead to increased accessibility and diminishing debt.

> Writer's idea

> Evidence

> Interpretation

> Evidence

> Interpretation

> Evidence

> Writer's conclusion

°See "Grammar Terms," page 272.

1e Using sources responsibly

Using the ideas and information in sources carries the responsibility to acknowledge those sources fully. Failure to acknowledge sources undermines the incremental construction of knowledge on which academic work depends. It also opens you to charges of plagiarism, which can be punishable. (See Chapter 40.)

Perspective on sources

Considering your own perspective on a subject before you start to research will allow you to recognize others' views and to treat them fairly in your writing, whether or not you agree with them.

- **Gauge what you already know and think about your subject.** If you know your own mind before you look at sources, you'll be able to reflect on how they reinforce, contradict, or expand on your knowledge.
- **Evaluate sources carefully.** You need to recognize and weigh other writers' biases and positions and consider multiple perspectives. See pages 140–48 for a discussion on evaluating sources.
- **Treat sources fairly.** Be careful not to misrepresent the source author's meaning when quoting, paraphrasing, or summarizing.

Handling of sources

You can avoid plagiarism by keeping close track of the sources you consult, the ideas that influence your thinking, and the words and sentences you borrow.

- **Keep track of source information.** Always record the publication information of sources you consult: author, title, date, and so on. See pages 127–28 for a list of what to record.
- **Be careful with quotations.** If you cut and paste a portion of a source into your document, put quotation marks around it so that you don't mix up your words and the source's words. For more on quoting sources, see page 151.
- **Use your own words in paraphrases and summaries.** You will be less likely to use the source author's words if you look away from the source while you write down what you remember from it. You must still cite the source (see next page). For more on summarizing and paraphrasing sources, see pages 150–51.

Citation of sources

As you draft, be conscious of when you're using source information and be conscientious about clearly marking where the borrowed material came from. In your final draft, you'll use a particular style of citation within your text to refer to a detailed list of sources at the end.

Most disciplines have a preferred style of source citation. For lists of disciplines' style guides, see pages 164–65. For documentation guidelines and samples, see pages 166–205 (MLA style), 205–23 (APA style), 223–37 (Chicago style), and 237–45 (CSE and IEEE styles).

ESL Cultures have varying definitions of a writer's responsibilities to sources. In Canada, a writer must cite all sources, even if they are well known.

1f Language

In ordinary conversation with friends, and in informal written communication such as notes, blogs, and text messages, you probably use slang or dialect words as well as nonstandard, ungrammatical sentences, confident that you will still communicate your message. But just as you probably change from torn jeans into a clean suit for a job interview, so too you should use a slightly more formal (or standard) version of English to communicate in an academic environment.

Formal does not mean pretentious or stuffy. You should aim to convey your ideas clearly and plainly so that your readers will focus on your arguments rather than on your style or your personality. To do so, follow the rules of the dialect called **standard English** used by academic writers throughout the English-speaking world. This handbook will help you to write clear and correct standard English.

This means avoiding words and expressions, such as slang and ethnic or regional dialect, that are labelled "nonstandard." As well, you should translate any essential terms from a language other than English. (Note, however, that in English Canadian academic discourse, many writers assume that their readers can understand French.)

Academic writing has some further specific style conventions:

- **Write objectively, not subjectively,** maintaining some distance between you and your reader. Generally, use the third person (*he, she, it, they*) rather than the first (*I, me*) or second (*you*).

1f

- **Write authoritatively and neutrally.** Do not apologize for, or overly qualify, statements that you intend to support with strong logic and evidence. (If your sentence begins, *I feel that* ..., then your sentence is about your feelings rather than about an argument that can be demonstrated or debated.) Avoid gushing enthusiasm or hostile criticism.
- **Avoid false passives.** Use the **passive voice**° (p. 63) only when you intend to convey that an outside agency has acted upon the passive subject, as in *He was prevented by the government* or *He was arrested*. Use **active**° rather than passive verbs to indicate who is performing the action: not *His actions were believed to be illegal* but *CSIS believed that his actions were illegal*.

Checklist for academic language

Rapid communication by email and text messaging encourages some informalities that are inappropriate in academic writing. Check your academic papers especially for the following:

Sentences

☑ Does every sentence have a subject and a verb? (pp. 82–83)
☑ Have you avoided fragments and run-on sentences? (pp. 82–84)

Punctuation

☑ Have you used standard punctuation between and within sentences? Check especially for missing or misplaced commas and apostrophes. (pp. 89–98)

Spelling (pp. 109–11)

☑ Have you used correct, standard spellings?
☑ Have you avoided social media spellings such as *cuz* for *because* and *u* for *you*?

Capital letters (pp. 113–14)

☑ Does each sentence begin with a capital?
☑ Have you capitalized all proper nouns?

Abbreviations and contractions (pp. 117–18)

☑ Have you avoided using contractions such as *I've* rather than *I have*?
☑ Have you avoided informal abbreviations such as *b4* for *before*?
☑ Have you used only conventional abbreviations for the discipline you are writing in?

°See "Grammar Terms," page 272.

1g Revision

In revising, you adopt a critical eye toward your writing, examining it as readers will for ideas and evidence, their relationships and arrangement, and the degree to which they work or don't work for your thesis.

Whenever possible, let a draft rest for a while to get some distance from it and perhaps to gather comments from others, such as your classmates or instructor. Then revise the draft using the checklist for revising academic writing below, concentrating on the effectiveness of the whole. (Leave style, correctness, and other specific issues for the separate step of editing, discussed below.)

Checklist for revising academic writing

Assignment (p. 3)

☑ How have you responded to the assignment for this writing?
☑ Do your subject, purpose, and genre meet the requirements of the assignment?

Purpose, audience, and genre (pp. 4–5)

☑ What is your purpose? Does it conform to the assignment?
☑ Who are your readers? Will your purpose be clear to them?
☑ How does your writing conform to the conventions of the genre you are writing in?

Thesis (p. 5)

☑ What is your thesis, or central claim?
☑ Where in the paper does your thesis become clear?

Development

☑ What are the main points supporting the thesis?
☑ How well do the facts, examples, and other evidence support each main point?

Use of sources

☑ Have you used sources to support—not substitute for—your own ideas? (See pp. 8, 10, 142–43.)
☑ Have you integrated borrowed material into your own sentences? (See pp. 149–52.)
☑ Have you fully cited each use of a source? (See pp. 163–245.)

Unity

☑ What does each paragraph contribute to the thesis?
☑ Within paragraphs, what does each sentence contribute to the paragraph's idea? (This paragraph idea is often expressed in a **topic sentence**.)

> ## Coherence
> ☑ Will the organization be clear to readers?
> ☑ How smoothly does the paper flow?
> ☑ Have you used transitions to link paragraphs and sentences? (See p. 282 for a list of transitional expressions, such as *first, however*, and *in addition*.)

1h Editing and proofreading

Much of this book concerns editing—tightening or clarifying sentences, polishing words, repairing mistakes in grammar and punctuation. Leave this work until after revision so that your content and organization are set before you tinker with your expression. For editing guidelines, see the essential learning objectives on pages 34 (effective sentences), 54 (grammatical sentences), 88 (punctuation), and 108 (spelling and mechanics).

Most writers find that they spot errors better on paper than on a computer screen, so edit a printout if you can. And be sure to proofread your final draft before you submit it, even if you have used a spelling checker or similar aid (see below).

Spelling checkers

A spelling checker can be a great ally: it will flag words that are spelled incorrectly and will usually suggest alternative spellings that resemble what you've typed. However, this ally has limitations:

- **The checker may flag a word that you've spelled correctly,** just because the word does not appear in its dictionary, or because your checker is set to "American" spelling but you have typed the word using Canadian spelling, or vice versa. See page 109.
- **The checker may suggest incorrect alternatives.** Before accepting any highlighted suggestion from the checker, you need to verify that the word is actually what you intend. Consult an online or printed dictionary when you aren't sure of the checker's recommendations.
- **Most important, a spelling checker will not flag words that appear in its dictionary but that you have misused.** The paragraph in the following screen shot contains eleven errors that a spelling checker failed to catch. Can you spot all of them?

To correct misused homonyms (*whose* or *who's, their* or *they're*) consult "Commonly Misused Words" on pages 261–71.

> The whether effects all of us, though it's affects are
> different for different people. Some people love a fare
> day with warm temperatures and sunshine. They revel in
> spending a hole day outside. Other people enjoy dark,
> rainy daze. They like to slow down and here they're inner
> thoughts. Most people agree, however, that to much of
> one kind of weather makes them board.

Grammar/style checkers

Grammar/style checkers can flag incorrect grammar or punctuation and wordy or awkward sentences. You may be able to customize a checker to suit your needs and habits as a writer—for instance, instructing it to look for problems with subject-verb agreement or for passive verbs.

Like spelling checkers, however, grammar/style checkers are limited:

- **They miss many errors** because they are not yet capable of analyzing language in all its complexity.
- **They often question passages that don't need editing,** such as an appropriate passive verb or a deliberate and emphatic use of repetition.

Each time a grammar/style checker questions something, you must determine whether a change is needed at all and what change will be most effective, and you must read your papers carefully on your own to find any errors the program missed.

2 Writing Arguments

Argument is writing that attempts to solve a problem, introduce and defend a particular interpretation, shape or change readers' opinions, or move readers to action. Most of the academic papers you write in college and university courses will be arguments.

2a Elements of argument

All arguments have four main elements: subject, claims, evidence, and assumptions.

MyWritingLab

Visit MyWritingLab for more help with writing arguments.

2a

Subject

A subject for argument should meet the following requirements:

- **It can be disputed:** reasonable people can disagree over it.
- **It *will* be disputed:** it is controversial.
- **It is narrow enough:** it can be researched and argued in the space and time available.

Claims

Claims are statements that require support. In an argument, the central claim is the thesis, asserted outright in the thesis statement. (See p. 5.) An argumentative thesis statement is always an opinion, a judgment you have made based on facts and logic and arguable on the basis of facts and logic. It may be one of the following:

- **A claim about past or present reality,** such as *Academic cheating increases with students' economic insecurity.*
- **A claim of value,** such as *The new residence fees are unfair given the condition of the facilities.*
- **A recommendation for a course of action,** such as *The campus can relieve parking problems by providing better and cheaper access via public transport.*

The backbone of the argument consists of specific claims that support the thesis statement. These claims may also state opinions, or they may state facts or beliefs.

Evidence

Evidence shows the validity of your claims. There are several kinds of evidence.

- **Facts:** statements whose truth can be verified.
- **Statistics:** facts expressed as numbers.
- **Examples:** specific instances of the point being made.
- **Expert opinions:** the judgments formed by authorities on the basis of their own analyses of the facts.

Evidence must be reliable to be convincing. Ask these questions about your evidence:

- **Is it accurate**—trustworthy, exact, undistorted?
- **Is it relevant**—authoritative, pertinent, and current?
- **Is it representative**—true to its context, neither under- nor overrepresenting any element of the sample it's drawn from?
- **Is it adequate**—plentiful and specific?

Assumptions

An **assumption** is an opinion, a principle, or a belief that ties evidence to claims: the assumption explains why a particular piece of evidence is relevant to a particular claim. For example:

Claim	The university needs a new chemistry lab.
Evidence (in part)	The testimony of chemistry professors.
Assumption	Chemistry professors are reliable evaluators of the present lab's quality.

Assumptions are always present in arguments, even when they are not stated. In writing an argument, you need to recognize your own assumptions and remember that your readers may hold different assumptions. (For example, someone might assume that chemistry professors want a new state-of-the-art lab even if the existing one is functional.) If you think that readers may not agree with an assumption, you should make it explicit and establish its validity.

2b Balance in argument

Balance is essential if an argument is to establish common ground between you and your readers. You need to make appropriate appeals to readers and treat opposing views fairly.

Appeals

In presenting your claims and evidence, you'll make three kinds of appeals to readers:

- **A *rational* appeal calls on readers' sense of logic.** It requires reasonable claims and sound evidence to support the claims.
- **An *emotional* appeal calls on readers' feelings.** You strengthen support for your claims by encouraging readers to feel empathy, pride, anger, or some other emotion.
- **An *ethical* appeal is the sense you give of being reasonable, fair, and competent.**

Appeals require balance. Emotional appeals in particular can be risky if they misjudge readers' feelings or are inappropriate to the argument (for example, creating fear to force agreement with a claim or pity to override facts).

Opposing views

If your thesis is arguable, then others can provide their own evidence to support different views. Dealing

2d

with these views fairly, giving them their due, shows your responsibility and gives you a chance to deal with objections your readers may have. Find out what the opposing views are and what evidence supports them.

A common way to handle opposing views is to state them, refute those you can, grant the validity of others, and demonstrate why, despite their validity, the opposing views are less compelling than your own.

Another approach emphasizes the search for common ground. In a **Rogerian argument** you start by showing that you understand readers' views and by establishing points on which you and readers agree and disagree. Creating a connection in this way can be especially helpful when you expect readers to resist your argument.

2c Organization of argument

Argument papers all include the same parts:

- **Introduction:** Running a paragraph or two, the introduction establishes the significance of the subject, provides background, and generally includes the thesis statement. If readers are likely to resist the thesis statement, you may want to put it later in the paper, after the evidence.
- **Body:** In one or more paragraphs, the body develops each claim, supporting the thesis with sound evidence.
- **Response to opposing views:** Depending on what you think readers need, this response may come early or late in the paper, or may be covered point by point throughout.
- **Conclusion:** Usually one paragraph, the conclusion often restates the thesis, summarizes the supporting claims, and makes a final appeal to readers.

2d Sample argument

As you read the following essay by Craig Holbrook, a student, notice especially the structure, the relation of claims and supporting evidence, the kinds of appeals Holbrook makes, and the way he addresses opposing views.

TV Can Be Good for You

Television wastes time, pollutes minds, destroys brain cells, and turns some viewers into murderers. Thus runs the prevailing talk about the medium, supported by serious research as well as simple belief. Television, however, can also have strong virtues: it can ease loneliness, spark healthful laughter, and even educate young children by providing voices that supplement those of real people.

Almost everyone who has lived alone understands the curse of silence, when the only sound is the buzz of unhappiness or anxiety inside one's own head. Although people of all ages who live alone can experience intense loneliness, the elderly are especially vulnerable to solitude. For example, they may suffer increased confusion or depression when left alone for long periods but then rebound when they have steady companionship (Bondevik and Skogstad 329-30).

A study of elderly men and women in New Zealand found that television can actually serve as a companion by assuming "the role of social contact with the wider world," reducing "feelings of isolation and loneliness because it directs viewers' attention away from themselves" ("Television Programming"). Thus television's voices can provide comfort because they distract from a focus on being alone.

The absence of real voices can be most damaging when it means a lack of laughter. Here, too, research shows that television can have a positive effect on health. Laughter is one of the most powerful calming forces available to human beings, proven in many studies to reduce heart rate, lower blood pressure, and ease other stress-related ailments (Burroughs, Mahoney, and Lippman 172; Griffiths 18). Television offers plenty of laughter: the recent listings for a single Friday night included more than twenty comedy programs running on the networks and on basic cable.

A study reported in a health magazine found that laughter inspired by television and video is as healthful as the laughter generated by live comedy. Volunteers laughing at a video comedy routine "showed significant improvements in several immune functions, such as natural killer-cell activity" (Laliberte 78). Further, the effects of the comedy were so profound that "merely anticipating watching a funny video improved mood, depression, and anger as much as two days beforehand" (79). Even for people with plenty of companionship, television's voices can have healthful effects by causing laughter.

Television also provides information about the world. This service can be helpful to everyone but especially to children, whose natural curiosity can exhaust the knowledge and patience of their parents and caretakers. While the TV may be baby-sitting children, it can also enrich them. For example, educational programs such as those on the Discovery Channel, the Disney Channel, TV Ontario, Knowledge, and PBS offer a steady stream of information at various cognitive levels. Even many cartoons,

2d

which are generally dismissed as mindless or worse, familiarize children with the material of literature, including strong characters enacting classic narratives.

Three researchers conducting a review of studies involving children and television found that TV can inspire imaginative play, which psychologists describe as important for children's cognitive development (Thakkar, Garrison, and Christakis 2028). In the studies reviewed, children who watched *Mister Rogers' Neighborhood*, a show that emphasized make-believe, demonstrated significant increases in imaginative play (2029). Thus high-quality educational programming can both inform young viewers and improve their cognitive development.

The value of television voices should not be oversold. For one thing, almost everyone agrees that too much TV does no one any good and may cause much harm. Many studies show that excessive TV watching increases violent behaviour, especially in children, and can cause, rather than ease, other antisocial behaviours (Reeks 114; Walsh 34). In addition, human beings require the give and take of actual interaction. Steven Pinker, an expert in children's language acquisition, warns that children cannot develop language properly by watching television. They need to interact with actual speakers who respond directly to their needs (282). Television voices are not real voices and in the end can do only limited good.

Even limited good, however, is something, especially for those who are lonely or neglected. Television is not an entirely positive force, but neither is it an entirely negative one. Its voices stand by to provide company, laughter, and information whenever they're needed.

Works Cited

Bondevik, Margareth, and Anders Skogstad. "The Oldest Old, ADL, Social Network, and Loneliness." *Western Journal of Nursing Research*, vol. 20, no. 3, 1998, pp. 325-43. *Sage Journals Online,* wjn.sagepub.com/content/20/3/325.

Burroughs, W. Jeffrey, et al. "Attributes of Health-Promoting Laughter: Cross-Generational Comparison." *Journal of Psychology*, vol. 136, no. 2, 2004, pp. 171-81. *Taylor & Francis Online,* dx.doi.org/10.1080/00223980209604148.

Griffiths, Joan. "The Mirthful Brain." *Omni,* Aug. 1996, pp. 18-19.

Laliberte, Richard W. "The Benefits of Laughter." *Shape,* Sept. 2003, pp. 78-79.

Pinker, Steven. *The Language Instinct: How the Mind Creates Language.* Harper and Row, 1994.

Reeks, Anne. "Kids and TV: A Guide." *Parenting,* Apr. 2005, pp. 110-15.

"Television Programming for Older People: Summary Research Report."

   NZ on Air, 25 July 2001, www.nzonair.govt.nz/media

   /policyandresearch/researchpdfs/oldpeoplesreport.pdf.

Thakkar, Rupin R., et al. "A Systematic Review for the Effects of Television

   Viewing by Infants and Preschoolers." *Pediatrics,* vol. 18, no. 5,

   2006, pp. 2025-31.

Walsh, Teri. "Too Much TV Linked to Depression." *Prevention,* Feb. 2001,

   pp. 34-36.

—Craig Holbrook (student)

3a

3 Writing in the Disciplines

Chapters 1 and 2 discuss features of academic writing in any discipline. This chapter outlines key differences among the disciplines.

3a Literature

Works of literature include novels, short stories, poems, plays, and forms of creative nonfiction. Writing about a literary work requires close reading of the text with particular attention to the words in order to form an interpretation of meaning or an analysis of aesthetic structure and style. In turn, the evidence for the interpretation is mainly quotations from the work that support the ideas about it. Literary analysis may employ primary (historical) sources to establish contexts. Literary analysis also sometimes draws on secondary sources—that is, the comments of critics, theoreticians, biographers, and others on the work, its contexts, or its author.

Writing assignments

You may be asked to write one or more of the following types of papers. The first two are the most common.

- **Literary analysis paper:** your ideas about a work of literature, interpreting its meaning, context, or representations based on your rigorous analysis of specific words, passages, characters, and events.
- **Literary research paper:** analysis of a literary work based on research about the work, its contexts, and perhaps its author.

MyWritingLab

Visit MyWritingLab for more help with writing in the disciplines.

3b

- **Personal response or reaction paper:** your thoughts or feelings about a literary work.
- **Book review:** a summary and evaluation of a book, usually for readers who have not read it.
- **Theatre review:** a summary and evaluation of a theatrical performance.

Source documentation

Unless your instructor specifies otherwise, follow the guidelines in the *MLA Handbook,* detailed on pages 165–205.

3b Other humanities

The humanities include literature, discussed above, as well as the visual arts, music, film, dance, history, philosophy, and religion. Writers in the humanities explain, analyze, and reconstruct human experience by drawing on written words, works of art, and other human creations. The evidence in humanities writing comes largely from primary sources, such as eyewitness accounts of events, news reporting, works of art, and religious texts. Evidence may also come from secondary sources, such as a historian's interpretation of events or a critic's review of a painting.

Writing assignments

Papers in the humanities generally perform one or more of the following operations, often in combination with one another:

- **Explanation:** for instance, showing how a painter developed a particular technique or clarifying a general's role in a battle.
- **Analysis:** examining the elements of a philosophical argument or breaking down the causes of a historical event.
- **Interpretation:** inferring the meaning of a film from its images or the significance of a historical event from contemporary accounts of it.
- **Synthesis:** finding a pattern in a historical period or a composer's works.
- **Evaluation:** judging the quality of an architect's design or a historian's conclusions.

Source documentation

Writers in the humanities generally use the recommendations in either the *MLA Handbook* (pp. 165–205) or the *Chicago Manual of Style* (pp. 223–37). Ask your

Style (pp. 223–37). Ask your instructor whether you should use MLA or Chicago (CMS) style.

3c Social sciences

The social sciences include anthropology, economics, education, management, political science, psychology, and sociology. Researchers in the social sciences examine the way human beings relate to themselves, to one another, and to their environment. Using the scientific method, they pose a question, formulate a hypothesis (a generalization that can be tested), collect and analyze data, and draw conclusions to support, refine, or disprove the hypothesis. The data may be numerical or qualitative, and they may come from firsthand observations, interviews, surveys, or controlled experiments. When writing, social scientists explain their research methods and procedures carefully and document their evidence so that readers can check the sources and replicate the research.

Writing assignments

Depending on the courses you take, you may be asked to write one or more of the following assignments:

- **Summary or review of research:** a report on the available research literature on a subject.
- **Case analysis:** an explanation of the components of a phenomenon, such as a factory closing.
- **Problem-solving analysis:** an explanation of the elements of a problem with suggestions for how to solve it.
- **Research paper:** an interpretation, analysis, or evaluation of the writings of experts on a subject.
- **Research report:** a description of your own original research or your attempt to replicate someone else's research.

Source documentation

The most widely used style guide in the social sciences is the *Publication Manual of the American Psychological Association* (APA). See pages 205–23 for a description of this style. Other social science style guides are listed on page 237.

3d Natural and applied sciences

The natural and applied sciences include biology, chemistry, physics, mathematics, engineering, computer science, and their branches. Researchers in these fields strive to understand natural and technological phenomena and, often, to apply the knowledge to solving problems. Like social scientists, natural and applied scientists gather evidence using the scientific method, a process of continually testing and refining a hypothesis. Scientific evidence is almost always numerical data obtained from measurement in a controlled laboratory setting or in the natural world. In their writing, scientists, like social scientists, explain their research carefully and document their evidence so that readers can check the sources and replicate the research.

Writing assignments

Assignments in the natural and applied sciences include the following:

- **Summary:** a distillation of a research article in a brief, concise form.
- **Critique:** a summary and evaluation of a scientific report.
- **Lab report:** an explanation of the methodology, procedure, and results of an experiment you conduct.
- **Research report:** a report on the research of other scientists and your own methods, findings, and conclusions.
- **Research proposal:** a report of relevant literature on a subject and a plan for further research.

Source documentation

The most widely used style guide in the natural and applied sciences is *Scientific Style and Format: The CSE Manual for Authors, Editors, and Publishers* (CSE). See pages 237–45 for a description of this style. Other science style guides are listed on page 245.

4 Presenting Writing

Legible, consistent, and attractive papers serve your readers and reflect well on you. This chapter covers the basics of formatting any document clearly and effectively.

4a Formats for academic papers

Many academic disciplines prefer specific formats for students' papers. This book details three such formats:

MyWritingLab

Visit **MyWritingLab** for more help with presenting writing.

- **MLA,** used in English, foreign languages, and some other humanities (pp. 165–205).
- **APA,** used in the social sciences and some natural sciences (pp. 205–23).
- **Chicago,** used in history, art history, religion, and some other humanities (pp. 223–37).

The design guidelines in this chapter extend the range of elements and options covered by most academic styles and in some cases contradict those styles. Your instructors may want you to adhere strictly to a particular style or may allow some latitude in design. Ask them for their preferences.

4b Clear and effective documents

Your papers must of course be neat and legible. But you can do more to make your work accessible and attractive by taking care with margins, text, lists, and headings.

Margins

Provide minimum one-inch (2.5 cm) margins on all sides of a page to prevent unpleasant crowding. If your document will be presented in a binder, provide a larger left margin—say, 1½ inches or 4 cm.

Text

Line spacing

Double-space most academic documents, with an initial indention for paragraphs.

Type fonts and sizes

The readability of text derives partly from the type fonts (or faces) and their sizes. For academic documents, choose a standard font and a type size of 10 or 12 points, as in the samples below.

10-point Times New Roman
12-point Times New Roman

Highlighting

Within a document's text, *italic*, **boldface**, underlined, or even colour type can emphasize key words or sentences. Underlining is rarest these days, having been replaced by italics in most academic writing. Boldface can give strong emphasis—for instance, to a term being defined. Colour can highlight headings and illustrations.

Note, however, that these effects can appear unprofessional. Many instructors prefer students to use a single font size without colour or boldface.

Lists

Lists visually reinforce the relations between like items—for example, the steps in a process or the elements of a proposal. A list is easier to read than a paragraph and adds white space to the page.

When wording a list, work for parallelism among items—for instance, use all complete sentences or all phrases (see also p. 43). Set the list with space above and below and with numbering or bullets (indented dots or other devices, such as the small squares in the lists below and on the next page).

Headings

Headings are signposts. In a long or complex document, they direct the reader's attention by focusing the eye on a document's most significant content. Most academic documents use headings functionally, to divide text, orient readers, and create emphasis. Note, however, that many instructors do not want headings in short papers (less than 5,000 words). Follow these guidelines:

- **Use one, two, or three levels of headings** depending on the needs of your material and the length of your document. Some level of heading every two or so pages may help keep readers on track.
- **Create an outline of your document** to plan where headings should go. Reserve the first level of heading for the main points (and sections) of your document. Use a second and perhaps a third level of heading to mark subsections of supporting information.
- **Keep headings as short as possible** while making them specific about the material that follows.
- **Word headings consistently**—for instance, all questions (*What Is the Scientific Method?*), all phrases with *-ing* words (*Understanding the Scientific Method*), or all phrases with nouns (*The Scientific Method*).
- **Indicate the relative importance of headings** with type size, positioning, and highlighting, such as capital letters, italics, or boldface.

FIRST-LEVEL HEADING
Second-Level Heading
Third-Level Heading

- **Keep the appearance simple**, using the same type font and size for headings as for the text.
- **Don't break a page immediately after a heading.** Move the heading to the next page.

Note Document format in many social sciences requires a particular treatment of headings. MLA style discourages elaborate formatting and prefers a simplified heading design. See pages 165–205.

4c Visuals and other media

An illustration can often make a point more efficiently and effectively than words can. Tables present data. Figures (such as graphs or charts) usually recast data in visual form. Images (such as drawings and photographs) can explain processes, represent what something looks like, add emphasis, or convey a theme.

Responsible use of visuals and other media

Media require care to ensure honest use of others' material.

- **Create and evaluate media carefully.** Verify that the data you use are accurate. Be skeptical of images that you find on the Web—altered photographs are often posted and circulated widely.
- **Provide a source note.** You must credit the source when you use someone else's data to create a visual, when you embed someone else's media in your document, or when you link to someone else's media file (see pp. 137–38). Each discipline has a slightly different style for such source notes; those in the illustrations on the next two pages reflect MLA style for English and some other humanities.
- **Obtain permission if it is required**—for instance, if your project will be posted on the Web. See page 157 on copyright and permissions.

Effective use of visuals and other media

Follow these guidelines when using media in academic writing.

- **Focus on a purpose.** Ensure that any media relate directly to points in your writing. Otherwise, readers may find the media distracting, irrelevant, or confusing.
- **Connect visuals to your text.** Direct readers to visuals in your text with references—for instance, "See Fig. 2." Number and label tables separately from graphs, diagrams, and other figures (Table 1, Table 2, and so on; Fig. 1, Fig. 2, and so on). Always include a caption that ties the visual to your text and provides source information.
- **Work audio and video links into online projects.** Whether you link to photographs, sound, or video, tell your audience how the media relate to your ideas and what you intend them to show.

4c

Tables

Tables usually summarize raw data, displaying the data concisely and clearly to show how variables relate to one another, how variables change over time, or how two or more groups contrast.

- **Provide a self-explanatory title above the table.**
- **Provide self-explanatory headings for horizontal rows and vertical columns.** Use abbreviations only if you are certain readers will understand them.
- **Lay out rows and columns for maximum clarity.** In the sample below, for instance, lines divide the table into parts, headings align with their data, and numbers align vertically down columns.

Table 1

Census families in private households by family structure and presence of children, by census metropolitan area (2011 Census)
(*St. John's, Halifax, Moncton, Saint John*)

	2011			
	St. John's (N.L.)	Halifax (N.S.)	Moncton (N.B.)	Saint John (N.B.)
	Number			
All families	56,995	109,765	40,300	37,340
Without children at home	21,870	46,825	18,465	15,420
With children at home	35,125	62,945	21,835	21,920
Families of married couples	38,845	74,470	26,920	25,700
Without children at home	16,725	35,450	13,905	12,690
With children at home	22,120	39,025	13,020	13,010
Families of common-law couples	8,140	16,930	7,280	4,680
Without children at home	5,150	11,375	4,565	2,735
With children at home	2,990	5,550	2,715	1,945
Lone-parent families	10,015	18,365	6,100	6,965
Male parent	1,790	3,375	1,180	1,310
Female parent	8,225	14,990	4,915	5,655

Source: Statistics Canada; *2011 Census of Population*; Catalogue no. 98-312-XCB; Statistics Canada, 13 Feb. 2013; table, www.statcan.gc.ca/tables-tableaux/sum-som/l01/cst01/famil121a-eng.htm.

Figures

Figures represent data or show concepts graphically. They include charts, graphs, and diagrams.

Pie charts

Pie charts show the relations among the parts of a whole. The whole totals 100 percent, and each pie slice is proportional in size to its share of the whole. Use a pie chart to emphasize shares rather than underlying data.

- **Use colour to mark segments of the chart.** Use distinct shades of grey, black, and white if your paper will not be read in colour.
- **Clearly label every segment.**
- **Provide a self-explanatory caption below the chart.**

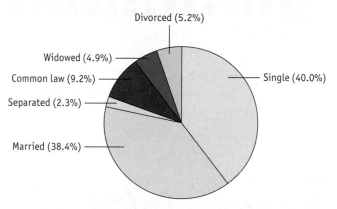

Fig.1 Marital status of Canadians in 2014. Data from Statistics Canada; "Estimates of population, by marital status or legal marital status, age and sex for July 1, Canada, provinces and territories"; 12 Nov. 2014; CANSIM table 051-0042.

Bar charts

Bar charts compare groups or time periods on a measure such as quantity or frequency.

Line graphs

Line graphs show change over time in one or more subjects.

- **Label the vertical scale and include a zero point** to clarify the values being measured.
- **Label the horizontal scale** to show the groups being compared.
- **Provide a self-explanatory caption below the chart.**

Statistics Canada also offers a guide to using and creating graphs called Statistics: Power from Data! at *http://www.statcan.gc.ca/edu/power-pouvoir/toc-tdm/5214718-eng.htm*.

EUse with caution

Fig.2   Use of child care highest among parents of children between the ages of 2 and 4. Data from Statistics Canada; "Child Care in Canada"; *General Social Survey, 2011*; Statistics Canada, 30 Oct. 2014; chart 1.

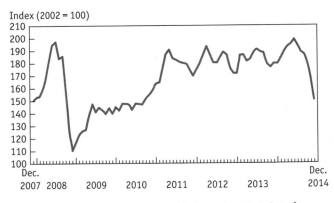

Fig.3   Gasoline prices continue to fall in December 2014. Data from Statistics Canada; "Consumer Price Index, 2014"; *The Daily*, 23 Jan. 2015; CANSIM table 326-0020; chart 2.

When in doubt about how to prepare tables and figures, ask your instructor or supervisor.

Diagrams

Diagrams show concepts visually, such as the structure of an organization, the way something works or looks, or the relations among subjects. Use a diagram to show what can't be described economically in words.

4e

- Clearly label important parts of the diagram.
- Provide a self-explanatory caption below the diagram.

Fig.4 Marketing department organizational chart.

4d Websites

When you create a website, be aware that readers generally alternate between skimming pages for highlights and focusing intently on sections of text.

4e *PowerPoint* or *Prezi* presentations

Many speakers use software such as *PowerPoint* or *Prezi* to show summaries, images, and multimedia during oral presentations. When using such programs, don't try to put your entire presentation onscreen. Instead, select the key points, words, and images that you want listeners to remember. Be aware, however, that when your audience is reading your text or looking at your images, they are not listening to your words.

4f Readers with vision loss

Your audience may include readers who have low vision, problems with colour perception, or difficulties processing visual information. If so, consider adapting your design to meet these readers' needs. Here are a few pointers:

- **Use large type fonts.** Most guidelines call for 14 points or larger.
- **Use standard type fonts.** Avoid decorative fonts with unusual flourishes, even in headings.
- **Avoid words in all-capital letters.**
- **Avoid relying on colour alone to distinguish elements.** Label elements and distinguish them by position or size.
- **Use contrasting colours.** To make colours distinct, choose them from opposite sides of the colour spectrum—violet and yellow, for instance, or orange and blue.
- **Use red and green selectively.** To readers who are red-green colourblind, these colours will appear in shades of grey, yellow, or blue.
- **Use only light colours for tints behind type.** Make the type itself black or a very dark colour.

PART 2

Effective Sentences

Effective Sentences

Emphasis

- Make subjects and verbs of sentences focus on key actors and actions. (See opposite.)
- Stress main ideas by placing them first or last in a sentence. (See p. 36.)
- Link equally important ideas with coordination. (See p. 37.)
- De-emphasize less important ideas with subordination. (See p. 38.)

Conciseness

- Use the active voice to focus on key actors and actions. (See p. 39.)
- Cut empty words and unneeded repetition. (See p. 40.)
- Avoid unneeded *there is* and *it is* constructions. (See p. 41.)
- Tighten word groups to their essence, and combine sentences where appropriate. (See pp. 41–42.)

Parallelism

- Use parallel constructions to show the equivalence of elements that are connected by *and, or, not only ... but also,* and similar words. (See pp. 42–43.)
- Use parallelism in lists, headings, and outlines. (See p. 43.)

Variety and details

- Vary sentence lengths and structures to stress your main ideas and hold readers' attention. (See pp. 44–46.)
- Provide details that make your sentences clear and interesting. (See p. 46.)

Appropriate words

- Use language appropriate for your writing situation. (See pp. 46–48.)
- Avoid sexist and other biased language. (See pp. 48–50.)

Exact words

- Choose words that are suited to your meaning and are concrete and specific. (See pp. 51–52.)
- Make words correct in idiom and also fresh, not clichéd. (See p. 52.)

5 Emphasis

Emphatic writing leads readers to see your main ideas immediately, without having to puzzle out meanings or importance. Besides the following strategies for achieving emphasis, see also the discussions of conciseness (p. 39) and variety (p. 44).

5a Subjects and verbs

The heart of every sentence is its **subject**° and its **verb**.° The subject is the person or thing that acts, and the verb is what the subject does: *Children* [subject] *grow* [verb]. When these elements do not identify the key actor and action in the sentence, readers must find that information elsewhere and the sentence may be wordy and unemphatic. In the following sentences, the subjects and verbs are underlined:

Unemphatic   The <u>intention</u> of the company <u>was</u> to expand its workforce. A <u>proposal</u> <u>was</u> also <u>made</u> to diversify the backgrounds and abilities of employees.

These sentences are unemphatic because their key ideas do not appear in their subjects and verbs. Revised, the sentences are not only clearer but also more concise:

Revised   The <u>company</u> <u>intended</u> to expand its workforce. <u>It</u> also <u>proposed</u> to diversify the backgrounds and abilities of employees.

Now the *actual* subject of the sentence is also the *grammatical* subject. The unemphatic constructions shown below and on the next page usually drain meaning from the subject and verb of a sentence.

Nouns made from verbs

Nouns made from verbs can obscure the key actions of sentences and add words. These nouns include *intention* (from *intend*), *proposal* (from *propose*), *decision* (from *decide*), *expectation* (from *expect*), *persistence* (from *persist*), *argument* (from *argue*), and *inclusion* (from *include*).

Unemphatic   After the company made a <u>decision</u> to hire more workers with disabilities, its next step was the <u>construction</u> of wheelchair ramps and other facilities.

°See "Grammar Terms," page 272.

MyWritingLab

Visit **MyWritingLab** for more help with emphasis.

| Revised | After the company <u>decided</u> to hire more workers with disabilities, it next <u>constructed</u> wheelchair ramps and other facilities. |

Weak verbs

Weak verbs don't express much action. They include *made* and *was* in the second unemphatic example on the previous page. Such verbs tend to stall sentences just where they should be moving, and they often bury key actions:

5b

| Unemphatic | The company <u>is</u> now the leader among businesses in complying with the 2005 Accessibility for Ontarians with Disabilities Act. Its officers <u>make</u> speeches on the act to business groups. |

| Revised | The company now <u>leads</u> other businesses in complying with the 2005 Accessibility for Ontarians with Disabilities Act. Its officers <u>speak</u> on the act to business groups. |

Passive voice

Verbs in the **passive voice**° state actions received by, not performed by, their subjects. Thus the passive voice de-emphasizes the true actor of the sentence, sometimes omitting it entirely. Generally, use the **active voice**,° in which the subject performs the verb's action. (See p. 63 for more on passive and active voice.)

| Unemphatic | The 2005 <u>law is seen</u> by most businesses as fair, but the <u>costs</u> of complying <u>have</u> sometimes <u>been objected to</u>. |

| Revised | Most <u>businesses see</u> the 2005 law as fair, but <u>some</u> <u>have objected to</u> the costs of complying. |

5b Sentence beginnings and endings

The beginning and ending of a sentence are the most emphatic positions, and the ending is usually more emphatic than the beginning. To emphasize information, place it first or last, reserving the middle for incidentals.

| Unemphatic | Education remains the single best means of economic advancement, despite its shortcomings. |

| Revised | Education remains, despite its shortcomings, the single best means of economic advancement. |

Generally, readers expect the beginning of a sentence to contain information that they already know or that you have already introduced. They then look to the ending for

°See "Grammar Terms," page 272.

new information. In the unemphatic passage below, the second and third sentences both begin with new topics (underlined), while the old topics from the first sentence (the controversy and education) appear at the end.

Unemphatic   Education often means controversy these days, with rising costs and constant complaints about its inadequacies. But the <u>value of schooling</u> should not be obscured by the controversy. The <u>single best means of economic advancement</u>, despite its shortcomings, remains education.

In the revised version, old information (underlined) begins each sentence and new information ends it.

Revised   Education often means controversy these days, with rising costs and constant complaints about its inadequacies. But the <u>controversy</u> should not obscure the value of schooling. <u>Education</u> remains, despite its shortcomings, the single best means of economic advancement.

5c Coordination and subordination

Clear sentences show the relationships between ideas and stress the more important ideas over the lesser ones. Two techniques, **coordination**° and **subordination**,° can help you achieve such clarity.

Coordination

Use coordination to show that two or more elements in a sentence are equally important in meaning.

■ **Link two complete sentences (main clauses°) with a comma and a coordinating conjunction** (*and, but, or, nor, for, so, yet*).

<u>The first Calgary Stampede in 1912 was a great success</u>, but <u>a second one was not held until 1919</u>. (*But* is a coordinating conjunction and must follow the comma.)

■ **Link two main clauses with a semicolon alone or a semicolon and a transitional expression°** such as *however, indeed,* or *therefore.*

<u>The early Stampedes were cowboy shows</u>; since 1923, however, <u>the Stampede has included an agricultural exhibition</u>. (*However* is a conjunctive adverb and can move around within its clause. It usually sounds better in the middle of the clause, set off by a pair of commas. See pp. 85–86.)

■ **Within clauses, link words and word groups with a coordinating conjunction** such as *and, but, or,* and *nor.*

° See "Grammar Terms," page 272.

<u>Cowboys</u> and <u>city folk</u> alike <u>flocked to the bronco riding</u> or <u>thronged the chuckwagon racing events</u>.

■ **Link main clauses, words, or phrases° with a correlative conjunction°** such as *not only … but also* and *either … or*.

Families not only <u>had fun</u> but also <u>learned about cattle ranching</u>.

Coordination clarifies meaning and smooths choppy sentences.

5c

Choppy sentences	We should not rely so heavily on oil. Coal and uranium are also overused. We have a substantial energy resource in the moving waters of our rivers. Smaller streams add to the total volume of water. The resource renews itself. Coal and oil are irreplaceable. Uranium is also irreplaceable. The cost of water does not increase much over time. The costs of coal, oil, and uranium rise dramatically.
Ideas coordinated	We should not rely so heavily on coal, oil, <u>and</u> uranium, <u>for</u> we have a substantial energy resource in the moving waters of our rivers <u>and</u> streams. Coal, oil, <u>and</u> uranium are irreplaceable <u>and</u> thus subject to dramatic cost increases; water, <u>however</u>, is self-renewing <u>and</u> more stable in cost.

Notes A string of main clauses connected by *and* implies that all ideas are equally important and creates a dull, plodding rhythm. Use subordination (see the next section) to revise such excessive coordination.

Two punctuation errors—comma splices and fused sentences—occur when you link main clauses without punctuation or a conjunction.

Subordination

Use subordination to indicate that some elements in a sentence are less important than others for your meaning. Usually, the main idea appears in the main clause,° and supporting information appears in subordinate structures:

■ **Use a subordinate clause° beginning with a subordinating word** such as *although, because, before, if, since, that, when, where, which,* and *who (whom)*.

<u>Although production costs have declined</u>, they are still high. [Stresses that costs are still high.]

Costs, <u>which include labour and facilities</u>, are difficult to control. [Stresses that costs are difficult to control.]

°See "Grammar Terms," page 272.

■ Use a phrase.

Despite some decline, production costs are still high.

Costs, including labour and facilities, are difficult to control.

■ **Use a single word.**

Declining costs have not matched prices.

Labour costs are difficult to control.

Subordination can transform a monotonous string of main clauses into a more emphatic and interesting passage. (See also p. 40.)

String of main clauses	In recent years computer prices have fallen, and production costs have fallen more slowly, and computer manufacturers have had to struggle, for their profits have been shrinking.
Revised	Because production costs have fallen more slowly than computer prices in recent years, computer manufacturers have had to struggle with shrinking profits.

Generally, subordinate clauses give the most emphasis to secondary information, phrases give less, and single words give the least.

Note A subordinate clause or a phrase is not a complete sentence and should not be set off and punctuated as one. See pages 82–84 on sentence fragments.

6 Conciseness

Concise writing makes every word count. Conciseness is not the same as brevity: detail and originality should not be cut along with needless words. Rather, the length of an expression should be appropriate to the thought.

6a Focusing on the subject and verb

Using the **subjects°** and **verbs°** of your sentences for the key actors and actions will tighten sentences. See page 35 for help identifying the subject and verb and for a discussion of how to stress them:

■ **Avoid nouns made from verbs,** such as *intention* (from *intend*) and *decision* (from *decide*).

°See "Grammar Terms," page 272.

MyWritingLab

Visit **MyWritingLab** for more help with writing concisely.

6a

- **Strengthen weak verbs,** such as *is* and *make.*
- **Rewrite the passive voice as active**—for instance, changing *The star was seen by astronomers* to *Astronomers saw the star.*

6b Cutting empty words

Cutting words that contribute nothing to your meaning will make your writing move faster and work harder.

Wordy	In my opinion I think that the situation of the production of genetically modified food at this point in time is no different from the kind of plant breeding, namely through hybridization, for the purpose of improvement that has been going on more or less for centuries.
Concise	Today's genetically modified food is not so different from yesterday's hybridized plants.

The underlining in the wordy example above highlights these kinds of empty words:

- **Phrases that add nothing to meaning:**

all things considered	in a manner of speaking
a person by the name of	in my opinion
as far as I'm concerned	last but not least
for all intents and purposes	more or less

- **Abstract or general words that pad sentences (and usually require additional words such as *of* and *the*):**

area	element	kind	situation
aspect	factor	manner	thing
case	field	nature	type

- **Word groups that mean the same thing as single words:**

For	Substitute
at all times	always
at the present time	now
at this point in time	now
for the purpose of	for
due to the fact that	because
because of the fact that	because
in the final analysis	finally

6c Cutting unneeded repetition

Repeating or restating key words from sentence to sentence can link the sentences and emphasize information the reader already knows (see p. 36). But unnecessary repetition weakens sentences and paragraphs.

Wordy	Many unskilled workers <u>without training in a particular job</u> are unemployed <u>and do not have any work</u>.
Concise	Many unskilled workers are unemployed.

Be especially alert to phrases that say the same thing twice. In the following examples, only the underlined words are needed:

<u>circle</u> around	the <u>future</u> to come
<u>consensus</u> of opinion	important <u>essentials</u>
<u>continue</u> on	<u>repeat</u> again
<u>cooperate</u> together	<u>return</u> again
<u>few</u> in number	<u>square</u> [<u>round</u>] in shape
final <u>completion</u>	surrounding <u>circumstances</u>

6e

6d Tightening modifiers

Modifiers° can be expanded or contracted depending on the emphasis you want to achieve. When editing your sentences, consider whether any modifiers can be reduced without loss of emphasis or clarity.

Wordy	The weight-loss industry faces new competition from lipolysis, <u>which is</u> a cosmetic procedure <u>that is</u> noninvasive.
Concise	The weight-loss industry faces new competition from lipolysis, <u>a noninvasive cosmetic procedure</u>.

6e Revising *there is* or *it is*

Sentences beginning *there is* or *it is* (called **expletive constructions°**) are sometimes useful to emphasize a change in direction, but usually they just add needless words.

Wordy	<u>There is a noninvasive laser treatment that</u> makes people thinner by rupturing fat cells and releasing the fat into the spaces between cells. <u>It is the expectation of some doctors</u> that the procedure will replace liposuction.
Concise	<u>A noninvasive laser treatment</u> makes people thinner by rupturing fat cells and releasing the fat into the spaces between cells. <u>Some doctors expect</u> that the procedure will replace liposuction.

°See "Grammar Terms," page 272.

6f Combining sentences

Often the information in two or more sentences can be combined into one tight sentence.

Wordy	People who receive fat-releasing laser treatments can lose centimetres from their waists. They can also lose centimetres from their hips and thighs. They do not lose weight. The released fat remains in their bodies.
Concise	People who receive fat-releasing laser treatments can lose centimetres from their <u>waists, hips, and thighs,</u> <u>but</u> they do not lose weight <u>because</u> the released fat remains in their bodies.

7 Parallelism

Parallelism matches the form of your sentence to its meaning: when your ideas are equally important, or parallel, you express them in similar, or parallel, grammatical form.

The air is dirtied by <u>factories belching smoke</u> and <u>vehicles spewing exhaust</u>.

Parallelism can work like glue to link the parts of a sentence and also the sentences of a paragraph:

<u>Pulleys are ancient machines</u> for transferring power. Unfortunately, <u>they are also inefficient machines</u>.

7a Parallelism with *and, but, or, nor, yet*

The **coordinating conjunctions**° *and, but, or, nor,* and *yet* signal a need for parallelism.

The industrial base was <u>shifting</u> and <u>shrinking</u>.

Politicians seldom <u>acknowledged the problem</u> or <u>proposed alternatives</u>.

Industrial workers were understandably disturbed <u>that they were losing their jobs</u> and <u>that no one seemed to care</u>.

Nonparallel	Steel companies kept losing money because <u>their plants were inefficient</u>, <u>high labour costs</u>, and <u>foreign competition was increasing</u>.

MyWritingLab

Visit **MyWritingLab** for more help with parallelism.

°See "Grammar Terms," page 272.

| Revised | Steel companies kept losing money because of <u>inefficient plants</u>, <u>high labour costs</u>, and <u>increasing foreign competition</u>. |

Note Parallel elements match in structure, but they need not match word for word.

Be careful not to omit needed words in parallel structures.

| Nonparallel | Given training, workers can acquire the <u>skills</u> and <u>interest in</u> other jobs. [Idiom dictates different prepositions with *skills* and *interest*.] |
| Revised | Given training, workers can acquire the skills <u>for</u> and interest in other jobs. |

7b Parallelism with *both … and, either … or,* and so on

Correlative conjunctions° stress equality and balance between elements. The correlative conjunctions include *both … and, either … or, neither … nor, not only … but also,* and *whether … or.* Parallelism confirms the equality between elements: the words after the first and second connectors must match.

| Nonparallel | Huck Finn learns not only <u>that human beings have an enormous capacity for folly</u> but also <u>enormous dignity</u>. [The first element includes *that human beings have;* the second element does not.] |
| Revised | Huck Finn learns <u>that human beings have</u> not only <u>an enormous capacity for folly</u> but also enormous dignity. [Repositioning *not only* makes the two elements parallel.] |

7c Parallelism with lists, headings, and outlines

The items in a list or outline should be parallel. Parallelism is essential in the headings that divide a paper into sections. (See p. 26.)

Nonparallel	Revised
Changes in Renaissance England	Changes in Renaissance England
1. Extension of trade routes	1. Extension of trade routes
2. Merchant class became more powerful	2. <u>Increased power</u> of the merchant class
3. The death of feudalism	3. <u>Death</u> of feudalism
4. Upsurging of the arts	4. <u>Upsurge</u> of the arts
5. Religious quarrels began	5. <u>Rise</u> of religious quarrels

°See "Grammar Terms," page 272.

8 Variety and Details

To make your writing interesting as well as clear, use varied sentences that are well textured with details.

8a

8a Varied sentence lengths and structures

In most contemporary writing, sentences tend to vary from about ten to about forty words, with an average of fifteen to twenty-five words. If your sentences are all at one extreme or the other, your readers may have difficulty locating main ideas and seeing the relations among them.

- **Long sentences.** Break a sequence of long sentences into shorter, simpler ones that stress key ideas.
- **Short sentences.** Combine a sequence of short sentences with coordination (p. 37) and subordination (p. 38) to show relationships and stress main ideas.

A good way to focus and hold readers' attention is to vary the structure of sentences so that they do not all follow the same pattern.

Varied sentence structures

A long sequence of **main clauses**° can make all ideas seem equally important and create a plodding rhythm, as in the unvaried passage below. You want to emphasize your key subjects and verbs, moving in each sentence from old information to new (see pp. 36–37). Subordinating less important information (bracketed in the revised passage) can help you achieve this emphasis.

Unvaried

The moon is now drifting away from the earth. It moves away about 2.5 cm a year. This movement is lengthening our days, and they increase about a thousandth of a second every century. Forty-seven of our present days will someday make up a month. We might eventually lose the moon altogether. Such great planetary movement rightly concerns astronomers, but it need not worry us. It will take 50 million years.

Revised

The moon is now drifting away from the earth [about 2.5 cm a year.] [At a thousandth of a second every century,] this movement is lengthening our days. Forty-seven of our present days will someday make up a month, [if we don't

°See "Grammar Terms," page 272.

eventually lose the moon altogether.] Such great planetary movement rightly concerns astronomers, but it need not worry us. It will take 50 million years.

Varied sentence beginnings

An English sentence often begins with its subject, which generally captures old information from a preceding sentence (see pp. 36–37):

> Canadian hip-hop artist K'naan was born in Mogadishu, Somalia, in 1978. He moved with his family to Toronto when he was thirteen.

8a

However, an unbroken sequence of sentences beginning with the subject quickly becomes monotonous:

Monotonous
K'naan could not speak English when he arrived in Toronto. He learned to rap phonetically by listening to records. Canadian promoter Sol Guy invited K'naan to perform at the United Nations in 1999. K'naan had experienced the civil war in Somalia as well as urban violence in Toronto, and he has consistently performed on behalf of human rights. He has received many awards for his humanitarian work, his music, and his spoken words.

Revised
K'naan could not speak English when he arrived in Toronto. By listening to records, however, he learned to rap phonetically. In 1999, Canadian promoter Sol Guy invited K'naan to perform at the United Nations. Having experienced the civil war in Somalia as well as urban violence in Toronto, K'naan has consistently performed on behalf of human rights. In recognition, he has received many awards for his humanitarian work, his music, and his spoken words.

The underlined expressions represent the most common choices for varying sentence beginnings:

- **Adverb modifiers,** such as *In 1999* (modifies the verb *invited*).
- **Adjective modifiers,** such as *Having experienced the civil war in Somalia* (modifies *K'naan*).
- **Transitional expressions,** such as *however*. (See transitional expression, p. 282, for a list.)

Varied word order

Occasionally, to achieve special emphasis, reverse the usual word order of a sentence.

K'naan's hit single, "Wavin' Flag: The Celebration Mix," was chosen as the official anthem for the 2010 FIFA World Cup in

South Africa. <u>The song, he hoped, would cause celebration</u>.
[Compare with normal word order: *He hoped the song would cause celebration*.]

8b Details

Relevant details such as facts and examples create the texture and life that keep readers alert and help them grasp your meaning. For instance:

Flat

Built in Montreal harbour, the former Expo '67 site is a popular place for sports and also features other attractions.

Detailed

Built <u>on a green archipelago of natural and artificial islands</u> in Montreal harbour, the former Expo '67 site is a popular place for <u>walking, cycling, rowing, swimming, and ice skating</u>, and also features <u>international gardens, a casino, a theatre, and a museum</u>.

9 Appropriate Words

English-speaking Canadians use their common language in different ways. The spoken English of Newfoundland, Quebec, and the Ottawa Valley varies in vocabulary, syntax, and pronunciation. Canadians who speak indigenous languages such as Cree, Mohawk, and Inuktitut may flavour their English with syntax and idiom borrowed from their languages. Canadians from many regional and ethnic backgrounds have enriched our common English language.

Nevertheless, most academic and business writing calls for **standard English**, usually defined as the English expected and used by educated English-speaking people. Therefore, in academic and business writing, use regional and ethnic dialect words and phrases cautiously, only when you are aiming for a particular effect with a particular audience. In all cases, avoid words and expressions that your readers might find confusing, hurtful, or insulting.

9a Nonstandard dialect

Like many countries, Canada includes several regional, social, and ethnic groups that have their own distinct **dialects**, or versions of English: standard English,

MyWritingLab

Visit **MyWritingLab** for more help with appropriate words.

Newfoundland English, West Indian English, and Ottawa Valley English are examples. English-speaking Quebecers frequently use words and expressions borrowed from French, giving their English a unique flavour.

If you normally speak a dialect version of English, be aware that in academic or business writing, where audiences usually expect standard English, your dialect words and expressions may be misunderstood or perceived as mistakes.

9d

Edit your drafts to eliminate dialect expressions, especially those that dictionaries label "nonstandard," such as *this here school, that there building, them books, knowed, throwed, eh, didn't ought, hadn't ought, didn't never, could of, would of, should of, that house there, I think me, I done it, I seen it.*

9b Slang

Slang is the insider language used by a group, such as musicians or football players, to reflect common experiences or to make technical references efficient. The slang you use when texting with friends is not appropriate for an academic essay.

Though valuable within a group, slang is often too private or imprecise for academic or business writing.

9c Colloquial language

Colloquial language is the everyday spoken language, including expressions such as *go crazy, get along with, a lot, kids* (for *children*), and *stuff* (for possessions or other objects). Colloquial language suits informal writing, and an occasional colloquial word can help you achieve a desired emphasis in otherwise formal writing. But most colloquial language is not precise enough for academic or business writing.

9d Technical words

All disciplines and professions rely on specialized language that allows members to communicate precisely and efficiently with each other. Chemists, for instance, have their *phosphatides,* and literary critics have their *subtexts.* Use the terms of a discipline or profession when you are writing within it. When you are writing for a nonspecialist audience, however, avoid unnecessary technical terms and carefully define the terms you must use.

9e Indirect and pretentious writing

Small, plain, and direct words are usually preferable to big, showy, or evasive words. Take special care to avoid the following:

- **Euphemisms** are presumably inoffensive words that substitute for words deemed potentially offensive or too blunt, such as *passed away* for *died* or *misspeak* for *lie*. Use euphemisms only when you know that blunt, truthful words would needlessly hurt or offend members of your audience.
- **Double talk** (at times called **doublespeak** or **weasel words**) is language intended to confuse or to be misunderstood: the *revenue enhancement* that is really a tax, the *biodegradable* bags that still last decades. Double talk has no place in honest writing.
- **Pretentious writing** is fancy language that is more elaborate than its subject requires. Choose your words for their exactness and economy. The big, ornate word may be tempting, but pass it up. Your readers will be grateful.

Pretentious	To perpetuate our endeavour of providing funds for our elderly citizens as we do at the present moment, we will face the exigency of enhanced contributions from all our citizens.
Revised	We cannot continue to fund the Canada Pension Plan for the elderly unless we raise taxes.

9f Sexist and other biased language

Even when we do not mean it to, our language can reflect and perpetuate hurtful prejudices toward groups of people. Such biased language can be obvious—words such as *nigger, honky, mick, kike, fag, dyke, squaw, raghead,* and *broad*. But it can also be subtle, generalizing about groups in ways that may be familiar but that are also inaccurate or unfair.

Biased language reflects poorly on the user, not on the person or persons whom it mischaracterizes or insults. Unbiased language does not submit to false generalizations. It treats people respectfully as individuals and labels groups as they wish to be labelled.

Stereotypes of race, ethnicity, and other characteristics

A **stereotype** characterizes and judges people simply on the basis of their membership in a group: *Men are uncommunicative. Women are emotional. Liberals want to raise taxes. Conservatives are rednecks.*

In your writing, avoid statements about the traits of whole groups that may be true of only some members. Be especially cautious about substituting such statements for the evidence you should be providing instead.

Stereotype	Elderly drivers should have their licences limited to daytime driving only. [Asserts that all elderly people are poor night drivers.]
Revised	Drivers with impaired night vision should have their licences limited to daytime driving only.

Some stereotypes have become part of the language, but they are still potentially offensive.

Stereotype	The administrators are too blind to see the need for a new gymnasium.
Revised	The administrators do not understand the need for a new gymnasium.

Sexist language

Sexist language distinguishes needlessly between men and women in matters such as occupation, ability, behaviour, temperament, and maturity. It can wound or irritate readers and indicates the writer's thoughtlessness or unfairness. The following guidelines can help you eliminate sexist language from your writing.

- **Avoid demeaning and patronizing language**—for instance, identifying women and men differently or trivializing either gender.

Sexist	Dr. Keith Kim and Lydia Hawkins collaborated.
Revised	Dr. Keith Kim and Dr. Lydia Hawkins collaborated.
Revised	Keith Kim and Lydia Hawkins co-authored the article.
Sexist	Ladies are entering almost every occupation formerly filled by men.
Revised	Women are entering almost every occupation formerly filled by men.

- **Avoid occupational or social stereotypes that assume a role or profession is exclusively male or female.**

Sexist	A doctor should commend a nurse when she provides his patients with good care.
Revised	A doctor should commend a nurse who provides good care for patients.

- **Avoid using *man* or words containing *man* to refer to all human beings.** Some alternatives:

businessman	businessperson
chairman	chair, chairperson
craftsman	craftsperson, artisan
layman	layperson
mankind	humankind, humanity, human beings, people
manpower	personnel, human resources
policeman	police officer
salesman	salesperson

Sexist	<u>Man</u> has not reached the limits of social justice.
Revised	<u>Humankind</u> [or <u>Humanity</u>] has not reached the limits of social justice.
Sexist	The furniture consists of <u>manmade</u> materials.
Revised	The furniture consists of <u>synthetic</u> materials.

■ **Avoid using *he* to refer to both genders.** (See also p. 72.)

Sexist	The newborn <u>child</u> explores <u>his</u> world.
Revised	Newborn <u>children</u> explore <u>their</u> world. [Use the plural for the pronoun and the word it refers to.]
Revised	The newborn <u>child</u> explores <u>the</u> world. [Avoid the pronoun altogether.]
Revised	The newborn <u>child</u> explores <u>his or her</u> world. [Substitute male and female pronouns.]

Use the last option sparingly—only once in a group of sentences and only to stress the singular individual.

Inappropriate labels

Labels for groups of people can be shorthand stereotypes and can be discourteous when they ignore readers' preferences. Although sometimes dismissed as "political correctness," sensitivity in applying labels hurts no one and helps gain your readers' trust and respect.

■ **Avoid labels that (intentionally or not) insult the person or group you refer to.** A person with emotional problems is not a *mental patient*. A person using a wheelchair is not *wheelchair-bound*.

■ **Use names for racial, ethnic, and other groups that reflect the preferences of each group's members, or at least many of them.** Examples of current preferences include *First Nations* (for Canadians descended from Aboriginal peoples), *Inuit* (rather than Eskimo), and *people with disabilities* (rather than *the handicapped*). But the acceptability of labels changes often. To learn how a group's members wish to be labelled, ask them directly, attend to usage in reputable periodicals, or check a recent dictionary.

■ **Identify a person's group only when it is relevant to the point you're making.** Consider the context of the label: Is it a necessary piece of information? If not, don't use it.

10 Exact Words

To write clearly and effectively, you will want to find the words that fit your meaning exactly and convey your attitude precisely.

10a The right word for your meaning

10b

One key to helping readers understand you is to use words according to their established meanings.

- Consult a dictionary whenever you are unsure of a word's meaning.
- Distinguish between similar-sounding words that have widely different meanings.

Inexact	Older people often suffer infirmaries [places for the sick].
Exact	Older people often suffer infirmities [disabilities].

Some words, called **homonyms**, sound exactly alike but differ in meaning: for example, *principal/principle* or *rain/reign/rein*. (Many homonyms and near-homonyms are listed in "Commonly Misused Words," p. 261.)

- Distinguish between words with related but distinct meanings.

Inexact	Television commercials continuously [unceasingly] interrupt programming.
Exact	Television commercials continually [regularly] interrupt programming.

- Distinguish between words that have similar basic meanings but different emotional associations, or *connotations*.

It is a daring plan. [The plan is bold and courageous.]
It is a reckless plan. [The plan is thoughtless and risky.]

Many dictionaries list and distinguish such synonyms, words with approximately, but often not exactly, the same meanings.

10b Concrete and specific words

Clear, exact writing balances abstract and general words, which outline ideas and objects, with concrete and specific words, which sharpen and solidify.

> MyWritingLab
> Visit **MyWritingLab** for more help with exact words.

- **Abstract words** name qualities and ideas: *beautiful, management, culture, freedom, awesome.* **Concrete words** name things we can know by our five senses of sight, hearing, touch, taste, and smell: *sleek, humming, rough, bitter, musty.*
- **General words** name classes or groups of things, such as *buildings, weather,* or *birds,* and they include all the varieties of the class. **Specific words** limit a general class, such as *buildings,* by naming one of its varieties, such as *skyscraper, Victorian courthouse, ranch house,* or *hut.*

10d

Abstract and general statements need development with concrete and specific details. For example:

| Vague | The size of his hands made his smallness real. [How big were his hands? How small was he?] |
| Exact | Not until I saw his delicate, doll-like hands did I realize that he stood a full head shorter than most other men. |

10c Idioms

Idioms are expressions in any language that do not fit the rules for meaning or grammar—for instance, *put up with, plug away at, make off with.*

Because they are not governed by rules, idioms usually cause particular difficulty for people learning to speak and write a new language. But even native speakers of English can confuse idioms involving **prepositions**,° such as *agree <u>on</u> a plan, agree <u>to</u> a proposal,* and *agree <u>with</u> a person* or *occupied <u>by</u> a person, occupied <u>in</u> study,* and *occupied <u>with</u> a thing.*

When in doubt about an idiom, consult your dictionary under the main word (*agree* and *occupy* in the examples). (See also p. 59 on verbs with particles.)

Note Many speakers of Quebec English use an English translation from a French idiom: e.g., *close the lights* instead of *turn off the lights.*

10d Clichés

Clichés, or **trite expressions**, are phrases so old and so often repeated that they have become stale. Examples include *better late than never, beyond the shadow of a doubt, face the music, green with envy, ladder of success, point with pride, sneaking suspicion,* and *as wise as an owl.*

Clichés may slide into your drafts. In editing, be wary of any expression you have heard or used before. Substitute fresh words of your own, or restate the idea in plain language.

°See "Grammar Terms," page 272.

Grammatical Sentences

Essential
Grammatical Sentences

This list focuses on the grammatical errors that most often confuse or distract readers. See "Detailed Contents" inside the back cover for a complete guide to this part.

Verbs

- Use the correct forms of irregular verbs such as *has broken* [not *has broke*]. (See opposite.)

- Use helping verbs where required, as in *she has been* [not *she been*]. (See p. 56.)

- Use consistent verb tense, as in *While she was jogging, she tripped* [not *trips*]. (See p. 60.)

- Make verbs agree with their subjects, as in *The list of items is* [not *are*] *long.* (See p. 65.)

Pronouns

- Make pronouns agree with the words they refer to, as in *Each of the women had her* [not *their*] *say.* (See p. 70.)

- Make pronouns refer clearly to the words they substitute for, avoiding uncertainties such as *Jill thanked Tracy when she* [Jill or Tracy?] *arrived.* (See p. 72.)

- Use pronouns consistently, avoiding shifts such as *When one enters university, you encounter new ideas.* (See p. 74.)

Modifiers

- Place modifiers close to the words they describe, as in *Trash cans without lids invite animals* [not *Trash cans invite animals without lids*]. (See p. 79.)

- Make each modifier clearly modify another word in the sentence, as in *Jogging, she pulled a muscle* [not *Jogging, a muscle was pulled*]. (See p. 81.)

Sentence faults

- Make every sentence complete, with its own subject and verb: *But first she called the police.* [Not *But first called the police.*] *New stores open weekly.* [Not *New stores weekly.*] (See p. 82.)

- A freestanding subordinate clause is not a complete sentence: *Jamal stayed home because he was sick.* [Not *Jamal stayed home. Because he was sick.*] (See p. 83.)

- Within sentences, link main clauses correctly. (See pp. 84–86.)

  Use a comma and a coordinating conjunction: *Cars jam the roads, and they add to smog.*

  Use a semicolon: *Many students attended the rally; the room was packed.*

  Use a semicolon and a transitional expression: *The snow fell heavily; however, it melted quickly.*

Parts of speech

Traditionally, English grammarians divided words into categories based on how those words functioned in an English sentence. These categories are called **parts of speech**. A word can serve as more than one part of speech depending on its form and its place in a sentence.

> The strike [noun] ended the game.
> Why did he strike [verb] the bell?
> That dress looks striking [adjective] on you.

Below is a sentence with parts of speech labelled. Each part of speech is defined in "Grammar Terms" on pages 272–83.

definite article	adverb	adjective	noun (subject)	adverb	verb	indefinite article
The	stylishly	dressed	server	carefully	handed	a

adjective	noun (direct object)	preposition	proper noun (indirect object)
brimming	glass	to	Carl.

VERBS

11 Verb Forms

Verb forms may give you trouble when the verb is irregular, when you omit certain endings, or when you need to use helping verbs.

11a *Sing/sang/sung* and other irregular verbs

Most verbs are **regular**: their **past-tense form**° and **past participle**° end in *-d* or *-ed*:

> Today the birds migrate. [**Plain form**° of verb.]
> Yesterday the birds migrated. [Past-tense form.]
> In the past the birds have migrated. [Past participle.]

MyWritingLab

Visit **MyWritingLab** for more help with verb forms.

About two hundred **irregular verbs** in English create their past-tense form and past participle in some way other than adding *-d* or *-ed*.

> Today the birds <u>fly</u>. They <u>begin</u> migration. [Plain form.]
>
> Yesterday the birds <u>flew</u>. They <u>began</u> migration. [Past-tense form.]
>
> In the past the birds have <u>flown</u>. They have <u>begun</u> migration. [Past participle.]

You can find a verb's forms by looking up the plain form in a dictionary. For a regular verb, the dictionary will give the *-d* or *-ed* form. For an irregular verb, the dictionary will give the past-tense form and then the past participle. If the dictionary gives only one irregular form after the plain form, then the past-tense form and past participle are the same (*think, thought, thought*).

11b Helping verbs

Helping verbs combine with some verb forms to indicate time and other kinds of meaning, as in <u>can</u> *run,* <u>might</u> *suppose,* <u>will</u> *open, was sleeping,* <u>had been</u> *eaten.* The **main verb**° in these phrases is the one that carries the main meaning (*run, suppose, open, sleeping, eaten*).

Required helping verbs

Standard English requires helping verbs in the situations listed below.

- **The main verb ends in *-ing*:**

  Archaeologists <u>are</u> conducting fieldwork all over the world. [Not *Archaeologists conducting. . . .*]

- **The main verb is *been* or *be*:**

  Many <u>have</u> been fortunate in their discoveries. [Not *Many been. . . .*]

  Some <u>could</u> be real-life Indiana Joneses. [Not *Some be. . . .*]

- **The main verb is a past participle,°** such as *given, talked, begun,* or *thrown:*

  The researchers <u>have</u> given interviews on radio and TV. [Not *The researchers given. . . .*]

In these examples, omitting the helping verb would create an incomplete sentence, or **sentence fragment** (p. 82).

Combinations of helping and main verbs ESL

Helping verbs and main verbs combine in specific ways.

°See "Grammar Terms," page 272.

Note The main verb in a verb phrase (the one carrying the main meaning) does not change to show a change in subject or time: *she has sung, you had sung*. Only the helping verb may change, as in these examples.

Form of *be* + present participle

Create the **progressive tenses**° with *be, am, is, are, was, were,* or *been* followed by the main verb's **present participle**° (ending in *-ing*).

Faulty   She is work on a new book.
Revised   She is working on a new book.

Faulty   She has been work on it several months.
Revised   She has been working on it several months.

Note Verbs that express mental states or activities rather than physical actions do not usually appear in the progressive tenses. These verbs include *adore, appear, believe, belong, have, hear, know, like, love, need, see, taste, think, understand,* and *want*.

Faulty   She is wanting to understand contemporary ethics.
Revised   She wants to understand contemporary ethics.

Form of *be* + past participle

Create the **passive voice**° with *be, am, is, are, was, were, being,* or *been* followed by the main verb's **past participle**° (usually ending in *-d* or *-ed* or, for irregular verbs, in *-t* or *-n*).

Faulty   Her last book was complete in four months.
Revised   Her last book was completed in four months.

Faulty   It was bring to the manager's attention.
Revised   It was brought to the manager's attention.

Note Only **transitive verbs**° may form the passive voice.

Faulty   A philosophy conference was occurred that week.
          [*Occur* is not a transitive verb.]
Revised   A philosophy conference occurred that week.

Form of *have* + past participle

To create one of the **perfect tenses,**° use the main verb's past participle preceded by a form of *have,* such as *has, had, have been,* or *will have had*.

Faulty   Some students have complain about the lab.
Revised   Some students have complained about the lab.

Faulty   Money has not been spend on the lab in years.
Revised   Money has not been spent on the lab in years.

°See "Grammar Terms," page 272.

Form of *do* + plain form

Always with the **plain form**° of the main verb, three forms of *do* serve as helping verbs: *do, does, did.*

Faulty   Safety concerns <u>do exists</u>.
Revised   Safety concerns <u>do exist</u>.

Faulty   <u>Didn't</u> the lab <u>closed</u> briefly last year?
Revised   <u>Didn't</u> the lab <u>close</u> briefly last year?

Modal + plain form

Most **modal** helping verbs combine with the plain form of the main verb to convey ability, possibility, necessity, and other meanings. The modals include *be able to, be supposed to, can, could, had better, have to, may, might, must, ought to, shall, should, used to, will,* and *would.*

Faulty   The lab equipment <u>may causes</u> injury.
Revised   The lab equipment <u>may cause</u> injury.
Faulty   The school <u>ought to replaced</u> it.
Revised   The school <u>ought to replace</u> it.

Note When a modal combines with another helping verb, the main verb generally changes from the plain form to a past participle:

Faulty   The equipment <u>could have fail</u>.
Revised   The equipment <u>could have failed</u>.

11c Verb + gerund or infinitive ESL

A **gerund** is the *-ing* form of a verb used as a noun (*Smoking kills*). An **infinitive** is the **plain form**° of the verb plus *to* (*Try to quit*). Gerunds and infinitives may follow certain verbs but not others. And sometimes the use of a gerund or infinitive with the same verb changes the meaning of the verb.

Either gerund or infinitive

A gerund or an infinitive may follow certain verbs with no significant difference in meaning: *begin, can't bear, can't stand, continue, hate, hesitate, like, love, prefer, start.*

The pump began <u>working</u>. The pump began <u>to work</u>.

Meaning change with gerund or infinitive

A gerund and an infinitive have quite different meanings when they follow four verbs: *forget, remember, stop,* and *try.*

The engineer stopped <u>watching</u> the pump. [She no longer watched.]

°See "Grammar Terms," page 272.

The engineer stopped to watch the pump. [She stopped in order to watch.]

Gerund, not infinitive

Do not use an infinitive after these verbs: *admit, adore, appreciate, avoid, consider, deny, detest, discuss, dislike, enjoy, escape, finish, imagine, keep, mind, miss, practise, put off, quit, recall, resent, resist, risk, suggest, tolerate, understand.*

Faulty   She suggested to check the pump.
Revised   She suggested checking the pump.

Infinitive, not gerund

Do not use a gerund after these verbs: *agree, allow, ask, assent, beg, claim, decide, expect, have, hope, manage, mean, offer, plan, pretend, promise, refuse, say, wait, want, wish.*

Faulty   She decided checking the pump.
Revised   She decided to check the pump.

Noun or pronoun + infinitive

Some verbs may be followed by an infinitive alone or by a **noun°** or **pronoun°** and an infinitive: *ask, beg, choose, dare, expect, help, need, promise, want, wish, would like.* A noun or pronoun changes the meaning.

She expected to watch.
She expected her workers to watch.

Some verbs *must* be followed by a noun or pronoun before an infinitive: *advise, allow, cause, challenge, command, convince, encourage, forbid, force, hire, instruct, order, permit, persuade, remind, require, teach, tell, warn.*

She instructed her workers to watch.

When these verbs are used in the **passive voice,°** they still require infinitives, not gerunds:

Faulty   He's allowed crossing the street.
Revised   He's allowed to cross the street.

Do not use *to* before the infinitive when it comes after one of the following verbs and a noun or pronoun: *feel, have, hear, let, make* ("force"), *see, watch.*

She let her workers learn by observation.

11d Verb + particle ESL

Some verbs consist of two words: the verb itself and a particle, a **preposition°** or **adverb°** that affects the meaning of the verb, as in *Look up the answer* (research the

°See "Grammar Terms," page 272.

answer) or _Look over_ the answer (check the answer). Many of these two-word verbs, also called idioms, are defined in dictionaries. (For more on idioms, see p. 52.)

Some two-word verbs may be separated in a sentence; others may not.

Inseparable two-word verbs

Verbs and particles that may not be separated by any other words include the following: _catch on, get along, give in, go out, grow up, keep on, look into, run into, run out of, speak up, stay away, take care of._

> Faulty   Children <u>grow</u> quickly <u>up</u>.
> Revised Children <u>grow up</u> quickly.

Separable two-word verbs

Most two-word verbs that take **direct objects**° may be separated by the object.

> Parents <u>help out</u> their children.
> Parents <u>help</u> their children <u>out</u>.

If the direct object is a **pronoun**,° the pronoun _must_ separate the verb from the particle.

> Faulty   Parents <u>help out</u> them.
> Revised Parents <u>help</u> them <u>out</u>.

The separable two-word verbs include the following: _call off, call up, fill out, fill up, give away, give back, hand in, help out, look over, look up, pick up, point out, put away, put back, put off, take out, take over, try on, try out, turn down._

12 Verb Tenses

The **tense** of a verb expresses the time its action occurred. Definitions and examples of the verb tenses appear on pages 281–82. The following are the most common trouble spots.

12a Uses of the present tense (_sing_)

The present tense has several distinctive uses:

Action occurring now
We <u>define</u> the problem differently.

Habitual or recurring action
Banks regularly <u>undergo</u> audits.

MyWritingLab

Visit **MyWritingLab** for more help with verb tenses.

°See "Grammar Terms," page 272.

12a (margin)

A general truth
The earth <u>is</u> round.

Discussion of literature, film, and so on
Hagar Shipley <u>realizes</u> that pride and fear prevent her from experiencing love and joy.

Future time
Funding <u>ends</u> in less than a year.

12b Uses of the perfect tenses (*have/had/will have sung*)

The **perfect tenses**° generally indicate an action completed before another specific time or action. The **present perfect tense**° also indicates action begun in the past and continued into the present.

present perfect
The dancer <u>has performed</u> here only once.
present perfect
The dancer <u>had trained</u> in Asia before his performance here ten years ago.
future perfect
He <u>will have danced</u> here again by the end of the year.

12c Consistency in tense

Within a sentence, the tenses of verbs and verb forms need not be identical as long as they reflect actual changes in time: *Carlo <u>will graduate</u> from university twenty years after his father <u>arrived</u> in Canada.* In speech we often shift tenses even when they don't reflect changes in time. But in writing such needless shifts in tense will confuse or distract readers.

Inconsistent	After weeks of preparation, the Canadian Corps <u>attacked</u> the German trenches at Vimy Ridge during Easter 1917. The Canadian troops, who <u>fight</u> together for the first time at Vimy, <u>lose</u> over ten thousand men in the battle.
Revised	After weeks of preparation, the Canadian Corps <u>attacked</u> the German trenches at Vimy Ridge during Easter 1917. The Canadian troops, who <u>fought</u> together for the first time at Vimy, <u>lost</u> over ten thousand men in the battle.

12d Sequence of tenses

When the tenses in a sentence are in **sequence**, the verbs in the **main clause**° and the **subordinate clause**° relate appropriately for meaning. Problems with tense sequence often occur with the past tense and **past perfect tense.**°

°See "Grammar Terms," page 272.

12d

Faulty   Researchers <u>tried</u> to review the study, but many of the original participants <u>died</u>.
past
past

Revised   Researchers <u>tried</u> to review the study, but many of the original participants <u>had died</u>. [The deaths had occurred before the review.]
past
past perfect

Faulty   Because other participants <u>refused</u> interviews, the review <u>had been terminated</u>.
past
past perfect

Revised   Because other participants <u>had refused</u> interviews, the review <u>was terminated</u>. [The refusal occurred before the termination.]
past perfect
past

13a

Other tense-sequence problems occur with the distinctive verb forms of **conditional sentences**, in which a subordinate clause begins *if*, *when*, or *unless* and the main clause states the result.

Faulty   If voters <u>have</u> more confidence, they <u>would vote</u> more often.
present
would + verb

Revised   If voters <u>had</u> more confidence, they <u>would vote</u> more often.
past
would + verb

See the next chapter for more on conditional sentences.

13 Verb Mood

The **mood** of a verb indicates whether a sentence is a statement or a question (*The theatre <u>needs</u> help. <u>Can</u> you <u>help</u> the theatre?*), a command (*<u>Help</u> the theatre*), or a suggestion, desire, or other nonfactual expression (*I wish I <u>were</u> an actor*).

13a Subjunctive mood: *I wish I were*

The **subjunctive mood** expresses a suggestion, requirement, or desire, or it states a condition that is contrary to fact (that is, imaginary or hypothetical).

- Suggestion or requirement with the verb *ask, insist, urge, require, recommend,* or *suggest*: use the verb's **plain form**° with all subjects.

Rules require that every donation <u>be</u> mailed.

MyWritingLab

Visit **MyWritingLab** for more help with verb mood.

°See "Grammar Terms," page 272.

- **Desire or present condition contrary to fact**: use the verb's **past-tense form**;° for *be,* use the past-tense form *were* with all subjects.

If the theatre <u>were</u> in better shape and <u>had</u> more money, its future would be guaranteed.

I wish I <u>were</u> able to donate money.

- **Past condition contrary to fact**: use the verb's **past perfect form**° (*had* + **past participle**°).

The theatre would have been better funded if it <u>had been</u> better managed.

Note In a sentence expressing a condition contrary to fact, (1) use *have,* not *of,* after *would* or *could* in the main clause; and (2) do not use *would* or *could* in the subordinate clause:

Faulty	People <u>would of</u> helped if they <u>would have</u> known.
Revised	People <u>would have</u> helped if they <u>had</u> known.

13b Consistency in mood

Shifts in mood within a sentence or among related sentences can be confusing. Such shifts occur most frequently in directions.

Inconsistent	<u>Dissolve</u> the crystals in the liquid. Then <u>you should heat</u> the solution to 120°C. [The first sentence is a command, the second a statement.]
Revised	<u>Dissolve</u> the crystals in the liquid. Then <u>heat</u> the solution to 120°C. [Consistent commands.]

14 Verb Voice

The voice of a verb tells whether the **subject**° of the sentence performs the action (**active voice**) or is acted upon (**passive voice**).

Active voice	The administration <u>increased</u> the library's budget.
Passive voice	The library's budget <u>was increased</u> by the administration.

MyWritingLab

Visit **MyWritingLab** for more help with verb voice.

°See "Grammar Terms," page 272.

14a Active voice vs. passive voice

The active voice always names the actor in a sentence, whereas the passive voice puts the actor in a phrase after the verb or even omits the actor altogether. Thus the active voice is usually more clear, emphatic, and concise than the passive voice.

Weak passive   The <u>library</u> <u>is used</u> by both students and teachers for studying and research, and the <u>plan</u> to expand it <u>has been praised</u> by many.

Strong active   Both <u>students and teachers</u> <u>use</u> the library for studying and research, and <u>many</u> <u>have praised</u> the plan to expand it.

The passive voice is useful in two situations: when the actor is unknown and when the actor is unimportant or less important than the object of the action.

14b

The Internet <u>was established</u> in 1969 by the US Department of Defense. The network <u>has been extended</u> internationally. [In the first sentence the writer wishes to stress the Internet. In the second sentence the actor is unknown or too complicated to name.]

After the solution <u>had been cooled</u> to 10°C, the acid <u>was added</u>. [The person who cooled and added, perhaps the writer, is less important than the actions. Passive sentences are common in scientific writing.]

Note Some writers use the passive voice because they mistakenly believe it sounds more sophisticated than the active voice or because they want to avoid assigning responsibility for an action: *The library hours were reduced.* (In fact, the manager cut the hours.) The passive voice conveys the passivity of the subject: *He was crushed by the bus.* (He didn't crush himself.)

The passive voice can be useful, however, when naming the actor is undesirable. Particularly in sensitive correspondence, this use of the passive can avoid offending readers because a specific actor is not named.

The residents of the shelter <u>were turned away</u> from your coffee shop.

14b Consistency in voice

A shift in voice (and subject) within or between sentences can be awkward or even confusing.

Inconsistent   Internet <u>blogs</u> <u>cover</u> an enormous range of topics. <u>Opportunities</u> for people to discuss pet issues <u>are provided</u> on these sites.

Revised   Internet <u>blogs</u> <u>cover</u> an enormous range of topics <u>and provide</u> opportunities for people to discuss pet issues.

15 Subject-Verb Agreement

A **subject**° and its **verb**° should agree in **number**°—singular with singular, plural with plural.

Cape Breton artists excel at traditional Celtic music.
  subject verb

Natalie MacMaster is a superb fiddler.
  subject   verb

15a -s ending for noun *or* verb, but not both

An *-s* or *-es* ending does opposite things to nouns and verbs: it usually makes a noun *plural*, but it always makes a present-tense verb *singular*. Thus if the subject noun is plural, it will probably end in *-s* or *-es* and the verb will not. If the subject is singular, it will not end in *-s* and the verb will.

15b

Singular noun	Plural noun
The boy plays.	The boys play.
The bird soars.	The birds soar.
The street is busy.	The streets are busy.
The town has a school.	The towns have a school.
The new light does not [or doesn't] help.	The new lights do not [or don't] help.

ESL Most noncount nouns—those that do not form plurals—take singular verbs: *That information is helpful.* (See pp. 78–79 for more on noncount nouns.)

15b Words between subject and verb

The survival of hibernating frogs in freezing temperatures is [not are] fascinating.

A chemical reaction inside the cells of the frogs stops [not stop] the formation of ice crystals.

Phrases beginning with *as well as, together with, along with,* and *in addition to* do not change the number of the subject.

The president, together with the deans, has [not have] agreed to improve the computer labs.

MyWritingLab
Visit MyWritingLab for more help with subject-verb agreement.

°See "Grammar Terms," page 272.

15c Subjects with *and*

Frost and Roethke were American poets who died in the same year.

Note When *each* or *every* precedes the compound subject, the verb is usually singular.

Each man, woman, and child has a right to be heard.

15d Subjects with *or* or *nor*

When parts of a subject are joined by *or* or *nor*, the verb agrees with the nearer part.

Either the painter or the carpenter knows the cost.

The cabinets or the bookcases are too costly.

When one part of the subject is singular and the other is plural, the sentence will be awkward unless you put the plural part second.

Awkward   Neither the owners nor the builder agrees.

Improved   Neither the builder nor the owners agree.

15e *Everyone* and other indefinite pronouns

Indefinite pronouns° include *anybody, anyone, each, everybody, everyone, neither, no one, one,* and *somebody.* Most are singular in meaning and take singular verbs.

Something smells.   Neither is right.

A few indefinite pronouns such as *all, any, none,* and *some* may take a singular or plural verb depending on whether the word they refer to is singular or plural.

All of the money is reserved for emergencies.

All of the funds are reserved for emergencies.

15f *Team* and other collective nouns

A **collective noun°** such as *team* or *family* takes a singular verb when the group acts as a unit.

The team has won five of the last six meets.

But when the group's members act separately, use a plural verb.

The old team have gone their separate ways.

°See "Grammar Terms," page 272.

If the sentence above seems awkward, reword it: *The members of the old team have gone their separate ways.*

15g *Who, which,* and *that*

When used as subjects, *who, which,* and *that* refer to another word in the sentence. The verb agrees with this other word.

Mayor Garber ought to listen to the people who <u>work</u> for her.

Bardini is the only aide who <u>has</u> her ear.

Bardini is one of the aides who <u>work</u> unpaid. [Of the aides who work unpaid, Bardini is one.]

Bardini is the only one of the aides who <u>knows</u> the community. [Of the aides, only one, Bardini, knows the community.]

15h *News* and other singular nouns ending in *-s*

Singular **nouns**° ending in *-s* include *athletics, economics, mathematics, measles, mumps, news, physics, politics,* and *statistics.* They take singular verbs.

After so long a wait, the news <u>has</u> to be good.

Statistics <u>is</u> required of psychology majors.

These words take plural verbs when they describe individual items rather than bodies of activity or knowledge.

The statistics <u>prove</u> him wrong.

The mayor's politics <u>are</u> controversial.

15i Verb preceding subject

<u>Is</u> voting a right or a privilege?

<u>Are</u> a right and a privilege the same thing?

There <u>are</u> differences between them.

Here <u>are</u> some possible solutions.

15j *Is, are,* and other linking verbs

Make a **linking verb**° agree with its subject, usually the first element in the sentence, not with other words referring to the subject.

The child's sole support <u>is</u> her court-appointed guardians.

Her court-appointed guardians <u>are</u> the child's sole support.

°See "Grammar Terms," page 272.

PRONOUNS

16 Pronoun Forms

A **noun°** or **pronoun°** changes form to show the reader how it functions in a sentence. These forms—called **cases**—are **subjective** (such as *I, she, they, man*), **objective** (such as *me, her, them, man*), and **possessive** (such as *my, her, their, man's*). A list of the case forms appears on pages 272–73.

16a Compound subjects and objects: *she and I* vs. *her and me*

Subjects° and **objects°** consisting of two or more nouns and pronouns have the same case forms as they would if one pronoun stood alone.

compound subject
She and Ming discussed the proposal.

compound object
The proposal disappointed her and him.

To test for the correct form, try one pronoun alone in the sentence. The case form that sounds correct is probably correct for all parts of the compound.

The prize went to [he, him] and [I, me].
The prize went to him.
The prize went to him and me.

16b Subject complements: *it was she*

Both a subject and a **subject complement°** appear in the same form—the subjective case.

subject complement
The one who cares most is she.

If this construction sounds stilted to you, use the more natural order: *She is the one who cares most.*

16c *Who* vs. *whom*

The choice between *who* and *whom* depends on the use of the word.

MyWritingLab
Visit **MyWritingLab** for more help with pronoun forms.

°See "Grammar Terms," page 272.

Questions

At the beginning of a question, use *who* for a subject and *whom* for an object.

subject↘   object◀

<u>Who</u> wrote the policy? <u>Whom</u> does it affect?

Test for the correct form by answering the question with the form of *he* or *she* that sounds correct. Then use the same form in the question.

[<u>Who, Whom</u>] does one ask?
One asks <u>her</u>.
<u>Whom</u> does one ask?

Subordinate clauses

In a **subordinate clause**,° use *who* or *whoever* for a subject, *whom* or *whomever* for an object.

subject↘

Give old clothes to <u>whoever</u> needs them.

object◀

I don't know <u>whom</u> the mayor appointed.

Test for the correct form by rewriting the sub-ordinate clause as a sentence. Replace *who* or *whom* with the form of *he* or *she* that sounds correct. Then use the same form in the original subordinate clause.

Few people know [<u>who, whom</u>] they should ask.
They should ask <u>her</u>.
Few people know <u>whom</u> they should ask.

Note Don't let expressions such as *I think* and *she says* confuse you when they come between the subject *who* and its verb.

subject↘

He is the one <u>who</u> I think is best qualified.

16d Other constructions

We or *us* with a noun

The choice of *we* or *us* before a noun depends on the use of the noun.

object of preposition↗

Freezing weather is welcomed by <u>us</u> skaters.

subject↗

<u>We</u> skaters welcome freezing weather.

Pronoun in an appositive

An **appositive** is a word or word group that renames a noun or pronoun. Within an appositive the form of a pronoun depends on the function of the word the appositive renames.

°See "Grammar Terms," page 272.

object of verb

The class elected two representatives, Samir and me.

subject

Two representatives, Samir and I, were elected.

Pronoun after *than* or *as*

After *than* or *as* in a comparison, the form of a pronoun indicates what words may have been omitted. A subjective pronoun is the subject of the omitted verb:

subject

Some critics like Glass more than she [does].

An objective pronoun is the object of the omitted verb:

object

Some critics like Glass more than [they like] her.

Subject and object of an infinitive

An **infinitive** is the **plain form°** of the verb plus *to* (*to swim*). Both its object and its subject are in the objective form.

subject of
infinitive

The school asked him to speak.

object of
infinitive

Students chose to invite him.

Form before a gerund

A **gerund** is the *-ing* form of a verb used as a noun (*a runner's breathing*). Generally, use the possessive form of a pronoun or noun immediately before a gerund.

The coach disapproved of their lifting weights.

The coach's disapproving was a surprise.

17 Pronoun-Antecedent Agreement

The word a pronoun refers to is its **antecedent**.

Successful students complete their homework.

antecedent   pronoun

For clarity, a pronoun should agree with its antecedent in **person°** (first, second, third), **number°** (singular, plural), and **gender°** (masculine, feminine, neuter).

MyWritingLab

Visit **MyWritingLab** for more help
with pronoun-antecedent agreement.

°See "Grammar Terms," page 272.

17a Antecedents with *and*

The dean and my adviser have offered <u>their</u> help.

Note When *each* or *every* precedes the compound antecedent, the pronoun is singular.

Every girl and woman took <u>her</u> seat.

17b Antecedents with *or* or *nor*

When parts of an antecedent are joined by *or* or *nor*, the pronoun agrees with the nearer part.

Tenants or owners must present <u>their</u> grievances.

Either the tenant or the owner will have <u>her</u> way.

17c

When one subject is plural and the other singular, put the plural subject second to avoid awkwardness.

Neither the owner nor the tenants have made <u>their</u> case.

17c *Everyone, person,* and other indefinite words

Indefinite words do not refer to any specific person or thing. They include **indefinite pronouns**° (such as *anyone, everybody, everything, none, no one, somebody*) and **generic nouns**° (such as *person, individual, child, student*).

Most indefinite words are singular in meaning and take singular pronouns.

Everyone on the women's team now has <u>her</u> own locker.

Each of the men still has <u>his</u> own locker.

Though they are singular, indefinite words often seem to mean "many" or "all" rather than "one" and are mistakenly referred to with plural pronouns, as in *Everyone deserves <u>their</u> privacy.* Often, too, we mean indefinite words to include both masculine and feminine genders and thus resort to *they* instead of the **generic *he***—the masculine pronoun referring to both genders, which is generally regarded as sexist: *Everyone deserves <u>his</u> privacy.*

To achieve nonsexist agreement in such cases, you have several options:

- **Change the indefinite word to a plural, and use a plural pronoun to match.**

  Faulty   Each athlete is entitled to <u>his</u> own locker.

  Revised   <u>All athletes</u> are entitled to <u>their</u> own lockers. [*Is* changes to *are*, and *locker* changes to *lockers*.]

°See "Grammar Terms," page 272.

- **Rewrite the sentence to omit the pronoun.**

   Revised   Each athlete is entitled to <u>a</u> locker.

- **Use *he or she* (*him or her, his or her*) to refer to the indefinite word.**

   Revised   Each athlete is entitled to <u>his or her</u> own locker.

He or she can be awkward, so avoid using it more than once in several sentences. Also avoid the combination *he/she,* which many readers do not accept.

17d *Team* and other collective nouns

Use a singular pronoun with *team, family, group,* or another **collective noun°** when referring to the group as a unit.

   The committee voted to disband <u>itself</u>.

When referring to the individual members of the group, use a plural pronoun.

   The old team have gone <u>their</u> separate ways.

If such a sentence sounds awkward, reword it: *The <u>members</u> of the old team have gone their separate ways.*

18 Pronoun Reference

If a **pronoun°** does not refer clearly to the word it substitutes for (its **antecedent**), readers will have difficulty grasping the pronoun's meaning.

18a Single antecedent

When either of two nouns can be a pronoun's antecedent, the reference will not be clear.

   Confusing   Emily Dickinson is sometimes compared with Jane Austen, but <u>she</u> led a more reclusive life.

Revise such a sentence in one of two ways:

- **Replace the pronoun with the appropriate noun.**

°See "Grammar Terms," page 272.

Clear   Emily Dickinson is sometimes compared with Jane
             Austen, but <u>Dickinson</u> led a more reclusive life.

■ **Avoid repetition by rewriting the sentence.** If you use
the pronoun, make sure it has only one possible antecedent.

Clear   Despite occasional comparisons, Emily Dick-
             inson was more reclusive than Jane Austen.

Clear   Though sometimes compared with <u>her</u>, Emily

             Dickinson was more reclusive than Jane Austen.

18b Close antecedent

A **clause**° beginning *who, which,* or *that* should generally fall immediately after the word it refers to.

Confusing   Jody found a dress in the attic <u>that</u> her aunt
             had worn.

Clear   In the attic Jody found a dr<u>ess that</u> her aunt
             had worn.

18c Specific antecedent

A pronoun should refer to a specific **noun**° or other
pronoun. Readers can only guess at the meaning of a pronoun when its antecedent is not stated outright.

Vague *this, that, which,* or *it*

This, that, which, or *it* should refer to a specific noun,
not to a whole word group expressing an idea or situation.

Confusing   Lord Selkirk's attempt to establish the Red River
             Colony <u>was opposed</u> by the fur traders of the
             North West Company and their Metis allies,
             who <u>attacked</u> the colony. <u>This</u> led Selkirk to
             fight both on the battlefield and in the courts.

Clear   Lord Selkirk's attempt to establish the Red River
             Colony was opposed by the fur traders of the
             North West Company and their Metis allies,
             who attacked the colony. <u>This opposition</u> led
             Selkirk to fight both on the battlefield and in
             the courts.

Implied nouns

A pronoun cannot refer clearly to a noun that is
merely implied by some other word or phrase, such as
news in *newspaper* or *happiness* in *happy.*

°See "Grammar Terms," page 272.

18c

Confusing	In Cohen's report she made claims that led to a lawsuit.
Clear	In her report Cohen made claims that led to a lawsuit.
Confusing	Her reports on psychological development generally go unnoticed outside it.
Clear	Her reports on psychological development generally go unnoticed outside the field.

Indefinite *it, they,* or *you*

It and *they* should have definite antecedents.

| Confusing | In the average television drama they present a false picture of life. |
| Clear | The average television drama presents a false picture of life. |

You should clearly mean "you, the reader," and the context must support such a meaning.

| Inappropriate | In the fourteenth century you had to struggle to survive. |
| Revised | In the fourteenth century one [or a person or people] had to struggle to survive. |

18d Consistency in pronouns

Within a sentence or a group of related sentences, pronouns should be consistent. You may shift pronouns unconsciously when you start with *one* and soon find it too stiff.

| Inconsistent | One will find when reading that your concentration improves with practice, so that you comprehend more in less time. |
| Revised | You will find when reading that your concentration improves with practice, so that you comprehend more in less time. |

Inconsistent pronouns also occur when singular shifts to plural: *Everyone who reads regularly will improve his or her* [not *their*] *speed.* See pages 70–72.

18d

MODIFIERS

19 Adjectives and Adverbs

Adjectives modify **nouns**° (*good* child) and **pronouns**° (*special* someone). **Adverbs** modify **verbs**° (see *well*), adjectives (*very* happy), other adverbs (*not* very), and whole word groups (*Otherwise, the room was empty*). The only way to tell if a modifier should be an adjective or an adverb is to determine its function in the sentence.

19a Adjective vs. adverb

Use only adverbs, not adjectives, to modify verbs, adverbs, or other adjectives.

Not   They took each other <u>serious</u>. They related <u>good</u>.

But   They took each other <u>seriously</u>. They related <u>well</u>.

19b Adjective with linking verb: *felt bad*

A modifier after a verb should be an adverb only if it describes the verb. If the modifier follows a **linking verb**° and describes the subject, it should be an adjective.

Two word pairs are especially tricky. One is *bad* and *badly*:

The weather grew <u>bad</u>.
    linking adjective
    verb

She felt <u>bad</u>.
    linking adjective
    verb

Flowers grow <u>badly</u> in such soil.
   verb   adverb

The other word pair is *good* and *well*. *Good* serves only as an adjective. *Well* may serve as an adverb with a host of meanings or as an adjective meaning only "fit" or "healthy."

Decker trained <u>well</u>.
   verb   adverb

She felt <u>well</u>.
    linking adjective
    verb

Her health was <u>good</u>.
   linking   adjective
   verb

19b

°See "Grammar Terms," page 272.

19c Comparison of adjectives and adverbs

Comparison° allows adjectives and adverbs to show degrees of quality or amount by changing form: *red, redder, reddest; awful, more awful, most awful; quickly, less quickly, least quickly.* A dictionary will list the *-er* and *-est* endings if they can be used. Otherwise, use *more* and *most* or *less* and *least.*

Some modifiers are irregular, changing their spelling for comparison: for example, *good, better, best; many, more, most; badly, worse, worst.*

Comparisons of two or more than two

Use the *-er* form, *more,* or *less* when comparing two items. Use the *-est* form, *most,* or *least* when comparing three or more items.

19c

> Of the two tests, the litmus is <u>better</u>.
> Of all six tests, the litmus is <u>best</u>.

Double comparisons

A double comparison combines the *-er* or *-est* ending with the word *more* or *most.* It is redundant.

> Jacques was the <u>wisest</u> [not <u>most wisest</u>] person in town. He was <u>smarter</u> [not <u>more smarter</u>] than anyone else.

The adjective *unique* never takes an intensifier or modifier:

> His inventions were <u>unique</u> [not <u>very unique</u> or <u>quite unique</u>].

Complete comparisons

A comparison should be complete.

■ **The comparison should state a relation fully enough to ensure clarity.**

Unclear   Car makers worry about their industry more than environmentalists.

Clear   Car makers worry about their industry more than environmentalists <u>do</u>.

Clear   Car makers worry about their industry more than <u>they worry about</u> environmentalists.

■ **The items being compared should in fact be comparable.**

Illogical   The cost of a hybrid car can be greater than a gasoline-powered car. [Illogically compares a cost and a car.]

Revised   The cost of a hybrid car can be greater than <u>the cost of</u> [or <u>that of</u>] a gasoline-powered car.

°See "Grammar Terms," page 272.

19d Double negatives

In a **double negative** two negative words cancel each other out. Some double negatives are intentional, as *She was not unhappy* indicates with understatement that she was indeed happy. But most double negatives say the opposite of what is intended: *Jenny did not feel nothing* asserts that Jenny felt other than nothing, or something.

Faulty   The CRA cannot hardly audit all tax returns. None of its audits never touch many cheaters.

Revised   The CRA cannot audit all tax returns. Its audits never touch many cheaters.

19e Present and past participles as adjectives ESL

Both **present participles°** and **past participles°** may serve as adjectives: *a burning house, a burned house*. As in the examples, the two participles usually differ in the time they indicate.

But some present and past participles—those derived from verbs expressing feeling—can have altogether different meanings. The present participle refers to something that causes the feeling: *That was a frightening storm*. The past participle refers to something that experiences the feeling: *They quieted the frightened horses*. Similar pairs include the following:

annoying/annoyed	pleasing/pleased
boring/bored	satisfying/satisfied
confusing/confused	surprising/surprised
exciting/excited	tiring/tired
exhausting/exhausted	troubling/troubled
interesting/interested	worrying/worried

19f Articles: *a, an, the* ESL

Articles° usually trouble native English speakers only in the choice of *a* versus *an*: *a* for words beginning with consonant sounds (*a bridge*), *an* for words beginning with vowel sounds, including a silent *h* (*an apple, an hour*).

For nonnative speakers, *a, an,* and *the* can be difficult because many other languages use such words quite differently or not at all. In English, their uses depend on their context and the kinds of nouns they precede.

Singular count nouns

A **count noun** names something countable and can form a plural: *glass/glasses, mountain/mountains, child/children, woman/women*.

°See "Grammar Terms," page 272.

- *A* or *an* **precedes a singular count noun when your reader does not already know its identity**, usually because you have not mentioned it before.

    <u>A</u> scientist in our chemistry department developed <u>a</u> process to strengthen metals. [*Scientist* and *process* are being introduced for the first time.]

- *The* **precedes a singular count noun that has a specific identity for your reader**, usually because (1) you have mentioned it before, (2) you identify it immediately before or after you state it, (3) it is unique (the only one in existence), or (4) it refers to an institution or facility that is shared by the community.

19f

    A scientist in our chemistry department developed a process to strengthen metals. <u>The</u> scientist patented <u>the</u> process. [*Scientist* and *process* were identified before.]

    <u>The</u> most productive laboratory is <u>the</u> research centre in <u>the</u> chemistry department. [*Most productive* identifies *laboratory*. *In the chemistry department* identifies *research centre*. And *chemistry department* is a shared facility.]

    <u>The</u> sun rises in <u>the</u> east. [*Sun* and *east* are unique.]

    Some men and women aspire to <u>the</u> priesthood. [*Priesthood* is a shared institution.]

Plural count nouns

A or *an* never precedes a plural noun. *The* does not precede a plural noun that names a general category. *The* does precede a plural noun that names specific representatives of a category.

    <u>Men</u> and <u>women</u> are different. [*Men* and *women* name general categories.]

    <u>The</u> women joined a team. [*Women* refers to specific people.]

Noncount nouns

A **noncount noun** names something that is not usually considered countable in English, and so it does not form a plural. Examples include the following:

Abstractions: confidence, democracy, education, equality, evidence, health, information, intelligence, knowledge, luxury, peace, pollution, research, success, supervision, truth, wealth, work

Emotions: anger, courage, happiness, hate, love, respect, satisfaction

Food and drink: bread, flour, meat, milk, salt, water, wine

Natural events and substances: air, blood, dirt, gasoline, gold, hair, heat, ice, oil, oxygen, rain, smoke, wood

Groups: clergy, clothing, equipment, furniture, garbage, jewellery, junk, legislation, mail, military, money, police
Fields of study: architecture, accounting, biology, business, chemistry, engineering, literature, psychology, science

A or *an* never precedes a noncount noun. *The* does precede a noncount noun that names specific representatives of a general category.

Vegetation suffers from drought. [*Vegetation* names a general category.]

The vegetation in the park withered or died. [*Vegetation* refers to specific plants.]

Note Many nouns are sometimes count nouns and sometimes noncount nouns.

The library has a room for readers. [*Room* is a count noun meaning "walled area."]

The library has room for reading. [*Room* is a noncount noun meaning "space."]

Proper nouns

A **proper noun** names a particular person, place, or thing and begins with a capital letter: *February, Joe Allen. A* or *an* never precedes a proper noun. *The* does occasionally, as with oceans (*the* Pacific), regions (*the* Middle East), rivers (*the* Fraser), some countries (*the* United States), and some universities (*the* University of Toronto).

Ian lives in Fredericton and attends the University of New Brunswick.

20 Misplaced and Dangling Modifiers

For clarity, modifiers generally must fall close to the words they modify.

20a Misplaced modifiers

A **misplaced modifier** falls in the wrong place in a sentence. It may be awkward, confusing, or even unintentionally funny.

20a

MyWritingLab

Visit MyWritingLab for more help with misplaced and dangling modifiers.

Clear placement

Confusing	He served steak to the men on paper plates.
Revised	He served the men steak on paper plates.
Confusing	Many dogs are killed by autos and trucks roaming unleashed.
Revised	Many dogs roaming unleashed are killed by autos and trucks.

Only and other limiting modifiers

Limiting modifiers include *almost, even, exactly, hardly, just, merely, nearly, only, scarcely,* and *simply*. They should fall immediately before the word or word group they modify.

20a

Unclear	They <u>only</u> saw each other during meals.
Revised	They saw <u>only</u> each other during meals.
Revised	They saw each other <u>only</u> during meals.

Infinitives and other grammatical units

Some grammatical units should generally not be split by long modifiers. For example, a long **adverb**° between **subject**° and **verb**° can be awkward and confusing.

Awkward	The Canucks, after losing the first game, went on to win the series.
Revised	After losing the the first game, the Canucks went on to win the series.

A **split infinitive**—a modifier placed between *to* and the verb—can be especially awkward and will annoy many readers.

Awkward	Farmers expected temperatures to <u>not</u> rise.
Revised	Farmers expected temperatures <u>not</u> to rise.

A split infinitive may sometimes be unavoidable without rewriting, though it may still bother some readers.

Several industries expect to <u>more than</u> triple their use of robots.

Order of adjectives ESL

English follows distinctive rules for arranging two or three adjectives before a noun. (A string of more than three adjectives before a noun is rare.) The adjectives follow this order:

Determiner	Opinion	Size or shape	Colour	Origin	Material	Noun used as adjective	Noun
many						state	**laws**
	lovely		green	Thai			**birds**
a		square			wooden		**table**
all						business	**reports**
the			blue		litmus		**paper**

20b Dangling modifiers

A **dangling modifier** does not sensibly modify anything in its sentence.

Dangling   Passing the building, the vandalism became visible.

Like most dangling modifiers, this one introduces a sentence, contains a verb form (*passing*), and implies but does not name a subject (whoever is passing). Readers assume that this implied subject is the same as the subject of the sentence (*vandalism*). When it is not, the modifier "dangles" unconnected to the rest of the sentence.

Revise dangling modifiers to achieve the emphasis you want.

- Rewrite the dangling modifier as a complete clause with its own stated subject and verb. Readers can accept different subjects when they are both stated.

    Dangling   Passing the building, the vandalism became visible.

    Revised   As we passed the building, the vandalism became visible.

- Change the subject of the sentence to a word the modifier properly describes.

    Dangling   Trying to understand the causes, vandalism has been extensively studied.

    Revised   Trying to understand the causes, researchers have extensively studied vandalism.

20b

SENTENCE FAULTS

21 Sentence Fragments

A **sentence fragment** is part of a sentence that is set off as if it were a whole sentence by an initial capital letter and a final period or other end punctuation. Although writers occasionally use fragments deliberately and effectively, readers perceive most fragments as serious errors in standard English. Use the tests below to ensure that you have linked or separated your ideas both appropriately for your meaning and correctly, without creating sentence fragments.

ESL Some languages other than English allow the omission of the **subject**° or the **verb**.° Except in commands (*Close the door*), English always requires you to state the subject and verb.

21a Tests for fragments

Use the following tests to ensure that you have correctly set off word groups as sentences—without creating sentence fragments. A word group punctuated as a sentence should pass *all three* of the following tests. If it does not, it is a fragment and needs to be revised.

Test 1: Find the verb.

A complete sentence requires a predicate **verb**° that asserts something about the subject. Some sentence fragments lack any verb form:

Fragment	Millions of sites on the Web.
Revised	Millions of sites <u>make up</u> the Web.

Other sentence fragments contain a verb form, but it is not a predicate verb. Instead, it is often the *-ing* or *to* form (*walking, to walk*):

Fragment	The Web <u>growing</u> with new sites and users every day.
Revised	The Web <u>grows</u> with new sites and users every day.

(See also pp. 56–58 on the use of **helping verbs**° to prevent sentence fragments.)

MyWritingLab

Visit MyWritingLab for more help with sentence fragments.

°See "Grammar Terms," page 272.

21a

Test 2: Find the subject.

The subject of the sentence will usually come before the verb. If there is no subject, the word group is probably a fragment.

Fragment	The Web continues to grow. <u>And shows no sign of slowing down</u>.
Revised	The Web continues to grow. And <u>it</u> shows no sign of slowing down.

Note Commands, in which the subject *you* is understood, are not sentence fragments: [*You*] *Close the door.*

Test 3: Make sure the clause is not subordinate.

A **subordinate clause** begins with either a **subordinating conjunction**° (such as *because, if, when*) or a **relative pronoun**° (*who, which, that*). Subordinate clauses serve as parts of sentences, not as whole sentences.

Fragment	The Internet was greatly improved by Web technology. <u>Which allows users to move easily between sites</u>.
Revised	The Internet was greatly improved by Web technology, which allows users to move easily between sites. [The subordinate clause joins a main clause in a complete sentence.]
Revised	The Internet was greatly improved by Web technology. It allows users to move easily between sites. [Substituting *It* for *Which* makes the subordinate clause into a complete sentence.]

Note Questions beginning *who, whom,* or *which* are not sentence fragments: *Who rattled the cage?*

21b Revision of fragments

Correct sentence fragments in one of two ways, depending on the importance of the information in the fragment:

- **Rewrite the fragment as a complete sentence**. The information in the fragment will then have the same importance as that in other complete sentences.

Fragment	The Internet was a true innovation. <u>Because no expansive computer network existed before it</u>.
Revised	The Internet was a true innovation. No expansive computer network existed before it. [Deleting *Because* makes the fragment into a complete sentence.]

°See "Grammar Terms," page 272.

■ **Combine the fragment with the appropriate main clause**. The information in the fragment will then be subordinated to that in the main clause.

Fragment   The Web is easy to use. <u>Loaded with links and graphics</u>.

Revised   The Web, <u>loaded with links and graphics</u>, is easy to use.

22 Comma Splices and Fused Sentences

22a

When you combine two complete sentences (**main clauses**°) in one sentence, you need to give readers a clear signal that one clause is ending and the other beginning. Two common errors fail to give this signal. In a **comma splice** two main clauses are joined (or spliced) only by a comma, which is usually too weak to signal the link between main clauses.

Comma   The Stanley Cup playoffs are over, we'd better
splice   get back to the library.

In a **fused sentence** (or **run-on sentence**) the clauses are not separated at all.

Fused   The Stanley Cup playoffs are over we'd better
sentence   get back to the library.

You can repair comma splices and fused sentences with coordination or subordination (pp. 37–39) and at the same time clarify the relations between the clauses.

22a Main clauses without *and, but, or, nor, for, so, yet*

Two main clauses in a sentence are usually separated with a comma and a **coordinating conjunction**° such as *and* or *but*. These signals tell readers to expect another main clause. When one or both signals are missing, the sentence may be confusing and may require rereading. Revise it in one of the following ways:

■ **Insert a coordinating conjunction when the ideas in the main clauses are closely related and equally important**.

Comma   Some laboratory-grown foods taste good, they
splice   are nutritious.

MyWritingLab

Visit **MyWritingLab** for more help with comma splices and fused sentences.

°See "Grammar Terms," page 272.

Revised	Some laboratory-grown foods taste good, <u>and</u> they are nutritious.

In a fused sentence, insert a comma and a coordinating conjunction.

Fused sentence	Chemists have made much progress they still have a way to go.
Revised	Chemists have made much progress, <u>but</u> they still have a way to go.

- **Insert a semicolon between clauses if the relation between the ideas is very close and obvious without a conjunction to show the precise relationship.**

Comma splice	Good taste is rare in laboratory-grown vegetables, they are usually bland.
Revised	Good taste is rare in laboratory-grown vegetables; they are usually bland.

22b

- **Make the clauses into separate sentences when the ideas expressed are only loosely related.**

Comma splice	Chemistry has contributed to our understanding of foods, many foods such as wheat and beans can be produced in the laboratory.
Revised	Chemistry has contributed to our understanding of foods. Many foods such as wheat and beans can be produced in the laboratory.

- **Subordinate one clause to the other when one idea is less important than the other.** The subordinate clause will modify something in the main clause.

Comma splice	The vitamins are adequate, the flavour and colour are deficient.
Revised	<u>Even though</u> the vitamins are adequate, the flavour and colour are deficient.

22b Main clauses related by *however, for example,* and so on

However and *for example* are **transitional expressions**° that can describe how one main clause relates to another. (See page 282 for additional examples.)

When most transitional expressions relate two main clauses, the clauses must be separated by a period or by a semicolon. The connecting word or phrase is usually set off by a comma or commas.

Comma splice	Most Canadians refuse to give up unhealthful habits, consequently our medical costs are higher than necessary.

°See "Grammar Terms," page 272.

| Revised | Most Canadians refuse to give up unhealthful habits. Consequently, our medical costs are higher than necessary. |
| Revised | Most Canadians refuse to give up unhealthful habits; consequently, our medical costs are higher than necessary. |

To test whether a word or phrase is a transitional expression, try moving it around in its clause. A transitional expression can move, whereas coordinating conjunctions (such as *and* or *but*) cannot.

Most Canadians refuse to give up unhealthful habits; our medical costs, consequently, are higher than necessary.

22b

PART 4

Punctuation

Essential
Punctuation

This list focuses on the most troublesome punctuation marks and uses, showing correctly punctuated sentences with brief explanations. For the other marks and other uses covered in this part, see "Detailed Contents" inside the back cover.

The Comma

- Subways are convenient , but they are costly to build.
  Subways are convenient but costly.
  [With *and, but,* etc., only between main clauses. See opposite.]

- Because of their cost , new subways are rarely built.
  [With an introductory element. See opposite.]

- Light rail , which is less costly , is often more feasible.
  Those who favour mass transit often propose light rail.
  [With a nonessential element, not with an essential element. See p. 90.]

- In a few older cities, commuters can choose from subways , buses , light rail , and railroads.
  [Separating items in a series. See pp. 91.]

The Semicolon

- She chose carpentry ; she wanted manual work.

  She had a law degree ; however, she became a carpenter.
  [Between main clauses not joined by *and, but,* etc., and those joined by *however, for example,* etc. See pp. 94–95.]

The Colon

- The school has one goal : to train businesspeople.
  [With a main clause to introduce information. See p. 95.]

The Apostrophe

- Jay Smith 's dog saved the life of the Joneses ' child.
  [Showing possession: -'s for singular nouns; -' alone for plural nouns ending in -s. See pp. 96–97.]

- Its [for The dog 's] bark warned the family. It 's [for It is] an intelligent dog.
  They 're [for They are] happy that their [the Joneses'] child is safe.

  [Not with possessive pronouns, only with contractions. See pp. 97–98.]

Quotation marks

- She asked, " Why did you do it ?"
  Kate Chopin uses irony in " The Story of an Hour ."
  [With direct quotations, with certain titles, and with other punctuation marks. See pp. 99–101.]

23 The Comma

The comma helps to separate sentence elements and to prevent misreading. Its main uses (and misuses) appear in this chapter.

23a Comma with *and, but, or, nor, for, so, yet*

Comma between main clauses

Use a comma before *and, but, or, nor, for, so,* and *yet* (the **coordinating conjunctions**°) when they link **main clauses**.°

> Banks offer many services, but they could do more.
> Many banks offer investment advice, and they may help small businesses establish credit.

Note The comma goes before, not after, the coordinating conjunction.

No comma between words, phrases, or subordinate clauses

Generally, do not use a comma before *and, but, or,* and *nor* when they link pairs of words, **phrases**,° or **subordinate clauses**°—that is, elements other than main clauses.

> Not   One bank established special accounts for older depositors, and counselled them on investments.
> But   One bank established special accounts for older depositors and counselled them on investments.

23b Comma with introductory elements

Use a comma after most elements that begin sentences and are distinct from the main clause.

> When times are uncertain, futurists multiply.
> Fortunately, some news is good.

You may omit the comma after a short introductory element if there's no risk that the reader will run the introductory element and main clause together: *By 2020 we may have reduced pollution.*

Note The **subject**° of a sentence is not an introductory element but a part of the main clause. Never use a comma to separate the subject and its verb.

23b

MyWritingLab

Visit **MyWritingLab** for more help with the comma.

°See "Grammar Terms," page 272.

Not   Some <u>pessimists, may</u> be disappointed.

But   Some <u>pessimists ● may</u> be disappointed.

23c Comma or commas with interrupting and concluding elements

Use a comma or commas to set off information that could be deleted without altering the basic meaning of the sentence.

Note When such optional information falls in the middle of the sentence, be sure to use one comma *before* and one *after* it.

Commas around nonessential elements

A **nonessential** (or **nonrestrictive**) **element** adds information about a word in the sentence but does not limit (or restrict) the word to a particular individual or group. Omitting the underlined element from any sentence below would remove incidental details but would not affect the sentence's basic meaning.

Nonessential modifiers

My cousin Len ● <u>who lives in Red Deer</u> ● came for the wedding.

I hadn't seen Len ● <u>a busy engineer</u> ● in a decade.

Nonessential appositives

Appositives are words or word groups that rename nouns.

Len's company ● <u>an international consulting firm</u> ● sends him all over the world.

His wife ● <u>Françoise</u> ● sometimes joins him.
[Len has only one wife, so her name merely adds nonessential information about her.]

No commas around essential elements

Do not use commas to set off **essential** (or **restrictive**) **elements**: modifiers and appositives that contain information essential to the meaning of the sentence. Omitting the underlined element from any of the following sentences would alter the meaning substantially, leaving the sentence unclear or too general.

Essential modifiers

My cousin ● <u>from Red Deer</u> ● came, but my ● cousin ● <u>from Yellowknife</u> ● couldn't attend.

She couldn't come ● <u>because she had broken her leg</u>.

The motel ● <u>where Len stayed</u> ● had a great pool.

23c

Essential appositives
The band from the university played all afternoon.
My parents danced to the song "Yesterday."

Commas around absolute phrases

An **absolute phrase** usually consists of the *-ing* form of a verb plus a subject for the verb. The phrase modifies the whole main clause of the sentence.

Many students, their debts mounting, worry about student loans.

Commas around transitional or parenthetical expressions

A **transitional expression**° such as *however, for example,* or *of course* forms a link between ideas. It is nonessential and is usually set off with a comma or commas.

Some students, in fact, graduate owing thousands.

A **parenthetical expression**° provides supplementary information not essential for meaning. Examples are *fortunately, to be frank,* and *all things considered.* Such an expression may be enclosed in parentheses (see p. 103) or, for more emphasis, in commas.

Most students, fortunately, are able to repay their loans.

Note Do not add a comma after a **coordinating conjunction**° (*and, but,* and so on) or a **subordinating conjunction**° (*although, because,* and so on). To distinguish between these words and transitional or parenthetical expressions, try moving the word or expression around in its clause. Transitional or parenthetical expressions can be moved; coordinating and subordinating conjunctions cannot.

Commas around phrases of contrast

Students should focus on education, not work.

Commas around *yes* and *no*

Provinces should recognize that, yes, education is expensive.

Commas around words of direct address

Heed this lesson, readers.

23d Commas with series

Commas between series items

Use commas to separate the items in lists or series.

The names Belia, Beelzebub, and Lucifer sound ominous.

°See "Grammar Terms," page 272.

The comma before the last item in a series (before *and*), also known as the Oxford comma or the Harvard comma, is optional, but it is never wrong and it is usually clearer.

No commas around series

Do not use a comma *before* or *after* a series.

Not   The skills of, hunting, foraging, and agriculture, sustained the Plains Aboriginal people.

But   The skills of hunting, foraging, and agriculture sustained the Plains Aboriginal people.

23e Comma with adjectives

Comma between equal adjectives

Use a comma between two or more **adjectives**° when each one modifies the same word equally. As a test, such adjectives could be joined by *and*.

The book had a worn, cracked binding.

No comma between unequal adjectives

Do not use a comma between adjectives when one forms a unit with the modified word. As a test, the two adjectives could not sensibly be joined by *and*.

The study examined the eye movements of healthy young men.

The researchers watched for one specific movement.

23f Commas with dates, addresses, place names, numbers

When they appear within sentences, elements punctuated with commas are also ended with commas.

Dates

On July 1, 1967, Canada celebrated its centennial. [Note that commas appear before *and* after the year.]

The Canadian Expeditionary Force reached France in February 1915. [No comma is needed between a month or season and a year.]

Addresses and place names

Use the address 49 Front Street, St. John's, Newfoundland and Labrador A1E 2Y2, for all correspondence. [No comma is needed between the name of the province and the postal code.]

Numbers

In scientific usage, metric numbers require spaces instead of commas, but in nontechnical usage, some writers continue to use commas. (See also p. 118.)

°See "Grammar Terms," page 272.

When completed, the Trans Canada Trail will consist of over 17,000 km of linked recreational trails running from St. John's, NL, to Victoria, BC.

Our local organizing committee raised nearly $10,000 for our portion of the trail.

One anonymous donor contributed $2,000,000 to the project.

Note It is common in Quebec, even in English documents, to see numbers written in international style with a comma instead of a decimal point and the currency sign after the number:

The newer model costs 129,95$.

23g Commas with quotations

A comma or commas usually separate a quotation from a signal phrase that identifies the source, such as *she said* or *he replied*.

Marshall McLuhan said, "The medium is the message."

"Knowledge is power," wrote Francis Bacon.

"You don't need a weatherman," sings Bob Dylan, "to know which way the wind blows."

Exceptions Do not use commas with signal phrases in the following situations:

- **Use a semicolon or a period after a signal phrase that interrupts a quotation between main clauses.** The choice depends on the punctuation of the original:

  "That part of my life was over," she wrote; "his words had sealed it shut."

  "That part of my life was over," she wrote. "His words had sealed it shut."

- **Use a colon when a complete sentence introduces a quotation:**

  Her statement was clear: "I will not resign."

- **Omit commas when a quotation is integrated into your sentence structure,** including a quotation introduced by *that:*

  Vicki Crowchild said that "a lot of people got healed just by telling their story."

  Calvin Bruneau hopes that the Truth and Reconciliation Commission "leads to better all-around relations between First Nations people and the government."

23g

24 The Semicolon

The semicolon separates equal and balanced sentence elements, usually **main clauses**.°

24a Semicolon between main clauses not joined by *and, but, or, nor,* and so on

Semicolon between main clauses

Use a semicolon between **main clauses**° that are not connected by the coordinating conjunction *and, but, or, nor, for, so,* or *yet.* The semicolon signals that one clause is ending and another is beginning.

> Increased taxes are only one way to pay for programs**;** cost cutting also frees up money.
>
> A new ulcer drug has a mixed reputation**;** doctors find that the drug works but worry about its side effects.

24b No semicolon between main clauses and subordinate elements

Do not use a semicolon between a main clause and a subordinate element, such as a **subordinate clause**° or a **phrase**.°

> Not   <u>According to African authorities</u>; Pygmies today number only about 35,000.
>
> But   <u>According to African authorities</u>**,** Pygmies today number only about 35,000.
>
> Not   Anthropologists have campaigned; <u>for the protection of the Pygmies' habitat.</u>
>
> But   Anthropologists have campaigned <u>for the protection of the Pygmies' habitat.</u>

24b Semicolon with *however, for example,* and so on

Use a semicolon between **main clauses**° that are related by **transitional expressions**° such as *however, indeed, therefore, thus, after all, for example, in fact,* and *of course.*

> Blue jeans are fashionable all over the world**;** however, the American originators still wear more jeans than anyone else.

MyWritingLab

Visit **MyWritingLab** for more help with the semicolon.

°See "Grammar Terms," page 272.

A transitional expression may move around within its clause, so the semicolon will not always come just before the expression. The transitional expression itself is usually set off with a comma or commas.

> Blue jeans are fashionable all over the world; the American originators, however, still wear more jeans than anyone else.

24c Semicolons with series

Semicolons between series items

Use semicolons (rather than commas) to separate items in a series when the items contain commas.

> The custody case involved Amy Dalton, the child; Ellen and Mark Dalton, the parents; and Ruth and Hal Blum, the grandparents.

No semicolon before a series

Do not use a semicolon to introduce a series. (Use a colon or a dash instead.)

> Not Teachers have heard all sorts of reasons why students do poorly; psychological problems, family illness, too much work, too little time.
>
> But Teachers have heard all sorts of reasons why students do poorly: psychological problems, family illness, too much work, too little time.

25a

25 The Colon

The colon is mainly a mark of introduction, but it has a few other conventional uses as well.

25a Colon for introduction

Colon at the end of a main clause

The colon ends a **main clause°** and introduces various additions:

> The first warm days of spring, followed by cool nights, send an unmistakable message: it's time to visit the sugar bush. [Introduces an explanation.]

°See "Grammar Terms," page 272.

MyWritingLab

Visit MyWritingLab for more help with the colon.

We look forward to a variety of maple products: syrup, toffee, fudge, maple butter, and maple sugar. [Introduces a series.]

The sugaring-off meal provides an essential ingredient for the men and women who work in the sugar bush: calories to fuel hard labour. [Introduces an **appositive.**°]

A farmer in the Beauce gives his helpers plenty of food: "We serve maple-glazed ham, eggs poached in maple syrup, and maple-baked beans. For dessert we offer sugar pie." [Introduces a long quotation.]

No colon inside a main clause

Do not use a colon inside a main clause, especially after *such as* or a verb.

Not   The best-known maple product is: syrup. Outside of Canada, few people have tasted maple delicacies such as: toffee or *tire*.

But   The best-known maple product is syrup. Outside of Canada, few people have tasted maple delicacies such as toffee or *tire*.

25b Colon with salutation of business letter, title and subtitle, and divisions of time

26a

Salutation of a business letter
Dear Ms. Burak:

Title and subtitle
Anna Freud: Her Life and Work

Time
12:26   6:00

26 The Apostrophe

The apostrophe (') appears as part of a word to indicate possession, the omission of one or more letters, or (in a few cases) plural number.

26a Apostrophe with possessives

The **possessive form** of a word indicates that it owns or is the source of another word: *the dog's hair*, everyone's *hope*. For **nouns**° and **indefinite pronouns,**° such as

---

MyWritingLab

Visit **MyWritingLab** for more help with the apostrophe.

°See "Grammar Terms," page 272.

everyone, the possessive form always includes an apostrophe and often an *-s.* (Only personal pronouns such as *hers* and *its* do not use apostrophes for possession.)

Note The apostrophe or apostrophe-plus-*s* is an *addition.* Before this addition, always spell the name of the owner or owners without dropping or adding letters.

Singular words: Add -'s.

Some of the earth's forests are regenerating.

Everyone's fitness can be improved through daily exercise.

The *-'s* ending for singular words usually pertains to singular words ending in *-s.*

Francis's work is highly regarded.

The business's customers filed suit.

Some writers, however, add only the apostrophe to singular words ending in *-s,* especially when the additional *s* would make the word difficult to pronounce (*Moses'*) or when the name sounds like a plural (*Rivers'*).

Plural words ending in -s: Add -' only.

Workers' incomes have fallen slightly over the past year.

Many students take several years' leave after high school.

The Murphys' son lives at home.

Plural words not ending in -s: Add -'s.

Children's education is at stake.

We need to attract the media's attention.

Compound words: Add -'s only to the last word.

The brother-in-law's business failed.

Taxes are always somebody else's fault.

Two or more owners: Add -'s depending on possession.

Zimbale's and Mason's comedy techniques are similar. [Each comedian has his own technique.]

The child recovered despite her mother and father's neglect. [The mother and father were jointly neglectful.]

26b Misuses of the apostrophe

No apostrophe with plural nouns°

Not   The unleashed dog's belonged to the Jones'.

But   The unleashed dogs belonged to the Joneses.

°See "Grammar Terms," page 272.

No apostrophe with singular verbs°

Not   The subway <u>break's</u> down less often now.

But   The subway <u>breaks</u> down less often now.

No apostrophe with possessives of personal pronouns°

Not   The frog is <u>her's</u>, not <u>their's</u>. <u>It's</u> skin is speckled.

But   The frog is <u>hers</u>, not <u>theirs</u>. <u>Its</u> skin is speckled.

Note Don't confuse possessive pronouns and contractions: *its, your, their,* and *whose* are possessives. *It's, you're, they're,* and *who's* are contractions. See below.

26c Apostrophe with contractions

A **contraction** replaces one or more letters, numbers, or words with an apostrophe.

it is	it's	cannot	can't
you are	you're	does not	doesn't
they are	they're	were not	weren't
who is	who's	class of 2018	class of '18

Note The contractions *it's, you're, they're,* and *who's* are easily confused with the possessive pronouns° *its, your, their,* and *whose.* To avoid misusing any of these words, search for all of them in your drafts and test for correctness:

■ **Do you intend the word to contain the sentence verb *is* or *are*,** as in *It <u>is</u> a shame, They <u>are</u> to blame, You <u>are</u> right, Who <u>is</u> coming?* Then use an apostrophe (which indicates the missing letters): *it's, they're, you're, who's.*

■ **Do you intend the word to indicate possession,** as in *<u>Its</u> tail was wagging, <u>Their</u> car broke down, <u>Your</u> eyes are blue, <u>Whose</u> book is that?* Then don't use an apostrophe (no letters are missing).

26d Apostrophe with plural abbreviations, dates, and words or characters named as words

You'll sometimes see apostrophes used to form the plurals of abbreviations (*BA's*), dates (*1900's*), and words or characters used as words (*but's*). However, current style guides recommend against the apostrophe in these cases.

BAs   PhDs   1900s   2010s

The sentence has too many *but*s.

Two *3*s end the password.

Note Italicize a word or character named as a word (see p. 116), but not the added *-s.*

27 Quotation Marks

Quotation marks—either double (" ") or single (' ')—mainly enclose direct quotations from speech and from writing.

This chapter treats the main uses of quotation marks. Additional issues with quotations are discussed elsewhere in this book:

- **Using commas with signal phrases like *she said* introducing quotations.** See page 93.
- **Using brackets and the ellipsis mark to indicate changes in quotations.** See pages 104–06.
- **Quoting sources versus paraphrasing or summarizing them.** See pages 150–52.
- **Integrating quotations into your text.** See pages 149–57.
- **Avoiding plagiarism when quoting.** See pages 157–63.
- **Formatting long prose quotations and poetry quotations.** See pages 203 (MLA style), 221 (APA style), and 235 (Chicago style).

27a

Note Always use quotation marks in pairs, one at the beginning of a quotation and one at the end.

27a Quotation marks with direct quotations

Double quotation marks

A **direct quotation** reports what someone said or wrote, in the exact words of the original.

> *"*Life,*"* said the psychoanalyst Karen Horney, *"*remains a very efficient therapist.*"*

Note Do not use quotation marks with an **indirect quotation**, which reports what someone said or wrote but not in the exact words of the original: *Karen Horney remarked that life is a good therapist.*

Single quotation marks

Use single quotation marks to enclose a quotation within a quotation.

> "All the eyes of the world," Tommy Douglas told the House of Commons just before Good Friday in 1939, "will turn back to 'a green hill far away, without a city wall,' where the founder of Christianity was crucified by those forces of selfishness, greed, and lust for gain that are still at work in the world."

MyWritingLab

Visit MyWritingLab for more help with quotation marks.

Dialogue

When quoting a conversation, use double quotation marks and begin a new paragraph for each speaker.

> "What shall I call you? Your name?" Andrews whispered rapidly, as with a high squeak the latch of the door rose.
>
> "Elizabeth," she said. "Elizabeth."
>
> —Graham Greene, *The Man Within*

27b Quotation marks for titles of works

Do not use quotation marks for the titles of your own papers. Within your text, however, use quotation marks to enclose the titles of works that are published or released within larger works. Use italics for all other titles. (See p. 115.)

Short story	Essay
"The Loons"	"Joey: A 'Mechanical Boy'"
Short poem	Song
"Her Kind"	"Suzanne"
Article in a periodical	Episode of a television or radio program
"Does 'Scaring' Work?"	"Dieppe" (on *Canada at War*)
Page or document on a website	Subdivision of a book
"Reader's Page" (on the site *Friends of Prufrock*)	"The Mast Head" (Chapter 35 of *Moby-Dick*)

Note APA and CSE styles do not use quotation marks for titles within source citations. See pages 208 and 239.

27c Quotation marks with words used in a special sense

> On movie sets movable "wild walls" make a one-walled room seem four-walled on film.

Avoid using quotation marks to excuse slang or to express irony—that is, to indicate that you are using a word with a different or even opposite meaning than usual.

Not	Settlers <u>"justified"</u> their treatment of native people.
But	Settlers <u>attempted to justify</u> their treatment of native people.

Note Use italics to highlight words you are defining. See page 116.

27d Quotation marks with other punctuation

Commas and periods: Inside quotation marks

> Jonathan Swift wrote a famous satire, "A Modest Proposal," in 1729.
>
> "Swift's 'A Modest Proposal,'" wrote one critic, "is so outrageous that it cannot be believed."

Exception When a parenthetical source citation immediately follows a quotation, place any comma or period *after* the citation:

> One critic calls the essay "outrageous" (Olms 26).

Colons and semicolons: Outside quotation marks

> Some years ago the slogan in elementary education was "learning by playing"; now educators stress basic skills.
>
> We all know the meaning of "basic skills": reading, writing, and arithmetic.

Dashes, question marks, and exclamation points: Inside quotation marks only if part of the quotation

When a dash, exclamation point, or question mark is part of the quotation, place it *inside* quotation marks. Don't use any other punctuation, such as a period or comma.

27d

> "But must you—" Marcia hesitated, afraid of the answer.
>
> "Go away!" I yelled.
>
> Did you say, "Who is she?" [When both your sentence and the quotation would end in a question mark or exclamation point, use only the mark in the quotation.]

When a dash, question mark, or exclamation point applies only to the larger sentence, not to the quotation, place it *outside* quotation marks—again, with no other punctuation.

> Betty Friedan's question in 1963—"Who knows what women can be?"—encouraged others to seek answers.
>
> Who said, "Now cracks a noble heart"?

28 End Punctuation

End a sentence with one of three punctuation marks: a period, a question mark, or an exclamation point.

28a Period for most sentences and some abbreviations

Statement	Mild command
The airline went bankrupt.	Think of the possibilities.

Indirect question°
The article asks how we can improve math education.
It asks what cost we are willing to pay.

Abbreviations

Use periods with abbreviations that end in small letters. Otherwise, omit periods from abbreviations.

Dr.	Mr., Mrs.	e.g.	Feb.	ft.
St.	Ms.	i.e.	p.	a.m., p.m.
PhD	BC, AD	US	IBM	CRTC
BA	AM, PM	UBC	CBC	AIDS

Note When a sentence ends in an abbreviation with a period, don't add a second period: *My first class is at 8 a.m.*

28b Question mark for direct questions°

What is the result?
What is the difference between those proposals?

28c Exclamation point for strong statements and commands

No! We must not lose this election!
Stop the car!

Note Use exclamation points sparingly to avoid seeming overly dramatic.

°See "Grammar Terms," page 272.

28c

29 Other Marks

The other marks of punctuation are the dash, parentheses, the ellipsis mark, brackets, and the slash.

29a Dash or dashes: Shifts and interruptions

The dash (—) punctuates sentences, while the hyphen (-) punctuates words. Form a dash using two hyphens (--), with no extra space before, after, or between the hyphens. Or use the character called an em-dash on your word processor.

Note Be sure to use a pair of dashes when a shift or interruption falls in the middle of a sentence.

Shift in tone or thought

The novel — if one can call it that — appeared in 1994.

Nonessential element

The qualities Monet painted — sunlight, shadows, deep colours — typified the rivers and gardens he used as subjects. [Commas may also set off nonessential elements. See p. 90.]

Introductory series

Shortness of breath, skin discolouration, persistent indigestion — all these may signify cancer.

Concluding series or explanation

The patient undergoes a battery of tests — CAT scan, ultrasound, and biopsy. [A colon may also set off a concluding series. See p. 96.]

29b

29b Parentheses: Nonessential elements

Parentheses always come in pairs, one before and one after the punctuated material.

Parenthetical expressions

Parentheses de-emphasize explanatory or supplemental words or phrases. (Commas emphasize these expressions more, and dashes still more.)

Frederick Banting (later Sir Frederick Banting) and Charles Best discovered insulin in 1923.

MyWritingLab

Visit **MyWritingLab** for more help with the dash, parentheses, the ellipsis mark, brackets, and the slash.

Don't put a comma before an opening parenthesis. After a parenthetical expression, place any punctuation *outside* the closing parenthesis.

Not   Although he did not receive the Nobel Prize, Charles Best had worked very closely with Frederick Banting **,** (later Sir Frederick Banting.)

But   Although he did not receive the Nobel Prize, Charles Best had worked very closely with Frederick Banting (later Sir Frederick Banting).

If a complete sentence falls within parentheses, place the period *inside* the closing parenthesis.

Banting became a professor at the University of Toronto in 1923. **(** He was knighted in 1934. **)**

Labels for lists with in text

Today Type 1 diabetes is managed effectively with **(** 1 **)** glucose monitors, **(** 2 **)** insulin pens, and **(** 3 **)** insulin pumps.

Do not use parentheses for such labels when you set a list off (that is, indent it) from your text.

29c Ellipsis mark: Omissions from quotations

The ellipsis mark, consisting of three periods separated by space (. . .), generally indicates an omission from a quotation. The following examples quote from or refer to the passage below about environmentalism:

Original quotation
At the heart of the environmentalist world view is the conviction that human physical and spiritual health depends on sustaining the planet in a relatively unaltered state. Earth is our home in the full, genetic sense, where humanity and its ancestors existed for all the millions of years of their evolution. Natural ecosystems—forests, coral reefs, marine blue waters maintain the world exactly as we would wish it to be maintained. When we debase the global environment and extinguish the variety of life, we are dismantling a support system that is too complex to understand, let alone replace, in the foreseeable future.
                    —Edward O. Wilson, "Is Humanity Suicidal?"

1. Omission of the middle of a sentence
Wilson observes, "Natural ecosystems . . . maintain the world exactly as we would wish it to be maintained."

2. Omission of the end of a sentence, without source citation
Wilson writes, "Earth is our home . . . ." [The sentence period, closed up to the last word, precedes the ellipsis mark.]

3. Omission of the end of a sentence, with source citation

Wilson writes, "Earth is our home . . . " (27). [The sentence period follows the source citation.]

4. Omission of parts of two or more sentences

Wilson writes, "At the heart of the environmentalist world view is the conviction that human physical and spiritual health depends on sustaining the planet . . . where humanity and its ancestors existed for all the millions of years of their evolution."

5. Omission of one or more sentences

As Wilson puts it, "At the heart of the environmentalist world view is the conviction that human physical and spiritual health depends on sustaining the planet in a relatively unaltered state . . . . When we debase the global environment and extinguish the variety of life, we are dismantling a support system that is too complex to understand, let alone replace, in the foreseeable future."

6. Omission from the middle of a sentence through the end of another sentence

"Earth is our home . . . . When we debase the global environment and extinguish the variety of life, we are dismantling a support system that is too complex to understand, let alone replace, in the foreseeable future."

29c

7. Omission of the beginning of a sentence, leaving a complete sentence

a. Bracketed capital letter

"[H]uman physical and spiritual health," Wilson writes, "depends on sustaining the planet in a relatively unaltered state." [No ellipsis mark is needed because the brackets around the *H* indicate that the letter was not capitalized originally and thus that the beginning of the sentence has been omitted.]

b. Small letter

According to Wilson, "human physical and spiritual health depends on sustaining the planet in a relatively unaltered state." [No ellipsis mark is needed because the small *h* indicates that the beginning of the sentence has been omitted.]

c. Capital letter from the original

Hami comments, " . . . Wilson argues eloquently for the environmentalist world view." [An ellipsis mark *is* needed because the quoted part of the sentence begins with a capital letter and it's otherwise not clear that the beginning of the original sentence has been omitted.]

8. Use of a word or phrase

Wilson describes the earth as "our home." [No ellipsis mark needed.]

Note these features of the examples:

- **Use an ellipsis mark when it is not otherwise clear that you have left out material from the source**, as when you omit one or more sentences (examples 5 and 6) or when the words you quote form a complete sentence that is different in the original (examples 1–4 and 7c).
- **You don't need an ellipsis mark when it is obvious that you have omitted something**, such as when a bracketed capital letter or a small letter indicates omission (examples 7a and 7b) or when a phrase clearly comes from a larger sentence (example 8).
- **Place an ellipsis mark after the sentence period** *except* **when a parenthetical source citation follows the quotation**, as in example 3. Then the sentence period falls after the citation.

If your quotation omits one or more lines of poetry or paragraphs of prose, show the omission with an entire line of ellipsis marks across the full width of the quotation.

29d Brackets: Changes in quotations

Though they have specialized uses in mathematical equations, brackets mainly indicate that you have altered a quotation to fit it into your sentence or added your own comment.

"[T]hat Petro-Canada station [just outside Red Deer] is one of the busiest in the nation," said a company spokesperson.

29e Slash: Options, breaks in poetry lines, and URLs

Option
Some teachers oppose pass/fail courses.

Break in poetry lines run into your text
Many readers have sensed a reluctant turn away from death in Frost's lines "The woods are lovely, dark and deep, / But I have promises to keep."

URL
http://www.statcan.gc.ca/start-debut-eng.html

29e

PART 5

Spelling and Mechanics

Essential

This list covers the main conventions of spelling and mechanics. For a detailed guide to this part, see "Detailed Contents" inside the back cover.

Spelling and the hyphen

- Proofread for correct spelling. Don't rely on your spelling checker. (See opposite.)
- Follow spelling rules for *ie* vs. *ei*, attaching endings to words, and forming plurals. (See opposite.)
- Use the hyphen to form compound words and to divide words at the ends of lines. (See p. 111.)

Capital letters

- Use capital letters appropriately for proper nouns and proper adjectives and for the titles of works and persons. (See pp. 113–14.)

Italics

- Use italics primarily for the titles of works published separately from other works. Ensure that italics in source citations conforms to your discipline's or instructor's requirements. (See pp. 115–16.)

Abbreviations

- Use abbreviations appropriately for the discipline or field you are writing in. (See pp. 117–18.)

Numbers

- Express numbers in numerals or words appropriately for the discipline or field you are writing in. (See pp. 118–19.)

30 Spelling and the Hyphen

Spelling, including using the hyphen, is a skill you can acquire by paying attention to words and by developing three habits:

- **Carefully proofread your writing.**
- **Cultivate a healthy suspicion of your spellings.**
- **Check a dictionary every time you doubt a spelling.**

30a Spelling checkers

A spelling checker can help you find and track spelling errors in your papers. But its usefulness is limited, mainly because it can't spot the confusion of words with similar spellings, such as *their/they're/there*. A grammar/style checker may flag such words, but only the ones listed in its dictionary, and you still must select the correct spelling. Proofread your papers to catch spelling errors.

See pages 14–15 for more on spelling checkers.

30b Spelling rules

We often misspell syllables rather than whole words. The following rules focus on troublesome syllables.

ie and *ei*

Follow the familiar jingle: *i* before *e* except after *c* or when pronounced "ay" as in *neighbour* and *weigh*.

i before *e*	believe	thief
e before *i*	receive	ceiling
ei pronounced "ay"	freight	vein

30b

Exceptions Remember common exceptions with this sentence: *The weird foreigner neither seizes leisure nor forfeits height.*

Silent final *e*

Drop a silent *e* when adding an ending that begins with a vowel. Keep the *e* if the ending begins with a consonant.

advise + able = advisable   care + ful = careful

Exceptions Keep the final *e* before a vowel to prevent confusion or mispronunciation: *dyeing, changeable*. Drop the *e* before a consonant when another vowel comes before the *e: argument, truly*.

MyWritingLab

Visit **MyWritingLab** for more help with spelling and the hyphen.

Final *y*

When adding to a word ending in *y*, change *y* to *i* when it follows a consonant. Keep the *y* when it follows a vowel, precedes *-ing*, or ends a proper name.

beauty, beauties	day, days
worry, worried	study, studying
supply, supplier	Minsky, Minskys

Consonants

When adding an ending to a one-syllable word that ends in a consonant, double the consonant if it follows a single vowel. Otherwise, don't double the consonant.

slap, slapping	pair, paired

For words of more than one syllable, double the final consonant when it follows a single vowel (1) if the syllable ending with that consonant is stressed in the newly formed word, or (2) if the final consonant is *l*, even if that syllable is not stressed.

submit, submitted	despair, despairing
refer, referred	refer, reference
label, labelled	revel, revelled

Plurals

Most nouns form plurals by adding *s* to the singular form. Nouns ending in *s, sh, ch,* or *x* add *es* to the singular.

boy, boys	kiss, kisses
table, tables	lurch, lurches
Murphy, Murphys	tax, taxes

Nouns ending in a vowel plus *o* add *s*. Nouns ending in a consonant plus *o* add *es*.

ratio, ratios	hero, heroes

Form the plural of a compound noun by adding *s* to the main word in the compound. The main word may not fall at the end.

passersby	breakthroughs
fathers-in-law	city-states

Some English nouns that come from other languages form the plural according to their original language.

analysis, analyses	medium, media
crisis, crises	phenomenon, phenomena
criterion, criteria	piano, pianos

ESL Noncount nouns do not form plurals, either regularly (with an added *s*) or irregularly. Examples of noncount nouns include *equipment, intelligence,* and *wealth.* See pages 78–79.

30b

Canadian spelling

American and British spelling differ in ways such as the following.

American	British
color, humor	colour, humour
theater, center	theatre, centre
canceled, traveled	cancelled, travelled
judgment	judgement
realize, analyze	realise, analyse
defense, offense	defence, offence

Canadian spelling used to follow British usage. Over time, however, Canadians have adopted some aspects of American usage. Although it is usually acceptable (and very Canadian) to mix British and American spellings within one document, it is never acceptable to follow specific rules inconsistently.

For example, if you spell *theatre* with an *re* according to British spelling conventions, you should not then spell *metre* with an *er*, as in *meter*, which is American. Similarly, use both *colour* and *labour*, or *color* and *labor*, but not *colour* and *labor*. Many words that end in *re* and *our* in British spelling end in *er* and *or* in American spelling.

Be consistent as well with words that double their final *l*, that end in *ce* or *se*, or that end in *que*. Thus, *marvellous, defence*, and *cheque* are British (generally the preferred Canadian usage), while *marvelous, defense*, and *check* are American.

Some other words for which Canadians generally follow British spelling include *catalogue* (not *catalog*), *pyjamas* (not *pajamas*), and *whisky* (not *whiskey*).

Decide on the appropriate usage for your audience and stick to it, either by consistently following one dictionary's preferences or by setting your word processor's spelling-checker preference. This book, for example, follows the preferences of the *Canadian Oxford Dictionary*.

30c

30c The hyphen

Use the hyphen to form compound words and to divide words at the ends of lines.

Compound words

Compound words may be written as a single word (*breakthrough*), as two words (*decision makers*), or as a hyphenated word (*cross-reference*). Check a dictionary for the spelling of a compound word. Except as explained below, any compound not listed in the dictionary should be written as two words.

Sometimes a compound word comes from combining two or more words into a single **adjective**.° When such a compound adjective precedes a noun, a hyphen forms the words clearly into a unit.

> She is a well-known actor.
> Some French-speaking students work as translators.
> Alice reads eighteenth-century novels.

When a compound adjective follows the noun, the hyphen is unnecessary.

> The actor is well known.
> Many students are French speaking.
> Alice studies the eighteenth century.

The hyphen is also unnecessary in a compound modifier containing an *-ly* adverb, even before the noun: *clearly defined terms*.

Fractions and compound numbers

Hyphens join the parts of fractions: *three-fourths, one-half*. And the whole numbers *twenty-one* to *ninety-nine* are always hyphenated.

Prefixes and suffixes

Do not use hyphens with prefixes except as follows:

- **With the prefixes *self-*, *all-*, and *ex-*:** *self-control, all-inclusive, ex-student*.
- **With a prefix before a capitalized word:** *non-Aboriginal*.
- **With a capital letter before a word:** *T-shirt*.
- **To prevent misreading:** *de-emphasize, re-create a story*.

30c

The only suffix that regularly requires a hyphen is *-elect*, as in *president-elect*.

Word division at the end of a line

You can avoid short lines in your documents by setting your word processor to divide words automatically. To divide words manually, follow these guidelines:

- **Divide words only between syllables**—for instance, *win-dows*, not *wi-ndows*. Check a dictionary for correct syllable breaks.
- **Never divide a one-syllable word.**
- **Leave at least two letters on the first line and three on the second line.** If a word cannot be divided to follow this rule (for instance, *a-bus-er*), don't divide it.

°See "Grammar Terms," page 272.

If you must break an electronic address or URL—for instance, in a source citation—do not hyphenate, because readers may perceive any added hyphen as part of the address. The documentation styles differ in where they allow breaks in URLs. For example, MLA style allows a break only after a slash, while APA style allows a break before most punctuation marks.

31 Capital Letters

As a rule, capitalize a word only when a dictionary or conventional use says you must. Consult one of the style guides listed on pages 164–65 for special uses of capitals in the social, natural, and applied sciences.

31a First word of a sentence

No one expected the outcome.

31b Proper nouns° and proper adjectives°

Specific persons and things
Sidney Crosby   Rideau Canal

Specific places and geographical regions
Halifax   the North, the Maritimes

But: north of the city, a maritime climate

Days of the week, months, holidays
Monday   Yom Kippur
May   Christmas

But: winter, spring, summer, fall

Historical events, documents, periods, movements
the Meech Lake Accord   the Fenian Raids
the Early Modern period   Romanticism

Government offices, departments, and institutions
the Supreme Court   House of Commons
St. Joseph's Hospital   Department of National Defence

But: the court, the department, the hospital

Academic institutions and departments
University of New Brunswick Department of Nursing
Centennial College   Haven High School

But: the university, college course, high school diploma

31b

°See "Grammar Terms," page 272.

Organizations, associations, and their members

B'nai B'rith	New Democratic Party,
Girl Guides	New Democrats
Rotary Club	Greenpeace
Toronto Blue Jays	Montreal Symphony Orchestra

Races, nationalities, and their languages

First Nations	Germans
Indo-Canadian	Swahili
Caucasian	Italian

But: blacks, whites

Religions, their followers, and terms for the sacred

Christianity, Christians	God, Allah, Krishna
Judaism, Orthodox Jew	the Bible (but biblical)
Islam, Muslims	the Koran, the Qur'an

Common nouns as parts of proper nouns

Uncle Dan	Lake Superior
Professor Allen	Pacific Ocean
Main Street	Ford Motor Company

But: my uncle, the professor, the ocean, the company

31c Titles and subtitles of works

Capitalize all the words in a title and subtitle *except* **articles**° (*a, an, the*), *to* in **infinitives**,° **coordinating conjunctions**° (*and, but,* etc.), and **prepositions**° (*with, between,* etc.). Capitalize even these words when they are the first or last word in the title or when they fall after a colon or semicolon.

"The Albanian Virgin"	*Management: A New Theory*
Voyage of the Iceberg	"The Truth about AIDS"
"Knowing Whom to Ask"	*An End to Live For*

Note The preceding guidelines reflect MLA style for English and some other humanities. Other disciplines' style guides have different rules for capitals within source citations. See pages 205 (APA style) and 237 (CSE style).

31d Titles of persons

Title before name	Professor Jane Covington
Title after name	Jane Covington, a professor

31e Online communication

Online messages written in all-capital letters or with no capitals are difficult to read, and those in all-capitals are often considered rude. Use capital letters according to the rules in 31a–31d in all your online communication.

°See "Grammar Terms," page 272.

32 Italics

Italic type and underlining indicate the same thing: the word or words are being distinguished or emphasized. Italic type is now used almost universally in academic writing. Some instructors do recommend underlining, so ask your instructor for his or her preference.

Use italics consistently throughout a document. For instance, if you are using italics in source citations, use italics in the body of your paper as well. (If you are using underlining and you underline two or more words in a row, underline the space between the words, too: Criminal Statistics: Misuses of Numbers.)

32a Titles of works

Do not italicize the title of your own paper unless it contains an element (such as a book title) that requires highlighting.

Within your text, italicize the titles of works that are published, released, or produced separately from other works. Use quotation marks for all other titles. (See p. 100.)

Book
War and Peace

Play
Hamlet

Website
Friends of Prufrock
Google

Computer software
Microsoft Internet Explorer

Long musical work
The Beatles' *Revolver*
But: Symphony in C

Work of visual art
Emily Carr's *Wood Interior*

Long poem
Paradise Lost

Periodical
The Hamilton Spectator

Television or radio program
Dragon's Den

Movie
Maps to the Stars

Pamphlet
The Truth about Alcoholism

Published speech
Lincoln's *Gettysburg Address*

Exceptions Legal documents, the Bible, and parts of them are generally not italicized.

We studied the Book of Revelation in the Bible.

32b Ships, aircraft, spacecraft, trains

Challenger	the *Skeena*	*Queen Mary 2*
Apollo XI	HMCS *Charlottetown*	*Spirit of St. Louis*

32c Non-English words and phrases

Italicize a non-English expression that has not been absorbed into our language. A dictionary will say whether a word is still considered foreign to English.

> The scientific name for the brown trout is *Salmo trutta*. [The Latin scientific names for plants and animals are always italicized.]
>
> In Quebec, in vitro fertilization is covered by medicare. [In this example, *in vitro* is no longer italicized because it is now considered part of the English language.]

32d Words or characters named as words

Italicize words or characters (letters or numbers) that are referred to as themselves rather than used for their meanings, including terms you are defining.

> Some children pronounce *th*, as in *thought*, with an *f* sound.
>
> The word *syzygy* refers to a straight line formed by three celestial bodies, as in the alignment of the earth, sun, and moon.

32e Online alternatives

Some forms of online communication do not allow highlighting with italics for the purposes described in this chapter. If you can't use italics to distinguish book titles and other elements, type an underscore before and after the element: *Measurements coincide with those in _Joule's Handbook_*. You can also emphasize words with asterisks before and after: *I *will not* be able to attend*.

Don't use all-capital letters for emphasis; they yell too loudly. (See also pp. 113–14.)

32f Electronic addresses

Electronic addresses in essays and bibliographies should not be underlined or printed in a different colour from your text. Ensure that you turn off the Hyperlink option in your word processor's automatic formatting feature.

33 Abbreviations

The following guidelines on abbreviations pertain to the text of a nontechnical document. For any special requirements of the discipline you are writing in, consult one of the style guides listed on pages 164–65. In all disciplines, writers increasingly omit periods from abbreviations that end in capital letters. (See p. 103.)

If a name or term (such as *operating room*) appears often in a piece of writing, then its abbreviation (*OR*) can cut down on extra words. Spell out the full term at its first appearance, give the abbreviation in parentheses, and use the abbreviation thereafter.

33a Familiar abbreviations

Titles before names	Dr., Mr., Mrs., Ms., Rev., Gen.
Titles after names	MD, DDS, DVM, PhD, Sr., Jr.
Institutions	SFU, AGO, UNB, DFAIT
Organizations	CUPE, NDP, YMCA, IATA
Corporations	IBM, CBC, CN, GM
People, positions	JFK, FDR, ADM, CEO
Countries	US, UK
Specific numbers	no. 36 *or* No. 36
Specific amounts	$7.41, $1 million, $36K
Specific times	11:26 AM, 8:04 a.m., 2:00 PM, 8:05 p.m.
Specific dates	44 BC, AD 1492, 44 BCE, 1492 CE

Note The abbreviations BC ("before Christ"), BCE ("before the common era"), and CE ("common era") always follow the date. In contrast, AD (*anno domini*, "in the year of the Lord") always precedes the date.

33b Latin abbreviations

Generally, use the common Latin abbreviations (without italics) only in source citations and comments in parentheses.

i.e.	*id est*: that is
cf.	*confer*: compare
e.g.	*exempli gratia*: for example
et al.	*et alii*: and others

MyWritingLab

Visit **MyWritingLab** for more help with abbreviations.

etc.	*et cetera*: and so forth
NB	*nota bene*: note well

He said he would be gone a fortnight (i.e., two weeks).

Bloom et al., editors, *Anthology of Light Verse*

33c Words usually spelled out

Generally spell out certain kinds of words in the text of academic, general, and business writing. (In technical writing, however, abbreviate units of measurement.)

Units of measurement
The cottage is sixteen kilometres from town.

Geographical names
Margaret Laurence was born in Manitoba.

Names of days, months, and holidays
The truce was signed on Tuesday, April 16, and was ratified by Christmas.

Names of people
Robert Frost wrote accessible poems.

Courses of instruction
The writer teaches psychology and composition.

And

The new rules affect Vancouver and environs. [Use the ampersand, &, only in the names of business firms: *Lee & Sons*.]

34a

34 Numbers

This chapter addresses the use of numbers (numerals versus words) in the text of a nontechnical document. Usage does vary, so consult one of the style guides listed on pages 164–65 for the requirements of the discipline you are writing in.

34a Numerals, not words

Numbers requiring three or more words	Addresses
366 36,500	118 Sixth Street
	Prince Rupert, BC V8Z 3L7

Note "Sixth" is the *name* of the street, but "118" is the house *number*.

MyWritingLab

Visit **MyWritingLab** for more help with numbers.

Round numbers
over a million
26 million   2.45 billion

Exact amounts of money
$3.5 million $4.50

Days and years
June 18, 1985 AD 12
456 BC   12 CE

The time of day
9:00 AM   3:45 PM

Decimals, percentages,
and fractions
22.5   3½
48% (*or* 48 percent)

Scores and statistics
a ratio of 8 to 1   21 to 7
a mean of 26

Pages, chapters, volumes,
acts, scenes, lines
Chapter 9, page 123
Hamlet, act 5, scene 3

Note Two numbers in a row can be confusing. Rewrite to separate the numbers:

| Confusing | Out of 530 101 children caught the virus. |
| Clear | Out of 530 <u>children</u> 101 caught the virus. |

34b Words, not numerals

Numbers of one or two words
<u>sixty</u> days, <u>forty-two</u> laps, <u>one hundred</u> people

In business and technical writing, use words only for numbers under 11 (*ten reasons, four laps*).

Beginnings of sentences
<u>Seventy-five</u> riders entered the race.

If a number beginning a sentence requires more than two words to spell out, reword the sentence so that the number falls later.

34b

Faulty	<u>103</u> visitors returned.
Awkward	<u>One hundred three</u> visitors returned.
Revised	Of the visitors, <u>103</u> returned.

PART 6

Research and Documentation

Essential

This list covers the main considerations in using and documenting sources. For a detailed guide to this part, see "Detailed Contents" inside the back cover.

Developing a research strategy

- Formulate a question about your subject that can guide your research. (See opposite.)
- Set goals for your sources: library vs. Internet, primary vs. secondary, and so on. (See opposite.)

Tracking sources

- Prepare a working, annotated bibliography to locate and assess possible sources. (See pp. 127–28.)
- Use files, printouts, photocopies, and notes to keep track of promising sources. (See p. 129.)

Finding sources

- Develop keywords that describe your subject for searches of electronic sources. (See p. 130.)
- Consult appropriate sources to answer your research question. (See pp. 132–39.)

Evaluating and synthesizing sources

- Evaluate both print and online sources for their relevance and reliability. (See p. 140.)
- Synthesize sources to find their relationships and to support your own ideas. (See p. 148.)

Integrating sources into your text

- Summarize, paraphrase, or quote sources depending on the significance of the sources' ideas or wording. (See p. 150.)
- Work source material smoothly and informatively into your own text. (See p. 152.)
- Show clear boundaries where your borrowing of source material begins and ends. (See p. 156.)

Avoiding plagiarism

- Do not plagiarize, either deliberately or carelessly, by presenting the words or ideas of others as your own. (See p. 158.)

Documenting sources

- Using the style guide appropriate for your discipline, document your sources and format your paper. (See pp. 164–65 for a list of style guides and Chapters 42 for MLA style, 43 for APA style, 44 for Chicago style, and 45 for CSE and IEEE styles.)

35 Developing a Research Strategy

Research writing gives you a chance to work like a detective solving a case. The mystery is the answer to a question you care about. The search for the answer leads you to consider what others think about your subject, to build on that information, and ultimately to become an expert in your own right.

35a Subject, question, and thesis

Seek a research subject that you care about and want to know more about. Starting with such an interest will motivate you and will make you a participant in a dialogue when you begin examining sources.

Asking questions about your subject can give direction to your research by focusing your thinking on a particular approach. In asking questions, consider what about your subject intrigues or perplexes you, what you'd like to know more about. (See the next page for suggestions on using your own knowledge.)

Try to narrow your research question so that you can answer it in the time and space you have available. The question *How does human activity affect the environment?* is very broad, encompassing issues as diverse as pollution, climate change, population growth, land use, and biodiversity. In contrast, the question *How can buying environmentally friendly products help the environment?* or *How, if at all, should carbon emissions be taxed?* is much narrower. Each question also requires more than a simple yes-or-no answer, so that answering it, even tentatively, demands thought about pros and cons, causes and effects.

As you read and write, your question will probably evolve to reflect your increasing knowledge of the subject. Eventually its answer will become the thesis of your paper, the main idea that all the paper's evidence supports. (See also p. 5.)

35b

35b Goals for sources

Before you start looking for sources, consider what you already know about your subject and where you are likely to find information on it.

MyWritingLab

Visit MyWritingLab for more help with developing a research strategy.

Your own knowledge

Discovering what you already know about your topic will guide you in discovering what you don't know and thus need to research. Take some time to spell out facts you have learned, opinions you have heard or read elsewhere, and of course your own opinions. But remember that opinions are not facts, and that opinions, yours or a source's, are only as good as the logic and evidence used to support them.

When you've explored your thoughts, make a list of questions for which you don't have answers, whether factual (*How much do Canadians spend on environmentally friendly products?*) or more open-ended (*Are green products worth the higher prices?*). These questions will give you clues about the sources you need to look for first.

Kinds of sources

For many research projects, you'll want to consult a mix of sources, as described below. You may start by seeking the outlines of your subject—the range and depth of opinions about it—in reference works and articles in popular periodicals or through a search of the Web. Then, as you refine your views and your research question, you'll move on to more specialized sources, such as scholarly books and periodicals and your own interviews or surveys. (See pp. 130–38 for more on each kind of source.)

Library and Internet sources

The sources available at your library or through its website—mainly reference works, periodicals, and books—have two big advantages over most of what you'll find on the open Web: they are catalogued and indexed for easy retrieval; and they are generally reliable, having been screened first by their publishers and then by the library's staff. In contrast, the Internet's retrieval systems are more difficult to use effectively, and Web sources can be less reliable because many do not pass through any screening before being posted. (There are many exceptions, such as online scholarly journals and reference works. But these sources are generally available through your library's website as well.)

Most instructors expect research writers to consult library sources. But they'll accept online sources, too, if you have used them judiciously. Even with its disadvantages, the Internet can be a valuable resource for primary sources, scholarly work, current information, and diverse views. For guidelines on evaluating both print and online sources, see pages 140–48.

Primary and secondary sources

Use **primary sources** when they are available or are required by your assignment. These sources are first-hand accounts, such as historical documents (letters, legal records, and so on); eyewitness reports; works of literature, art, and philosophy; reports on experiments or surveys conducted by the writer; and your own interviews, experiments, observations, or correspondence.

Many assignments will allow you to use **secondary sources**, which report and analyze information drawn from other sources, often primary ones. Examples include a reporter's summary of a controversial issue, a historian's account of a battle, a critic's reading of a poem, and a psychologist's evaluation of several studies. Secondary sources may contain helpful summaries and interpretations that direct, support, and extend your own thinking. However, most research-writing assignments expect your own ideas to go beyond those in such sources.

Scholarly and popular sources

The scholarship of acknowledged experts is essential for depth, authority, and specificity. The general-interest views and information of popular sources can help you apply more scholarly approaches to daily life.

When looking for sources, you can gauge how scholarly or popular they are from bibliographic information:

- **Check the title.** Is it technical, or does it use a general vocabulary?
- **Check the publisher.** Is it a scholarly journal (such as *Education Forum*) or a publisher of scholarly books (such as University of Toronto Press), or is it a popular magazine (such as *Time* or *Maclean's*) or a publisher of popular books (such as Little, Brown)?
- **Check the length of periodical articles.** Scholarly articles are generally much longer than magazine and newspaper articles.
- **Check the author.** Look for biographical information that confirms the author's expertise.

35b

- **Check the URL.** A website's URL, or electronic address, includes a "tail" that tells you something about the source: *.edu* means the source comes from a US educational institution, *.gc.ca* from the government of Canada, *.ca* from a Canadian site, *.gov* from a US government body, *.org* from a nonprofit organization, *.com* from a commercial organization such as a corporation. Remember, however, that while a site ending in *.edu* may originate in a university, it might also be the personal webpage of a biased or ill-informed individual. Even sites sponsored by governments or by nonprofit organizations must be evaluated critically.

Older and newer sources

For most subjects a combination of older, established sources (such as books) and current sources (such as newspaper articles or interviews) will provide both background and up-to-date information. Only historical subjects or very current subjects require an emphasis on one extreme or another.

Impartial and biased sources

Seek a range of viewpoints. Sources that attempt to be impartial can offer an overview of your subject and trustworthy facts. Sources with clear biases can offer a diversity of opinion. Of course, to discover bias, you may have to read the source carefully (see p. 140); but you can infer quite a bit just from a bibliographic listing:

- **Check the author.** You may have heard of the author as a respected researcher (thus more likely to be objective) or as a leading proponent of a certain view (less likely to be objective).
- **Check the title.** It may reveal something about point of view. (Consider these contrasting titles: "Go for the Green" and "Where the Green Is: Examining the Paradox of Environmentally Conscious Consumption.")

Note Internet sources must be approached with particular care. See pages 141 and 144–48.

Sources with helpful features

Depending on your topic and how far along your research is, you may want to look for sources with features such as illustrations (which can clarify important concepts), bibliographies (which can direct you to other sources), and indexes (which can help you develop keywords for electronic searches; see p. 131).

36

36 Tracking Sources

Accurate record-keeping is essential for tracking where sources come from in order to cite them in your writing. As you search, compile the publication information for sources in a working bibliography, and make notes about a source's usefulness in an annotated bibliography. As you discover sources that look promising, keep track of

---

MyWritingLab

Visit MyWritingLab for more help with tracking sources.

them by saving them to files, making printouts or photocopies, or taking notes on useful information.

36a Working bibliography

To track where sources are, compile a working bibliography of possibilities. When you have a substantial file—say, ten to thirty sources—you can decide which ones seem most promising and look them up first.

Source information

Use the following lists to track sources. For source samples that show where you can find the required information, see pages 177, 180, 188, and 196.

For a print or electronic book
Library call number
Name(s) of author(s), editor(s), translator(s), or others listed

Title and subtitle
Publication data: (1) place of publication; (2) publisher's name; (3) date of publication; (4) title of any database or website used to reach the book; (5) sponsor and date of any website used to find the book
Other important data, such as edition or volume number
Medium (print, Web, Kindle file, etc.)
Date you consulted the book (if online)

For periodical articles in print, in online databases, or in Web journals
Name(s) of author(s)
Title and subtitle of article
Title of periodical
Publication data: (1) volume number and issue number (if any) in which the article appears; (2) date of issue; (3) page numbers on which article appears
Title of any database used to reach the source
Medium (print, Web, etc.)
Date you consulted the source (if online)

For Web material and other electronic sources
Name(s) of author(s)
Title and subtitle of source
Title of website
Publication data: sponsor and date of any website used to reach the source
Any publication data for the source in another medium (print, film, etc.)
Format of online source (website or page, podcast, email, etc.)
Date you consulted the source
Title of any database used to reach the source
Complete URL (see the note on the next page)
Digital Object Identifier, if any (see the note on the next page)
Medium (usually Web)

36a

For other sources
Name(s) of author(s) or others listed, such as a government
    department or a recording artist
Title of the work
Format, such as unpublished letter or live performance
Publication or production data: (1) publisher's or producer's
    name; (2) date of publication, release, or production;
    (3) identifying numbers (if any)
Medium (print, typescript, etc.)

Note Documentation styles vary in requiring URLs
and DOIs (Digital Object Identifiers) for citations of electronic sources. (See p. 209 for more on DOIs.) Even if you
don't need the complete URL or DOI in your final citation
of a source, record it anyway so that you'll be able to
track the source down if you want to consult it again.

36b Annotated bibliography

Creating annotations for the sources in your working
bibliography converts the list into a tool for assessing
sources. The annotations can help you discover gaps that
may remain in your sources and can help you decide
which sources to pursue in depth. As you discover and
evaluate each possible source, record not only its publication information but also the following:

- **What you know about the content of the source.** Periodical databases and book catalogues generally
  include abstracts, or summaries, of sources that can
  help with this part of the annotation.
- **How you think the source may be helpful in your
  research.** Does it offer expert opinion, statistics, an
  important example, or a range of views? Does it place
  your subject in a historical, social, or economic context?
- **Your assessment of the source.** Consider how reliable
  the source is and how it might fit into your research.
  (See pp. 140–49 for more on evaluating and synthesizing sources.)

As you become more familiar with your sources, you
can use your initial annotated bibliography to record
your evaluation of them and more detailed thoughts on
how they fit into your research. For example:

Cook, Tim. *At the Sharp End: Canadians Fighting the Great
    War, 1914–1916.* Vol. 1. Toronto: Viking Canada, 2007.
    Detailed military history of the Canadian Expeditionary
    Force in France and Belgium, with historic photos and
    military maps. Fully documented. Detailed index and
    bibliography. Print.

36b

Macdonald, Lyn. *They Called It Passchendaele: The Story of the Third Battle of Ypres and of the Men Who Fought in It.* London: Michael Joseph, 1978. Uses letters and interviews with soldiers to tell the story of the battle in their words. Some very moving personal stories. No Canadian content. Intended for a general audience, but sources are provided. With photos and maps. Print.

36c Files, printouts, photocopies, and notes

The following tips can help you keep track of potentially useful sources as you locate them in the library, in databases, and on the Web. For each type of source, consult the lists on pages 127–28 for the publication information to record on each photocopy, printout, or file so that you can track and cite the source.

- **Save or print out database sources.** As you locate database articles that look useful, save an electronic version (usually a PDF file). If you are unable to save a copy, consider printing the article. Include any pages that give publication information, such as journal name, publication date, volume number, author's name, and database name.

- **Save or print out Web and other online sources.** Save potentially useful online material to a file or print it, making sure to include the information for electronic sources in the list on page 127. For Web content, include the URL and/or the DOI so that you can find the source again.

- **Photocopy or take notes on print sources.** When you find a possible print source, such as a book, enter the key publication information into your working bibliography, or scan or photocopy the title page and the copyright page. For an article, scan or photocopy the periodical's table of contents. As you assess the usefulness of any print source, scan or photocopy the pages that relate to your topic, or take handwritten or typed notes.

36c

Note Whatever method you use to track and record source information, you'll need to take care not to plagiarize by confusing the words and ideas of sources with your own words and ideas. See pages 157–63 on avoiding plagiarism.

37 Finding Sources

This chapter discusses both using keywords to conduct electronic searches and taking advantage of the range of sources, both print and electronic, that you have access to: reference works, books, periodicals, the Web, other online sources, government publications, images, and your own sources.

37a Electronic searches

The library's website

As you conduct research, the Web will be your gateway to ideas and information. Always start with the library's website, not with a search engine such as *Google*. (*Google Scholar*, a tool that searches for scholarly articles, is discussed on p. 134.) The library site will lead you to vast resources that aren't available on the open Web. More important, its resources have been checked by editors and librarians to ensure their value. *Google* and other search engines may seem more user-friendly than the library site, but many more of their sources will be unreliable.

Databases and search engines

Keywords, or **descriptors**, name your subject for computer searches. To develop effective keywords, it helps to understand the different operations of library databases, library search engines, and public search engines:

- **A database matches your keywords to its index of authors, titles, and subject headings.** The subject headings reflect the database's directory of terms and are assigned by people who have read the sources. You can find these subject headings by using your own keywords until you locate a promising source. The information for the source will list the headings under which the database indexes the source and others like it. You can then use those headings for further searches.
- **A library's centralized search engine seeks your keywords among all the library's physical holdings and online offerings.** After your initial keyword search, the

MyWritingLab

Visit MyWritingLab for more help with finding sources.

engine will provide options to limit or expand your search within the library's available resources. The search engine will not return content from the open Web.

- **A Web search engine seeks your keywords in the titles and texts of sites on the public Web.** The results will depend on how well your keywords describe your subject and anticipate the words used in sources.

Keyword searches

With search engines such as *Google*, you can use everyday language to find sites—that is, you don't have to use special terms or symbols with your keywords to expand or narrow your search. Some library databases use natural-language searching as well, and most also provide a system that will improve the results of your search. The basic operators appear in the following list, but resources do differ. Use the Help or Advanced Search information to learn the system of any databases you are using.

- **Use *AND* or + to narrow the search** by including only sources that use all the given words. The keywords *green AND products* request only the sources that contain both words.
- **Use *NOT* or − ("minus") to narrow the search** by excluding irrelevant words. *Green AND products NOT guide* excludes sources that use the word *guide*.
- **Use *OR* to broaden the search** by giving alternative keywords. *Green AND products OR goods* allows for sources that use a synonym for *products*.
- **Use parentheses to form search phrases.** For instance, *(green products)* requests the exact phrase, not the separate words. (Some systems use quotation marks instead of parentheses for this purpose.)
- **Use wild cards to permit different versions of the same word.** In *consum**, for instance, the wild card * indicates that sources may include *consume, consumer, consumerism*, and *consumption* as well as *consumptive, consumedly*, and *consummate*. If a wild card opens up your search too much, you may be better off using *OR*: *consumption OR consumerism*. (Some systems use ?, :, or + for a wild card instead of *.)
- **Be sure to spell your keywords correctly.** Some search tools will look for close matches or approximations, but correct spelling gives you the best chance of finding relevant sources.

37a

37b Reference works

Reference works, often available online, include encyclopedias, dictionaries, digests, bibliographies, indexes, handbooks, atlases, and almanacs. Your research *must* go beyond these sources, but they can help you decide whether your subject really interests you, can help you develop your keywords for electronic searches, and can direct you to more detailed sources.

You'll find many reference works through your library and directly on the Web. The following list gives general Web references for academic research.

> *EDSITEment (edsitement.neh.gov)*
> *ipl2 (www.ipl.org)*
> *Library and Archives Canada (www.bac-lac.gc.ca)*
> *Library of Congress (www.loc.gov)*
> *LSU Libraries (www.lib.lsu.edu)*
> *Voice of the Shuttle (vos.ucsb.edu)*
> *WWW Virtual Library (vlib.org)*

Note The Web-based encyclopedia *Wikipedia* (found at *wikipedia.org*) is one of the largest reference sites on the Internet. Like any encyclopedia, *Wikipedia* can provide background information for research on a topic. But unlike other encyclopedias, *Wikipedia* is a wiki, a kind of website that can be contributed to or edited by anyone. Ask your instructor whether *Wikipedia* or any other wiki is an acceptable source before you use it. If you do use it, you must carefully evaluate any information you find, using the guidelines on pages 141 and 144–48.

37c Books

Depending on your subject, you may find some direction and information in so-called general or trade books, which include personal or popular views of culture, non-specialist explanations of scholarly work, and how-to guides. But usually the books you consult for academic research will be scholarly, intended for specialists, and will include detailed statements of theory or surveys of research.

You can search your library's online catalogue by authors' names, titles, or keywords. Using the tips on page 131, experiment with your own keywords until you locate a source that seems relevant to your subject. The book's detailed record will show Library of Congress or Library and Archives Canada subject headings that you can use to find similar books.

37d Periodicals

Periodicals include newspapers, academic journals, and magazines, either printed or online. Newspapers are useful for detailed accounts of past and current events. Journals and magazines can be harder to distinguish, but their differences are important. Most college and university instructors expect students' research to rely more on journals than on magazines.

Journals	Magazines
Examples	
American Anthropologist, Journal of Black Studies, Canadian Journal of Sociology	*The New Yorker, Maisonneuve, Rolling Stone, The Walrus*
Availability	
Mainly through college and university libraries, either on library shelves or in online databases	Public libraries, newsstands, bookstores, the open Web, and online databases
Purpose	
Advance knowledge in a particular field	Express opinion, inform, or entertain
Authors	
Specialists in the field	May or may not be specialists in their subjects
Readers	
Often specialists in the field	Members of the general public or a subgroup with a particular interest
Source citations	
Source citations always included	Source citations rarely included
Length of articles	
Usually long, ten pages or more	Usually short, fewer than ten pages
Frequency of publication	
Quarterly or less often	Weekly, biweekly, or monthly
Pagination of issues	
May be paged separately (like a magazine) or may be paged sequentially throughout an annual volume, so that issue number 3 (the third issue of the year) could open on page 373	Paged separately, each beginning on page 1

37d

Periodical databases

Periodical databases index the articles in journals, magazines, and newspapers. Often these databases include abstracts, or summaries, of the articles, and they may offer the full text of the articles as well. Your library subscribes to many databases, and you can search most of them through the library's website. They vary widely in what they index. To decide which ones to use, consider what you're looking for:

- **Does your research subject span more than one discipline?** Then start with a broad database such as *Academic Search Complete, JSTOR, Lexis-Nexis Academic Universe,* or *CQ Researcher.* A broad database covers many subjects and disciplines but does not index the full range of periodicals in each subject.
- **Does your research subject focus on a single discipline?** Then start with a discipline-specific database such as *Historical Abstracts, MLA International Bibliography, Biological Abstracts,* or *Education Research Complete.* A specific database covers few subjects but includes most of the available periodicals in each subject. If you don't know the name of an appropriate database, the library's website probably lists possibilities by discipline.
- **Which databases most likely include the kinds of resources you need?** Your library's website may provide a guide to databases, or it may allow you to search for databases by discipline. You can discover the focus of each database by checking its description (sometimes labelled "Help" or "Guide") or its list of indexed resources (sometimes labelled "Publications" or "Index"). The description should also tell you the time period the database covers, so you'll know whether you also need to consult older print indexes at the library.

37d

Note The search engine *Google* has developed *Google Scholar*, a search engine at *scholar.google.ca* that seeks out scholarly articles. It is particularly useful for subjects that range across disciplines, for which discipline-specific databases can be too limited. *Google Scholar* can connect to your library's holdings if you tell it to do so under Library Links. Keep in mind, however, that your library probably subscribes to most of the periodicals searched by *Google Scholar*, so begin there.

Database searches

The following screen shot shows partial results from a search of *EBSCOhost Academic Search Complete.* Clicking

Partial keyword search results

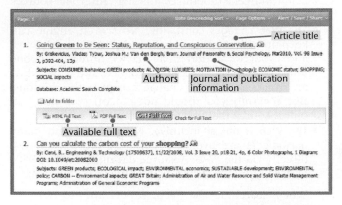

on either of these items would lead to a more detailed record containing two important kinds of information: a list of the subject headings the database uses for the source, which you can use to refine your search; and an abstract, or summary, of the article, which can tell you whether you want to pursue the article further. An abstract is not the article, however, and should not be used or cited as if it were.

Note Many databases allow you to limit your search to so-called peer-reviewed or refereed journals—that is, scholarly journals whose articles have been reviewed before publication by experts in the field and then revised by the author. Limiting your search to peer-reviewed journals can help you navigate huge databases that might otherwise return scores of unusable articles.

37e The Web

As an academic researcher, you enter the Web in two ways: through your library's website, and through public search engines such as *Bing* and *Google*. The library entrance is your main path to the books and periodicals that, for most subjects, should make up most of your sources. The public entrance, discussed here, can lead to a wealth of information and ideas, but it also has disadvantages that limit its usefulness for academic research:

- **The Web is a wide-open network.** Anyone with the right tools can place information on the Internet, and even a carefully conceived search can turn up sources with widely varying reliability: journal articles, government documents, scholarly data, term papers written by high school students, sales pitches masked

37e

as objective reports, wild theories. You must be especially diligent about evaluating Internet sources (see pp. 140–48).

■ **The Web changes constantly.** No search engine can keep up with the Web's daily additions and deletions, and a source you find today may be different or gone tomorrow. Some sites are designed and labelled as archives: they do not change except with additions. But generally you should not put off consulting an online source that you think you may want to use.

■ **The Web is not all-inclusive.** Most books and many periodicals are available only via the library, not directly via the Web. A source dating from the 1980s or even more recently may not appear on the Web.

When searching the Web, expect to use not just *Google* but three or four other search engines as well, so that you cover the range of sources. (For the latest information on Web search engines, see the links collected by *Easy Searcher* at *www.easysearcher.com*). Also expect to use trial and error to minimize the irrelevant hits and maximize the relevant ones. For example, a student researching consumption of environmentally friendly products first used the keywords *green consumption* and turned up 3.4 million items. Revising his terms to *"green consumption" "environmental issues,"* he cut the results to 2,400 items. Finally, he added *site:.org* to the end of his keywords, limiting the results to nonprofit organizations, and got just 387 results.

37f Social media

Online sources can connect you with experts and others whose ideas and information may inform your research. Because these sources, like websites, are unfiltered, you must always evaluate them carefully. (See pp. 147–48.)

■ **Email** allows you to communicate with others who may be interested in your subject, such as a teacher at your school or an expert in another province.

■ **Social-networking sites** are increasingly being used by organizations, businesses, individuals, and even scholars to communicate with others.

■ **Blogs (Web logs)** are personal sites on which an author posts time-stamped comments, generally centring on a common theme, in a format that allows readers to respond to the author and to each other. You can find directories of blogs at *www.blogcatalog .com*.

■ **Discussion lists** (or listservs) use email to connect sub-
scribers who are interested in a common subject.
Many have a scholarly or technical purpose. For an
index of discussion lists, see *tile.net/lists*.

■ **Newsgroups and Web forums** are more open than
discussion lists. See *www.delphiforums.com* and
groups.google.com/.

Note If your paper includes social media correspondence
that is not already public—for instance, an email or a
discussion-group posting—ask the author for permission
to use it.

37g Government publications

Government publications provide a vast array of
data, public records, and other historical and contemporary information. Consult *publications.gc.ca* to locate
federal government reports and publications on a wide
variety of subjects. Select "Search by Date" to access the
latest material. Many provinces also have websites with
catalogues of government reports and publications. Use a
search engine with the province's name as a keyword
along with terms like "Queen's Printer" or "government
publications." For example, a search on *Google* using the
keywords "Manitoba government publications" results in
www.gov.mb.ca/queensprinter/, the webpage of Manitoba's Queen's Printer, which lists Manitoba's provincial
statutory government publications along with links to
other provinces' publications.

For US government publications, consult the Government Printing Office's *GPO Federal Digital System*
at *www.gpo.gov/fdsys/*. Also helpful is *www.usa.gov*, a
portal to a range of US government documents. Many
federal, state, and local government agencies post important publications—legislation, reports, press releases—
on their own websites. You can find lists of sites for
various federal agencies by using the keywords *United
States federal government* with a search engine. Use the
name of a state, city, or town with *government* for state
and local information.

37h Visuals, audio, and video

Visuals, audio, and video can be used as both primary and secondary sources in academic writing. A
painting, an advertisement, or a video of a speech might
be the subject of a paper and thus a primary source. A
podcast of a radio interview or a university lecture might
serve as a secondary source. Because many Web sources

for multimedia are unfiltered—they can be posted by any-one—you must always evaluate them as carefully as you would any source on the open Web.

- **Visuals** such as charts, graphs, and photographs can be found in print or online. Online sources for images include public image databases such as *Digital Gallery* (New York Public Library); public directories such as *Art Project* by *Google*; and databases available through your library. For specifically Canadian images, *Images Canada* (*www.imagescanada.ca*) provides access to thousands of images found in the databases of many Canadian museums, libraries, and universities.
- **Video files** capture performances, public presentations and speeches, and news events, among other activities. They are available through the Web and through your library. Online sources of video include *American Memory;* search engines such as *Google;* and *YouTube*, which includes commercials, historical footage, current events, and much more.
- **Audio files** such as podcasts, webcasts, and CDs record radio programs, interviews, speeches, and music. They are available on the Web and through your library. Online sources of audio include *American Memory* and podcasts at *www.podcastdirectory .com*. A vast library of Canadian sources can be found at *www.CBC.ca*

37i Your own sources

Academic writing will often require you to conduct primary research for information of your own.

Observation

Observation can be an effective way to gather fresh information on your subject. You may observe in a controlled setting—for instance, watching the behaviour of children playing in a child-development lab. Or you may observe in a more open setting—for instance, watching the interactions among students at a cafeteria on your campus. Be sure your observation has a well-defined purpose that relates to your research project. Throughout the observation, take careful notes and always record the date, time, and location for each session.

Personal interviews

An interview can be especially helpful for a research project because it allows you to ask questions precisely geared to your subject. You can conduct an interview in person, over the telephone, or online. A personal interview is preferable because you can hear the person's tone and see his or her expressions and gestures.

Here are a few guidelines for interviews:

- **Prepare a list of open-ended questions to ask**—perhaps ten or twelve for a one-hour interview. Do some research for these questions to discover background on the issues.

- **Take care in interpreting answers,** especially if you are online and thus can't depend on facial expressions, gestures, and tone of voice to convey the subject's attitudes.

- **Keep thorough notes.** Take notes during an in-person or telephone interview, or record the interview if your subject agrees. For online interviews, save the discussion in a file of its own.

- **Verify quotations.** Before you quote your subject in your paper, check with him or her to ensure that the quotations are accurate.

Surveys

Asking questions of a defined group of people can provide information about respondents' attitudes, behaviour, backgrounds, and expectations. Use the following tips to plan and conduct a survey:

- **Decide what you want to find out.** The questions you ask should be dictated by your purpose. Formulating a hypothesis about your subject—a generalization that can be tested—will help you refine your purpose.

- **Define your population.** Think about the kinds of people your hypothesis is about—for instance, university students or preschool children—and sample this population.

- **Write your questions.** Surveys may contain closed questions (checklists and multiple-choice, true/false, or yes/no questions) or open-ended questions that allow brief, descriptive answers.

- **Test your questions on a few respondents.** Eliminate or recast questions that they find unclear, discomforting, or unanswerable.

- **Tally the results.** Count the actual numbers of answers, including any nonanswers.

- **Seek patterns in the raw data.** Such patterns may confirm or contradict your hypothesis. Revise the hypothesis or conduct additional research if necessary.

37i

38 Evaluating and Synthesizing Sources

Research writing is much more than finding sources and reporting their contents. The challenge and interest come from selecting appropriate sources and then interacting with and synthesizing them through **critical reading**. To read critically, you analyze a text, identifying its main ideas, evidence, bias, and other relevant elements; you evaluate its usefulness and quality; and you relate it to other texts and to your own ideas.

38a Evaluation of sources

Not all the sources you find will prove worthwhile: some may be irrelevant to your subject, and others may be unreliable. Gauging the relevance and reliability of sources is the essential task of evaluating them.

Note In evaluating sources you need to consider how they come to you. The sources you find through the library, both print and online, have been previewed for you by their publishers and by the library's staff. They still require your critical reading, but you can have some confidence in the information they contain. With online sources, however, you can't assume similar previewing, so your critical reading must be especially rigorous.

Library sources

To evaluate sources you find through the library, look at dates, titles, summaries, introductions, headings, author biographies, bibliographies, and any source citations. Try to answer the following questions about each source.

Evaluate relevance

- **Does the source devote some attention to your subject?** Check whether the source focuses on your subject or covers it marginally, and compare the source's coverage to that in other sources.
- **Is the source appropriately specialized for your needs?** Check the source's treatment of a topic you know something about, to ensure that it is neither too superficial nor too technical.

- **Is the source up to date enough for your subject?** Check the publication date. If your subject is current, your sources should be, too.

Evaluate reliability

- **Where does the source come from?** It matters whether you found the source through your library or directly on the Internet. (If on the Internet, see below and pp. 144–47.) Check whether a library source is popular or scholarly. Scholarly sources, such as refereed journals and university press books, are generally deeper and more reliable.
- **Is the author an expert in the field?** The authors of scholarly publications tend to be experts. To verify expertise, check an author's credentials in a biography (if the source includes one), in a biographical reference, or by using the author's name in a keyword search of the Web.
- **What is the bias of the source?** Every author has a point of view that influences the selection and interpretation of evidence. How do the author's ideas relate to those in other sources? What areas does the author emphasize, ignore, or dismiss? When you're aware of sources' biases, you can acknowledge and attempt to balance them.
- **Is the source fair and reasonable?** Even a strongly biased work should present sound reasoning, adequate evidence, and a fair picture of opposing views— all in an objective, calm tone. The absence of any of these qualities should raise a warning flag.
- **Is the source well written?** A coherent organization and clear, error-free sentences indicate a careful author.

See the next two pages for an example of how a student applied these criteria to two library sources.

38a

Websites

To a great extent, the same critical reading that serves you with library sources will help you evaluate websites. But most websites have not undergone prior screening by editors and librarians. On your own, you

(continued on p. 144)

Evaluating library sources

Below are a student's evaluations of the two library sources on the facing page. The student was researching consumption of environmentally friendly products.

Makower	Jackson
Origin	
Interview with Joel Makower published in *Vegetarian Times*, a popular magazine.	Article by Tim Jackson published in the *Journal of Industrial Ecology*, a scholarly journal sponsored by two reputable universities: MIT and Yale.
Author	
Gives Makower's credentials at the beginning of the interview: the author of a book on green products and of a monthly newsletter on green businesses.	Includes a biography at the end of the article that describes Jackson as a professor at the University of Surrey (UK) and lists his professional activities related to the environment.
Bias	
Describes and promotes green products. Concludes with an endorsement of a for-profit website that tracks and sells green products.	Gives multiple views of green consumerism. Argues that environmental solutions will involve green products and less consumption but differently than proposed by others.
Reasonableness and writing	
Presents Makower's data and perspective on distinguishing good from bad green products, using conversational writing in an informal presentation.	Presents and cites opposing views objectively, using formal academic writing.
Source citations	
Lacks citations for claims and data.	Lists scholarly and government sources in dozens of citations.
Assessment	
Probably unreliable: The article comes from a nonscholarly source, takes a one-sided approach to consumption, and depends on statistics credited only to Makower.	**Probably reliable:** The article comes from a scholarly journal, discusses many views and concedes some, and includes evidence from and citations of reliable sources.

38a

First and last pages
of an interview
with Joel Makower,
published in
Vegetarian Times

First and last pages
of an article by
Tim Jackson,
published in
the *Journal of
Industrial Ecology*

(continued from p. 141)

must distinguish scholarship from corporate promotion, valid data from invented statistics, well-founded opinion from clever propaganda.

To evaluate a website, add the following questions to those opposite and above.

- **What type of site are you viewing?** What does the type lead you to expect about the site's purpose and content?
- **Who is the author or sponsor?** How credible is the person or group responsible for the site?
- **What is the purpose of the site?** What does the site's author or sponsor intend to achieve? Can you detect bias?
- **What does context tell you?** What do you already know about the site's subject that can inform your evaluation? What kinds of support or other information do the site's links provide?
- **What does presentation tell you?** Is the site's design well thought out and effective? Is the writing clear and error-free?
- **How worthwhile is the content?** Are the site's claims well supported by evidence? Is the evidence from reliable sources?

The following discussion elaborates on each of these questions. Pages 146–47 illustrate how a student applied the questions to two websites.

Note To evaluate a Web document, you'll often need to refer to the site's home page to discover the author or sponsor, date of publication, and other relevant information. The page you're reading may include a link to the home page. If it doesn't, you can find it by editing the URL in the Address or Location field of your browser.

38a Determine the type of site

When you search the Web, you will encounter various types of sites. The URL is an important clue about what kind of site you have found.

For the purposes of evaluation, the most important part of any URL is the domain name, which generally contains the name of the sponsoring organization (for example, *www.CBC.ca* is owned by the Canadian Broadcasting Corporation, and *cpha.ca* by the Canadian Public Health Association) and an abbreviation that may describe the type of organization. In URLs for US websites, common abbreviations are *.org* for nonprofit organizations, *.edu* for educational institutions, *.gov* for government bodies, *.mil* for the military, and *.com* for commercial sites. Most institutional Canadian sites, including those of universities and colleges, end in *.ca.* Remember that a site with *.edu* could belong to a biased or unqualified individual who belongs to an educational institution, a site with *.org* or *.biz* might belong to an organization that advocates specific policies, and a site with *.com* might contain reliable information even though the site exists for commercial, not educational, purposes.

Identify the author or sponsor

A reputable site will list the author or group responsible for the site and will provide information or a link for contacting the author or sponsor. If none of this information is provided, you should not use the source. If you have only the author or group name, you may be able to discover more in a biographical dictionary or through a keyword search. Make sure the author and sponsor have expertise in the subject.

Gauge purpose

A website's purpose determines what ideas and information it offers. Inferring that purpose tells you how to interpret what you see on the site. If a site is intended to sell a product or an opinion, it may emphasize favourable ideas and information while ignoring or even distorting information and views that are unfavourable. In contrast, if a site is intended to build knowledge—for instance, a scholarly project or journal—it will likely acknowledge diverse views and evidence. Be suspicious of any site that does not describe its goals.

Consider context

Look outside the site itself. What do you already know about the site's subject and the prevailing views of it? Do the site's links support the site's credibility? Are they relevant to the site and reliable in themselves?

Look at presentation

38a

Considering both the look of a site and the way it's written can illuminate its intentions and reliability. Does the design reflect the apparent purpose of the site, or does it undercut or conceal that purpose in some way? Is the text clearly written, or is it difficult to understand?

Analyze content

With information about a site's author, purpose, and context, you're in a position to evaluate its content. Are the ideas and information slanted and, if so, in what direction? Are they up-to-date? Are the views and data authoritative, or do you need to balance them—or even reject them? Are claims supported by evidence from reliable sources?

(continued on p. 147)

Evaluating websites

Below is a student's comparative analysis of two Web-based sources he consulted during his research on environmentally friendly products. One source is an article published on the Environment Canada website, while the other (not shown) is an article ("What Is Global Warming?") published on the website Allianz Knowledge Partnersite.

Allianz Knowledge Partnersite	*Environment Canada*
Author and sponsor	
Site sponsor is the Allianz Group, a global insurance company. Author of article is identified as an editor, not a scientist.	Site sponsor is Environment Canada, a large government agency employing professionals who publish reports and scholarly articles in peer-reviewed journals.
Purpose and bias	
Educational page on a corporate-sponsored website with self-stated purpose of gathering information about global issues and making it available to an international audience.	Self-stated "science-based department" providing science and technology information for Canadians, supportive of environmental protection but also subject to government control.
Context	
One of many sites publishing current information on climate issues.	One of many sites publishing current research on climate issues.
Presentation	
Clean, professionally designed site with mostly error-free writing.	Professionally designed, academic tone, easy to read and navigate.
Content	
Article gives basic information about climate change and provides links to other pages that expand on its claims. The pages do not include citations of scholarly research.	Report is current (2014) with detailed methodology and analysis, and scholarly citations.
Assessment	
Probably unreliable: Despite the wealth of information in the article and its links, the material lacks the scholarly source citations necessary for its use as evidence in an academic paper.	**Probably reliable.** The agency is mandated to provide scientific evidence for policy-making, is staffed by scientists, and is accountable to Parliament, but the Minister has ultimate control over publications, and some reports emphasize the government's achievements.

38a

Article published on the *Environment Canada* website found in the *Environmental Indicators* section

Other online sources

Social media and multimedia require the same critical scrutiny as websites do. Social media—including email, blogs, and *Facebook* pages—can be sources of reliable data and opinions, but they can also contain misleading data and skewed opinions. Multimedia—visuals, audio, and video—can provide valuable support for your ideas, but they can also mislead or distort. For example, a *Google* or *YouTube* search using "Canadian minority parliaments" brings up the official website of the Parliament of Canada as well as media sites with editorials and commentaries strongly supporting or condemning the Conservative minority government elected in 2008, historic speeches by Tommy Douglas, and some Rick Mercer rants.

Use the following questions for evaluating social media and multimedia:

38a

- ■ **Who is the author or creator?** How credible is that person? You may be able to learn about the background of an author or creator with a keyword search of the Web or in a biographical dictionary. You can also get a sense of the interests and biases of an author or creator by tracking down his or her other work. If you can't identify the author or creator at all, you can't use the source.

- ■ **What is the author's or creator's purpose?** What can you tell about *why* the author/creator is publishing this work? Look for cues in the work—claims, use (or not) of evidence, and treatment of opposing views—to figure out how to position the source among your other sources.

- **What does the context reveal?** What do others' responses to the work indicate about the source's balance and reliability? Comments on a blog posting or the other messages in a discussion thread will give you a sense of how the author/creator is regarded.
- **How worthwhile is the content?** Are the claims made by the author/creator supported by evidence from reliable sources? If you don't see supporting information, ask the author/creator for it. Then verify the sources with your own research: are they reputable?
- **How does the source compare with other sources?** Do the claims seem accurate and fair given what you've seen in sources you know to be reliable? Always consider social media and multimedia in comparison to other sources so that you can distinguish singular, untested views from more mainstream views that have been subject to verification.

38b Synthesis of sources

Evaluating sources moves you into the most significant part of research writing: forging relationships for your own purpose. This **synthesis** is an essential step in reading sources critically and in creating new knowledge.

Respond to sources

Write down what your sources make you think. Do you agree or disagree with the author? Why do you agree or disagree? Does a source suggest new approaches to your subject? Is there anything in the source that you need to research further before you can understand it? Does the source prompt questions that you should keep in mind while reading other sources?

Connect sources

38b

When you notice a link between sources, record your ideas. Do two sources differ in their theories or their interpretations of facts? Does one source illuminate another—perhaps commenting or clarifying or supplying additional data? Do two or more sources report studies that support a theory you've read about or an idea of your own?

Heed your own insights

Apart from ideas prompted by your sources, you are sure to come up with independent thoughts: a conviction, a point of confusion that suddenly becomes clear, a question you haven't seen anyone else ask. These insights may occur at unexpected times, so it's good practice to keep a notebook or computer handy to record them.

Draw your own conclusions

As your research proceeds, the responses, connections, and insights you form through synthesis will lead you to answer your starting research question with a statement of your thesis (see p. 123). They will also lead you to the main ideas supporting your thesis—conclusions you have drawn from your synthesis of sources, forming the main divisions of your paper.

Use sources to support your conclusions

Effective synthesis requires careful handling of evidence from sources so that it meshes smoothly into your sentences and yet is clearly distinct from your own ideas. When drafting your paper, make sure that each paragraph focuses on an idea of your own, with the support for the idea coming from your sources. Generally, open each paragraph with your idea, provide evidence from a source or sources with appropriate citations, and close with an interpretation of the evidence. (For an example of such a paragraph, see p. 9.)

39 Integrating Sources into Your Text

Integrating source material into your sentences is key to synthesizing others' ideas and information with your own. Evidence drawn from sources should *back up* your conclusions, not *be* your conclusions: you don't want to let your evidence overwhelm your own point of view. The point of research is to investigate and go beyond sources in order to develop your own logical argument.

Integrating sources into your text may involve several conventions discussed elsewhere in this book of academic writing:

39

- **Using commas to punctuate signal phrases** (p. 93).
- **Placing other punctuation marks with quotation marks** (p. 101).
- **Using brackets and the ellipsis mark to indicate changes in quotations** (pp. 104–06).
- **Formatting long prose quotations and poetry quotations** (**MLA**, p. 203; **APA**, p. 221; and **CMS**, p. 235).

MyWritingLab

Visit **MyWritingLab** for more help with integrating sources into your text.

39a Summary, paraphrase, and direct quotation

As you take notes from sources or work source material into your draft, you can summarize, paraphrase, quote, or combine methods. The choice should depend on why you are using a source.

Note Summaries, paraphrases, and quotations all require source citations. A summary or paraphrase without a source citation or a quotation without quotation marks is plagiarism. See pages 157–63 for more on plagiarism.

Summary

When you summarize, you condense an extended idea or argument into a sentence or more in your own words. Summary is most useful when you want to record the gist of an author's idea without the background or supporting evidence. Here, for example, is a passage from a history of Canada's involvement in World War I, followed by a one-sentence summary.

Original quotation
The wealthy young men who enjoyed their socially-admired role as officers in the militia were quick to offer their services, displaying the leadership that was expected of the English-speaking, moneyed class who resided in "the Square Mile." One of the most notable among them was twenty-six-year-old Guy Melfort Drummond. Young Drummond, an officer in the 5th Royal Highlanders, seemed to have a glittering future. Handsome and very tall (six foot four), fluently bilingual and a millionaire, Drummond was being groomed for a career high in Conservative party politics, and there were those who whispered that the post of prime minister was not unlikely for Drummond some day.

—DANIEL D. DANCOCKS, *Welcome to Flanders Fields*, Toronto: McClelland & Stewart, 1988, 40.

39a

Summary
Assuming the leadership roles expected of them, rich young men like Guy Drummond, from the Montreal English-speaking establishment, volunteered for war in 1914.

Paraphrase

When you **paraphrase**, you follow the author's original presentation much more closely, but you still restate it in your own words. Paraphrase is most useful when you want to reconstruct an author's line of reasoning but don't feel the original words merit direct quotation. Here is a paraphrase of the final sentence in the passage quoted above:

Paraphrase

Tall, handsome, rich, and bilingual, Guy Drummond was thought by some to be a future Conservative prime minister.

Follow these guidelines when paraphrasing:

- **Read the material until you understand it.**
- **Restate the main ideas in your own words and sentence structures**. Use phrases if complete sentences seem cumbersome.
- **Be careful not to distort the author's meaning.**

For examples of poor and revised paraphrases, see page 162.

ESL If English is your second language, you may have difficulty paraphrasing the ideas in sources because synonyms don't occur to you or you don't see how to restructure sentences. Before attempting a paraphrase, read the original passage several times. Then, instead of "translating" line by line, try to state the gist of the passage without looking at it. Check your effort against the original to be sure you have captured the source author's meaning and emphasis without using his or her words and sentence structures. If you need a synonym for a word, look it up in a dictionary.

Direct quotation

Whether to quote a source instead of paraphrasing or summarizing it depends on the kind of source and on how important its exact words are. Quote extensively from primary sources that you are analyzing, such as historical documents or literary works. Quote selectively from secondary sources, such as other writers' views of primary sources. Summarize or paraphrase from secondary sources unless the material passes *both* of these tests:

- **The author's original satisfies one of these requirements:**
  The language is unusually vivid, bold, or inventive.
  The quotation cannot be paraphrased without distortion or loss of meaning.
  You take issue with the words themselves.
  The quotation represents and emphasizes the view of an important expert.
  The quotation is a graph, diagram, or table.

- **The quotation is as short as possible:**
  It includes only material relevant to your point.
  It is edited to eliminate examples and other unneeded material.

39a

When taking a quotation from a source, copy the material *carefully*. Take down the author's exact wording, spelling, capitalization, and punctuation. Proofread every direct quotation *at least twice,* and be sure you have supplied big quotation marks so that later you won't confuse the direct quotation with a paraphrase or summary.

39b Introduction and interpretation of source material

Note Most examples in the following pages use the documentation style of the Modern Language Association (MLA) and also **present-tense°** verbs that are typical of much writing in the humanities. For specific variations in the academic disciplines, see pages 155–56.

Introduction

Work all quotations, paraphrases, and summaries smoothly into your own sentences, adding words as necessary to mesh structures.

> Awkward   One editor disagrees with this view and "a good reporter does not fail to separate opinions from facts" (Lyman 52).
>
> Revised   One editor disagrees with this view, <u>maintaining that</u> "a good reporter does not fail to separate opinions from facts" (Lyman 52).

To mesh your own and your source's words, you may sometimes need to make a substitution or addition to the quotation, signalling your change with brackets:

> Words added
> "The tabloids [of England] are a journalistic case study in bad reporting," claims Lyman (52).

> Verb form changed
> A bad reporter, Lyman implies, is one who "[fails] to separate opinions from facts" (52). [The bracketed verb replaces *fail* in the original.]

> Capitalization changed
> "[T]o separate opinions from facts" is a goal of good reporting (Lyman 52). [In the original, *to* is not capitalized.]

> Noun supplied for pronoun
> The reliability of a news organization "depends on [reporters'] trustworthiness," says Lyman (52). [The bracketed noun replaces *their* in the original.]

Interpretation

Even when it does not conflict with your own sentence structure, source material will be ineffective if you merely dump it in readers' laps without explaining how

°See "Grammar Terms," page 272.

you intend it to be understood. In the following passage, we must figure out for ourselves that the writer's sentence and the quotation state opposite points of view.

Dumped Many news editors and reporters maintain that it is impossible to keep personal opinions from influencing the selection and presentation of facts. "True, news reporters, like everyone else, form impressions of what they see and hear. However, a good reporter does not fail to separate opinions from facts" (Lyman 52).

Revised Many news editors and reporters maintain that it is impossible to keep personal opinions from influencing the selection and presentation of facts. Yet not all authorities agree with this view. One editor grants that "news reporters, like everyone else, form impressions of what they see and hear." But, he insists, "a good reporter does not fail to separate opinions from facts" (Lyman 52).

Signal phrases

In the preceding revised passage, the words *One editor grants* and *he insists* are **signal phrases:** they tell readers who the source is and what to expect in the quotations. Signal phrases usually contain (1) the source author's name (or a substitute for it, such as *One editor* and *he*) and (2) a verb that indicates the source author's attitude or approach to what he or she says, as *grants* implies concession and *insists* implies argument.

Below are some verbs to use in signal phrases. For the appropriate **tense°** of such verbs (**present,°** as here, or **past°** or **present perfect°**) see pages 155–56.

Author is neutral	Author infers or suggests	Author argues	Author is uneasy or disparaging
comments	analyzes	claims	belittles
describes	asks	contends	bemoans
explains	assesses	defends	complains
illustrates	believes	disagrees	condemns
mentions	concludes	holds	deplores
notes	considers	insists	deprecates
observes	finds	maintains	derides
points out	predicts		laments
records	proposes	Author agrees	warns
relates	reveals	accepts	
reports	shows	admits	
says	speculates	agrees	
sees	suggests	concedes	
thinks	supposes	concurs	
writes		grants	

39b

°See "Grammar Terms," page 272.

Note that some signal verbs, such as *describes* and *assesses*, cannot be followed by *that*.

Vary your signal phrases to suit your interpretation of source material and also to keep readers' interest. A signal phrase may precede, interrupt, or follow the borrowed material:

Signal phrase precedes

<u>Lyman insists</u> that "a good reporter does not fail to separate opinions from facts" (52).

Signal phrase interrupts

"However," <u>Lyman insists</u>, "a good reporter does not fail to separate opinions from facts" (52).

Signal phrase follows

"[A] good reporter does not fail to separate opinions from facts," <u>Lyman insists</u> (52).

Background information

You can add information to source material to integrate it into your text and inform readers why you are using it. Often, you may want to provide the author's name in the text:

Author named

<u>Harold Lyman</u> grants that "news reporters, like everyone else, form impressions of what they see and hear." But, Lyman insists, "a good reporter does not fail to separate opinions from facts" (52).

If the source title contributes information about the author or the context of the borrowed material, you can provide the title in the text:

Title given

Harold Lyman, <u>in his book *The Conscience of the Journalist,*</u> grants that "news reporters, like everyone else, form impressions of what they see and hear." But, Lyman insists, "a good reporter does not fail to separate opinions from facts" (52).

39b

Finally, if the source author's background and experience reinforce or clarify the borrowed material, you can provide these credentials in the text:

Credentials given

Harold Lyman, <u>a newspaper editor for more than forty years,</u> grants that "news reporters, like everyone else, form impressions of what they see and hear." But, Lyman insists, "a good reporter does not fail to separate opinions from facts" (52).

You need not name the author, title, or credentials in your text when you are simply establishing facts or weaving together facts and opinions from varied sources to support a larger point. In the following passage, the information is more important than the source, so the author's name is confined to a parenthetical acknowledgment:

> The inexperienced Canadian troops at Saint-Julien, in their first major offensive of the Great War, achieved the only successful Allied attack of the Second Battle of Ypres (Dancocks 188).

Discipline styles for interpreting sources

The preceding guidelines for interpreting source material apply generally across academic disciplines, but there are differences in verb tenses and documentation style.

English and some other humanities

Writers in English, other languages, and related disciplines use MLA style for documenting sources (see Chapter 42) and generally use the **present tense°** of verbs in signal phrases. (See the list of signal-phrase verbs on p. 153.) In discussing sources other than works of literature, the **present perfect tense°** is also sometimes appropriate:

> Lyman insists ... [present].
> Lyman has insisted ... [present perfect].

In discussing works of literature, use only the present tense to describe both the work of the author and the action in the work:

> Kate Chopin builds irony into every turn of "The Story of an Hour." For example, Mrs. Mallard, the central character, finds joy in the death of her husband, whom she loves, because she anticipates "the long procession of years that would belong to her absolutely" (23).

Avoid shifting tenses in writing about literature. You can, for instance, shorten quotations to avoid their **past-tense°** verbs:

39b

Shift   Her freedom elevates her, so that "she carried herself unwittingly like a goddess of victory" (24).

No shift   Her freedom elevates her, so that she walks "unwittingly like a goddess of victory" (24).

History and other humanities

Writers in history, art history, philosophy, and related disciplines generally use the present tense or present perfect tense of verbs in signal phrases. (See the list of possible verbs on page 153.)

°See "Grammar Terms," page 272.

As Dancocks has noted, "The second Battle of Ypres was a relatively minor affair so far as the Great War was concerned."[6]

Eksteins claims, "For the Germans, this was a war to change the world; for the British this was a war to preserve a world."[7]

Eksteins sees the Christmas Truce of 1914 as the last European expression of traditional values such as honour, duty, and sportsmanship.[8]

The superscripted (raised) numbers after the quotations are part of the Chicago documentation style, used in history and other disciplines and discussed in Chapter 44.

Social and natural sciences

Writers in the sciences generally use a verb's present tense just for reporting the results of a study (*The data* suggest …). Otherwise, they use a verb's past tense or present perfect tense in a signal phrase, as when introducing an explanation, interpretation, or other commentary. (Thus, when you are writing for the sciences, generally convert the list of signal-phrase verbs on p. 153 from the present to the past or present perfect tense.)

In an exhaustive survey of the literature published between 1990 and 2013, Walker (2015) found "no proof, merely a weak correlation, linking place of residence and rate of illness" (p. 121).

Lin (2014) has suggested that preschooling may significantly affect children's academic performance through high school (p. 251).

These passages conform to the documentation style of the American Psychological Association (APA), discussed in Chapter 43. APA style or the similar CSE style (Chapter 45) is used in sociology, education, nursing, biology, and many other sciences.

39c

39c Clear boundaries for source material

Position source citations in your text to accomplish two goals: (1) make it clear exactly where your borrowing of source material begins and ends; (2) keep the citations as unobtrusive as possible. You can accomplish both goals by placing an in-text citation at the end of the sentence element containing the borrowed material. This sentence element may be a phrase or a clause, and it may begin, interrupt, or conclude the sentence. The following examples are in MLA style.

°See "Grammar Terms," page 272.

The inflation rate might climb as high as 30 percent (Kim 164), an increase that could threaten the small nation's stability.

The inflation rate, which might climb as high as 30 percent (Kim 164), could threaten the small nation's stability.

The small nation's stability could be threatened by its inflation rate, which, one source predicts, might climb as high as 30 percent (Kim 164).

In the last example the addition of *one source predicts* clarifies that Kim is responsible only for the inflation-rate prediction, not for the statement about stability.

When your paraphrase or summary of a source runs longer than a sentence, clarify the boundaries by using the author's name in the first sentence and placing the parenthetical citation at the end of the last sentence.

Juliette Kim studied the effects of acutely high inflation in several South American and African countries since World War II. She discovered that a major change in government accompanied or followed the inflationary period in 56 percent of cases (22-23).

40 Avoiding Plagiarism

The knowledge building that is the focus of academic writing rests on the honesty of all participants, including students, in using and crediting sources. This standard of honesty derives from the idea that the work of an author is his or her intellectual property: if you use that work, you must acknowledge the author's ownership. At the same time, source acknowledgments tell readers what your own writing is based on, creating the trust that knowledge building requires and permitting your readers to duplicate your research in order to test your conclusions.

40

Plagiarism (from a Latin word for "kidnapper") is the presentation of someone else's work as your own. Whether deliberate or accidental, plagiarism is a serious offence. It breaks trust, and it undermines or even destroys your credibility as a researcher and writer. In most colleges and universities, a code of academic honesty calls for severe consequences for plagiarism: a reduced or failing grade, suspension from school, or expulsion. Avoid plagiarism by

MyWritingLab

Visit **MyWritingLab** for more help with avoiding plagiarism.

recording and acknowledging all sources, including your classmates' and instructors' work.

40a Deliberate and careless plagiarism

Instructors usually distinguish between deliberate plagiarism, which is cheating, and careless plagiarism, which often stems from a writer's inexperience with managing sources.

Deliberate plagiarism

Deliberate plagiarism is intentional: the writer chooses to cheat by turning in someone else's work as his or her own. Students who deliberately plagiarize deprive themselves of an education in honest research. When their cheating is detected, the students often face stiff penalties, including expulsion.

Checklist for avoiding plagiarism

Know your source.

Are you using

☑ your own experience,
☑ common knowledge, or
☑ someone else's material?

You must acknowledge someone else's material.

Quote carefully.

☑ Check that every quotation exactly matches its source.
☑ Insert quotation marks around every quotation that you run into your text. (A quotation set off from the text does not need quotation marks. See pp. 203, 221, and 235.)
☑ Indicate any omission from a quotation with an ellipsis mark and any addition with brackets.
☑ Acknowledge the source of every quotation.

Paraphrase and summarize carefully.

☑ Use your own words and sentence structures for every paraphrase and summary. If you have used the author's words, add quotation marks around them.
☑ Acknowledge the source of the idea(s) in every paraphrase or summary.

Cite sources responsibly.

☑ Acknowledge every use of someone else's material in each place you use it.
☑ Include all your sources in your list of works cited. See Chapters 42–45 for citing sources in common documentation styles.

Deliberate plagiarism includes:

Copying a phrase, a sentence, or a longer passage from a source and passing it off as your own by not adding quotation marks and a source citation.

Summarizing or paraphrasing someone else's ideas without acknowledging the source in a citation.

Handing in as your own work a paper you have copied off the Web, had a friend write, or accepted from another student.

Handing in as your own work a paper you have purchased from a paper-writing service. **Paying for research or a paper does not make it your work.**

Careless plagiarism

Careless plagiarism is unintentional: grappling with complicated information and ideas in sources, the writer neglects to put quotation marks around a source's exact words or neglects to include a source citation for a quotation, paraphrase, or summary. Most instructors and schools do not permit careless plagiarism, but they may treat it less harshly than deliberate plagiarism—at least the first time.

Careless plagiarism includes:

Reading sources without taking notes on them and then not distinguishing what you recently learned from what you already knew.

Copying and pasting material from a source into your document without placing quotation marks around the other writer's work.

Forgetting to add a source citation for a paraphrase. Even though a paraphrase casts another person's idea in your own words, you still need to cite the source of the idea.

Omitting a source citation for another's idea because you are unaware of the need to acknowledge the idea.

40a

Plagiarism and the Internet

The Internet has made it easier to plagiarize than ever before, but it has also made plagiarism easier to detect. Instructors can use search engines to find specific phrases or sentences anywhere on the Web, including among scholarly publications, all kinds of websites, and term-paper collections. They can search term-paper sites as easily as students can, looking for similarities with papers they've received. They can also use detection software—such as *Turnitin, PlagiServe*, and *Glatt Plagiarism Services*—which compares students' work with other work anywhere on the Internet, seeking matches as short as a few words.

Some instructors suggest that their students use plagiarism-detection programs to verify that their own work does not include careless plagiarism, at least not from the Internet.

The way to avoid plagiarism is to acknowledge your sources by documenting them. This chapter discusses how to distinguish what doesn't require acknowledgment from what does and how to acknowledge online sources.

ESL The concept of intellectual property and the rules governing plagiarism are not universal. In some cultures, students may be encouraged to copy the words of scholars without acknowledgment in order to demonstrate their mastery of or respect for the scholars' work. In Canada, however, it is plagiarism to copy an author's work without quotation marks and a source citation. If you're unsure about plagiarism after reading this chapter, ask your instructor for advice.

40b What *not* to acknowledge

Your independent material

You are not required to acknowledge your own observations, thoughts, compilations of facts, or experimental results, expressed in your own words and format.

Common knowledge

You need not acknowledge common knowledge: the standard information of a field of study as well as folk literature and commonsensical observations.

If you do not know a subject well enough to determine whether a piece of information is common knowledge, make a record of the source. As you read more about the subject, the information may come up repeatedly without acknowledgment, in which case it is probably common knowledge. But if you are still in doubt when you finish your research, always acknowledge the source.

40c

40c What *must* be acknowledged

You must always acknowledge other people's independent material—that is, any facts or ideas that are not common knowledge or your own. The source may be anything, including a book, an article, a movie, an interview, a microfilmed document, a webpage, a computer program, a newsgroup posting, or an opinion expressed on the radio. You must acknowledge summaries or paraphrases of ideas or facts as well as quotations of the language and format in which ideas or facts appear: wording, sentence structures, arrangement, and special graphics (such as a diagram). You must acknowledge another's material no matter how you use it, how much of it you use, or how often you use it.

Note See pages 152–57 on integrating quotations into your own text without plagiarism. And see pages 163–64 on acknowledging sources.

Copied language: quotation marks and a source citation

The following example baldly plagiarizes the original quotation from Jessica Mitford's *Kind and Usual Punishment*, page 9. Without quotation marks or a source citation, the example matches Mitford's wording (underlined) and closely parallels her sentence structure:

Original quotation	"The character and mentality of the keepers may be of more importance in understanding prisons than the character and mentality of the kept."
Plagiarism	But <u>the character</u> of prison officials (<u>the keepers</u>) is <u>of more importance in understanding prisons than the character</u> of prisoners (<u>the kept</u>).

To avoid plagiarism, the writer has two options: (1) paraphrase and cite the source (see the examples on the next page) or (2) use Mitford's actual words *in quotation marks* and *with a source citation* (here, in MLA style):

Revision (quotation)	According to one critic of the penal system, "The character and mentality of the keepers may be of more importance in understanding prisons than the character and mentality of the kept" (Mitford 9).

Even with a source citation and with a different sentence structure, the next example is still plagiarism because it uses some of Mitford's words (underlined) without quotation marks:

40c

Plagiarism	According to one critic of the penal system, the psychology of <u>the kept</u> may say less about prisons than the psychology of <u>the keepers</u> (Mitford 9).
Revision (quotation)	According to one critic of the penal system, the psychology of "the kept" may say less about prisons than the psychology of "the keepers" (Mitford 9).

Paraphrase or summary: your own words and a source citation

The example below changes Mitford's sentence structure, but it still uses her words (underlined) without quotation marks and without a source citation:

> Plagiarism In understanding prisons, we should know more about the character and mentality of the keepers than of the kept.

To avoid plagiarism, the writer can use quotation marks and cite the source (previous page and above) or *use his or her own words* and still *cite the source* (because the idea is Mitford's, not the writer's):

> Revision Mitford holds that we may be able to learn
> (paraphrase) more about prisons from the psychology of the prison officials than from that of the prisoners (9).

> Revision We may understand prisons better if we focus
> (paraphrase) on the personalities and attitudes of the prison workers rather than those of the inmates (Mitford 9).

In the next example, the writer cites Mitford and does not use her words but still plagiarizes her sentence structure:

> Plagiarism One critic of the penal system maintains that the psychology of prison officials may be more informative about prisons than the psychology of prisoners (Mitford 9).

> Revision One critic of the penal system maintains that
> (paraphrase) we may be able to learn less from the psychology of prisoners than from the psychology of prison officials (Mitford 9).

40d Online sources

You should acknowledge online sources as you would any other source: whenever you use someone else's independent material in any form. But online sources may present additional challenges as well:

- **Record complete publication information each time you consult an online source.** Online sources may change from one day to the next or even disappear entirely. See page 127 for the information to record. If you do not have the proper information, you *may not* use the source.
- **Acknowledge linked sites.** If you use not only a website but also one or more of its linked sites, you must acknowledge the linked sites as well. One

person's using a second person's work does not release you from the responsibility to cite the second work.

- **Immediately put quotation marks around any text that you copy and paste into your document.** If you don't add quotation marks right away, you risk forgetting which words belong to the source and which are yours. If you don't know whose words you are using, recheck the source or *do not* use them.

- **Seek the author's permission before using an email message, discussion-group posting, or blog contribution.** Obtaining permission advises the author that his or her ideas are about to be distributed more widely and lets the author verify that you have not misrepresented the ideas.

If you want to use material in something you publish online, such as your own website, seek permission from the copyright holder in addition to citing the source. Generally, you can find information about copyright holders and permissions on the copyright page of a print publication (following the title page) and on a page labelled something like "Terms of Use" on a website. If you don't see an explicit release for student use, assume that you must seek permission.

41 Documenting Sources

Every time you borrow the words, facts, or ideas of others, you must document the source—that is, supply a reference (or document) telling readers that you borrowed the material and where you borrowed it from.

41a

41a Discipline styles for documentation

Editors and instructors in most academic disciplines require special documentation formats (or styles) in their scholarly journals and in students' papers. All the styles share two features:

- **Citations in the text signal that material is borrowed and refer readers to detailed information about the sources.**
- **Detailed source information, either in footnotes or at the end of the paper, tells how to locate the sources.**

MyWritingLab

Visit **MyWritingLab** for more help with documenting sources.

Aside from these essential similarities, the disciplines' documentation styles differ markedly in citation form, arrangement of source information, and other particulars. Each discipline's style reflects the needs of its practitioners for certain kinds of information presented in certain ways. For instance, the currency of a source is important in the social and natural sciences, where studies build on and correct each other; thus in-text citations in these disciplines usually include a source's date of publication. In the humanities, however, currency is less important, so in-text citations do not include date of publication.

The documentation formats of the disciplines are described in style guides, including those in the following list. This book presents the styles of the guides that are marked *.

Humanities

The Chicago Manual of Style. 16th ed. 2010. (See pp. 223–37.)

A Manual for Writers of Research Papers, Theses, and Dissertations. By Kate L. Turabian. 8th ed. Rev. Wayne C. Booth, Gregory G. Colomb, Joseph M. Williams, and the University of Chicago Press Editorial Staff. 2013. (See pp. 223–37.)

MLA Handbook. 8th ed. 2016. (See pp. 165–205.)

Social sciences

American Anthropological Association. *AAA Style Guide*. 2009. www.aaanet.org/publications/style_guide.pdf

American Political Science Association. *Style Manual for Political Science*. 2006. www.apsanet.org/Portals/54/APSA%20Files /publications/APSAStyleManual2006.pdf

Publication Manual of the American Psychological Association. 6th ed. 2009. (See pp. 205–23.)

American Sociological Association. *ASA Style Guide*. 4th ed. 2010.

Linguistic Society of America. "LSA Style Sheet." Published every December in *LSA Bulletin*.

A Uniform System of Citation (law). 19th ed. 2010.

Sciences and mathematics

American Chemical Society. *ACS Style Guide: A Manual for Authors and Editors*. 3rd ed. 2006.

American Institute of Physics. *Style Manual for Guidance in the Preparation of Papers*. 4th ed. 1997. kmh-lanl.hansonhub .com/AIP_Style_4thed.pdf

American Medical Association Manual of Style. 10th ed. 2007.

Council of Science Editors. Scientific Style and Format: The CSE Manual for Authors, Editors, and Publishers. 8th ed. 2014. (See pp. 237–45.)

*IEEE (formerly the Institute of Electrical and Electronics Engineers), *www.ieee.org*, has a number of specialized guides to standards and manuscript preparation available online, but students may find it easier to use the guide to IEEE style available as a PDF file at *ecp.engineering .utoronto.ca/online-handbook/accurate-documentation/* (See p. 245.)

Ask your instructor which style you should use. If no style is specified, use the guide from the preceding list that's most appropriate for the discipline in which you're writing. Do follow one system for citing sources—and one system only—so that you provide all the necessary information in a consistent format.

41b Bibliography software

Bibliography software—*Zotero, RefWorks, EndNote, ProCite,* and others—can help you format your source citations in the style of your choice. *Word* also has a reference management feature. Always ask your instructors if you may use such software for your papers. The programs prompt you for needed information (author's name, book title, and so on) and then format the information as required by the style. The programs remove some tedium from documenting sources, but they can't substitute for your own care and attention in giving your sources accurate and complete acknowledgment.

42 MLA Documentation and Format

MLA 42

English, other languages, and some humanities use the documentation style of the Modern Language Association, recently updated in the *MLA Handbook*, 8th ed. (2016). The MLA's website, at *www.mla.org*, offers occasional updates and answers to frequently asked questions about MLA style.

In MLA style, brief parenthetical citations in the text (on the following page) direct readers to a list of works cited at the end of the text (p. 170). This chapter also details the MLA format for papers (p. 203).

MyWritingLab

Visit **MyWritingLab** for more help with MLA documentation and format.

42a MLA parenthetical text citations

Citation formats

In-text citations of sources must include just enough information for the reader to locate both of the following:

- **The *source* in your list of works cited.**
- **The *place* in the source where the borrowed material appears.**

For any kind of print or electronic source, you can usually meet both these requirements by providing the author's last name and (if the source uses them) the page numbers where the material appears. The reader can find the source in your list of works cited and find the borrowed material in the source itself. If the source lacks a named author or page numbers, see models 6, 10, and 11.

1. Author not named in your text

When you have not already named the author in your sentence, provide the author's last name and the page number(s), with no punctuation between them, in parentheses.

After killing a German soldier, Elijah "pulls the man's hair back and removes his scalp . . ." (Boyden 193).

2. Author named in your text

When you have already given the author's name with the material you're citing, give just the page number(s) in parentheses.

Boyden describes how Elijah, after killing a German soldier, "pulls the man's hair back and removes his scalp . . ." (193).

3. A work with two authors

If the source has two authors, give last names in the text or in the citation.

"Most historians," Copp and McAndrew observe, "in their preoccupation with weapons, tactics, technology, and grand strategy . . . have ignored the vast human dimension of battle" (11).

Historians have tended to ignore the psychological impact of battle (Copp and McAndrew 11).

4. A work with three or more authors

If the source has more than two authors, give only the first author's name followed by et al. (the abbreviation for the Latin *et alii*, meaning "and others"). Do the same in your list of works cited (see p. 174).

Increased competition means that employees of public relations firms may find their loyalty stretched in more than one direction (Cameron et al. 417).

Increased competition means that employees of public relations firms may find their loyalty stretched in more than one direction (Cameron, Wilcox, Reber, and Shin 417).

5. A work by an author of two or more cited works

If your list of works cited includes two or more works by the same author, then your citation must tell the reader which of the author's works you are citing. Use the full title in the text. In parentheses, shorten the title to the first noun phrase (often a noun and adjectives that precede it) or its first one or two main words (excluding *A*, *An*, or *The*).

At about age seven, children begin to use appropriate gestures with their stories (Gardner, *Arts* 144-45).

6. An anonymous work

For a work with no named author or editor (whether an individual or an organization), use a full or shortened version of the title, as explained above.

One article notes that a death-row inmate may demand his own execution to achieve a fleeting notoriety ("Right" 16).

"The Right to Die" notes that a death-row inmate may demand execution to achieve a fleeting notoriety (16).

7. A work with a corporate author

Some works list as author a government body, committee, company, or other group. Cite such a work by the organization's name.

A 2015 report by the Department of Education provides evidence of an increase in graduation rates (12).

8. A nonprint source

Cite a nonprint source such as a webpage or a DVD just as you would any other source, by the name of the author or other contributor (first example) or by the title (second example). See model 10 on the omission of page or other reference numbers for entire works or for works lacking such numbers.

Business forecasts for the fourth quarter are optimistic (White 4).

Many decades after its release, *Citizen Kane* is still remarkable for its rich black-and-white photography.

9. A multivolume work

If you consulted only one volume of a multivolume work, your list of works cited will say so (see model 30 on p. 183), and you can treat the volume as you would any book. If you consulted more than one volume of a multivolume work, give the appropriate volume before the page number (here, volume 5):

After issuing the Emancipation Proclamation, Lincoln said, "What I did, I did after very full deliberations, and under a very heavy and solemn sense of responsibility" (5: 438).

10. An entire work or a work with no page or other reference numbers

When you cite an entire work rather than a part of it, you may omit any page or other reference number. If the work you cite has an author, try to give the author's name in your text. You will not need a parenthetical citation then, but the source still must appear in your list of works cited.

Richard Brown traces the history of the iceberg that struck *Titanic.*

Use the same format when you cite a specific passage from a work with no page, paragraph, or other reference numbers, such as a Web source.

If the author's name does not appear in your text, put it in a parenthetical citation.

Voyage of the Iceberg traces the history of the iceberg that struck *Titanic* (Brown).

11. A work with numbered paragraphs or sections instead of pages

Give the paragraph or section number(s) and distinguish them from page numbers: after the author's name, put a comma, a space, and par. (one paragraph), pars. (more than one paragraph), sec., or secs.

Twins reared apart report similar feelings (Palfrey, pars. 6-7).

12. A source referred to by another source (indirect source)

When you want to use material that is quoted or paraphrased by your source, try to find the original source and work from it. If you can't find the original source, indicate that your use of it is indirect.

F. G. Scott wrote of the battlefield of Messines, "This sordid life has been transfigured before me" (qtd. in Vance 42).

The list of works cited then includes only Vance (the work consulted), not Scott.

13. A literary work

Novels, plays, and poems are often available in many editions, so your instructor may ask you to provide information that will help readers find the passage you cite. For novels, follow the page number with the part, chapter, or other identifier.

Toward the end of James's novel, Maggie suddenly feels "the thick breath of the definite—which was the intimate, the immediate, the familiar, as she hadn't had them for so long" (535; pt. 6, ch. 41).

For poems that are not divided into parts, omit the page number and supply the line number(s) for the quotation, preceded by line or lines in the first citation.

In Shakespeare's Sonnet 73 the speaker identifies with the trees of late autumn: "Bare ruined choirs, where late the sweet birds sang" (line 4).
"In me," Shakespeare writes, "thou seest the glowing of such fire / That on the ashes of his youth doth lie . . ." (9-10).

For verse plays and poems that are divided into parts, replace the page number(s) with the part and the line number(s)—in the following example, act 3, scene 4, line 147.

Later in Shakespeare's *King Lear* the disguised Edgar says, "The prince of darkness is a gentleman" (3.4.147).

For a prose play, provide the page number followed by the act and scene, if any.

MLA
42a

14. The Bible

In a parenthetical citation of the Bible or other work of scripture, abbreviate the title of any book longer than four letters, and then give chapter and verse(s). In your list of works cited, give the edition you used, and the first time you cite it, mention the edition either in the text or in your parenthetical citation.

According to the Bible, at Babel God "did . . . confound the language of all the earth" (Gen. 11.9).

15. Two or more works in the same citation

When you refer to more than one work in a single citation, separate the references with a semicolon.

Two recent articles point out that a computer badly used can be less efficient than no computer at all (Gough and Hall 201; Richards 162).

Footnotes or endnotes in special circumstances

Footnotes or endnotes may supplement parenthetical citations when you cite several sources at once, when you comment on a source, or when you provide information that does not fit easily in the text. Signal a footnote or endnote in your text with a superscripted (raised) number above the appropriate line. Then write a note with the same number.

Text

The role of First Nations snipers in the Great War is well documented.[1]

Note

1. For further studies of First Nations snipers in the Great War, see Cook 289; Dancocks 125; Scott 3: 285-328.

MLA
42b

Indent a note one-half inch (1.25 cm), type the numeral on the text line, and follow the numeral with a period and a space. If the note appears as a footnote, place it at the bottom of the page on which the citation appears, set it off from the text with quadruple spacing, and double-space the note itself. If the note appears as an endnote, place it in numerical order with the other endnotes on a page between the text and the list of works cited. Double-space all the endnotes.

42b MLA list of works cited

On a new page at the end of your paper, a list titled Works Cited includes all the sources you quoted, paraphrased, or summarized in your paper. The format of the list is described below and illustrated on page 205.

Arrangement Arrange your sources in alphabetical order by the last name of the author (the first author if there is more than one). If an author is not given in the source, alphabetize the source by the first main word of the title (excluding *A*, *An*, or *The*).

Spacing and indention Double-space all entries. Type the first line of each entry at the left margin, and indent all subsequent lines one-half inch (1.25 cm).

The model for a works-cited list in the eighth edition of the *MLA Handbook* has nine core elements and a small number of optional elements. You should include only those elements that are relevant to your discussion of the work and useful to readers who wish to locate the same source. Note the period or comma that follows each element. Following these nine elements are any optional elements you wish to include.

①   ②   ③   ④
Author. Title of source. Title of container, Other contributors,
   ⑤   ⑥   ⑦   ⑧   ⑨
version, number, Publisher, publication date, location.
[optional elements]
Date of access / Medium or description / City

of publication / . . .

There is often more than one correct way to document a source. Items in your works-cited entry may differ depending on what you focus on in your discussion of the source (e.g., the work of the translator, of the editor, or of a performer). You can adapt these elements to document items that do not appear as models in this chapter.

Authors

The first MLA citation element is the author. The following models show how to handle authors' names in citing any kind of source.

1. One author

Boyden, Joseph. *Three Day Road*. Viking Canada, 2005.

MLA work-cited models

Authors

(continued)

MLA
42b

MLA work-cited models

(continued)

MLA
42b

MLA
42b

(*continued*)

Give the author's full name—last name first, a comma, first name, any middle name or initial, and a period. Omit any title, such as *Dr.* or *PhD*. The title of the source follows the author's name. It is the second MLA element.

2. Two authors

Copp, Terry, and Bill McAndrew. *Battle Exhaustion: Soldiers and Psychia-*
    trists in the Canadian Army, 1939-1945. McGill-Queen's UP, 1990.

Give the authors' names in the order provided on the title page. Reverse the first and last names of the first author *only*, not of the second author.

3. More than two authors

Wilcox, Dennis L., et al. *Think Public Relations.* Allyn & Bacon 2010.

Give only the first author's name followed by et al. (Latin abbreviation for "and others"). Do the same in your in-text citations of the source.

4. The same author(s) for two or more works

Frye, Northrop. *The Double Vision: Language and Meaning in Religion.*
    U of Toronto P, 1991.

---. *Fables of Identity: Studies in Poetic Mythology.* Harcourt, Brace &
    World, 1963.

Give the author's name only in the first entry. For the second and any subsequent works by the same author, substitute three hyphens for the author's name. Note that the three hyphens may substitute only for *exactly* the same name or names.

5. A corporate author

Vault Technologies. *Turnkey Parking Solutions.* Mills Publishing, 2008.

Corporate authors include companies, government bodies, and other groups. List the name of the group as author when a source gives only that name and not an individual's name. Do not include "The" before its name. If a corporate author is also the publisher, include it only as publisher and omit the author.

6. Author not named (anonymous)

The Dorling Kindersley World Reference Atlas. Dorling Kindersley, 2010.

"A Guardian and a Guide." *The Economist,* 4 Apr. 2012, p. 80.

List a work that names no author—neither an individual nor a group—by its full title. Alphabetize the work by the title's first main word, excluding *A, An,* or *The* (*Dorling* in the first example and Guardian in the second).

Periodical print sources

Print periodicals include scholarly journals, newspapers, and magazines that are published at regular intervals (quarterly, monthly, weekly, or daily). MLA style considers a journal to be the container of the articles it publishes; the container is the third citation element.

Articles in scholarly journals

7. An article in a journal with volume and issue numbers (print)

Bee, Robert. "The Importance of Preserving Paper-Based Artifacts in a Digital Age." *Library Quarterly,* vol. 78, no. 2, Apr. 2008, pp. 174-94.

See page 177 for the basic format for an article in a periodical (a journal) and the location of the required information in the journal.

8. An article in a journal with only issue numbers (print)

Rymhs, Deena. "David Collier's *Surviving Saskatoon* and New Comics." *Canadian Literature,* no. 194, 2007, pp. 75-92.

If a scholarly journal numbers only issues, not volumes, give the issue number alone.

9. An abstract of a journal article or a dissertation (print)

Lever, Janet. "Sex Differences in the Games Children Play." *Social Prob-*

>   *lems,* vol. 23, no. 2, 1996, pp. 478-87. *Psychological Abstracts,*

>   vol. 63, no. 5, 1996, item 1431.

For an abstract of a journal article, give the publication information for the article as in model 7 and then the information for the abstract.

For an abstract appearing in *Dissertation Abstracts* (*DA*) or *Dissertation Abstracts International* (*DAI*), use the following format:

Steciw, Steven K. "Alterations to the Pessac Project of Le Corbusier." U of

>   Cambridge, PhD dissertation, 1986. *DAI,* vol. 46, no. 10, 1986,

>   item 565C.

Articles in newspapers

10. An article in a national newspaper (print)

Curry, Bill. "EI Reform Set to Redefine 'Suitable' Work." *The Globe and*

>   *Mail,* 15 May 2012, Ottawa/Quebec ed., p. A4.

If the newspaper is divided into sections and makes the section label part of the page number, do the same (A1+, with the plus sign indicating that the article continues on a later page). If the section label is not part of the page number, provide it as, for instance, national ed., sec. 1, p. 3.

11. An article in a local newspaper (print)

Goldenberg, Joel. "Cineplex Commits to More Bilingual Signage." *The*

>   *Suburban* [Montreal], 11 Mar. 2015, p. 3.

If the city of publication does not appear in the title of a local newspaper, follow the title with the city name, not italicized, in brackets.

**MLA
42b**

Articles in magazines

12. An article in a weekly or biweekly magazine (print)

Geddes, John. "Death, Fear and Polling Data." *Maclean's,* 23 Mar. 2015,

>   pp. 16-17.

Follow the magazine title with the day, the month, and the year of publication. Abbreviate all months except May, June, and July. Include volume and issue number, if the magazine uses them.

13. An article in a monthly or bimonthly magazine (print)

Wyatt, Kyle Carsten. "A Better Place to Skin a Seal." *The Walrus,*

>   Apr. 2015, pp. 63-65.

Format for a print journal article

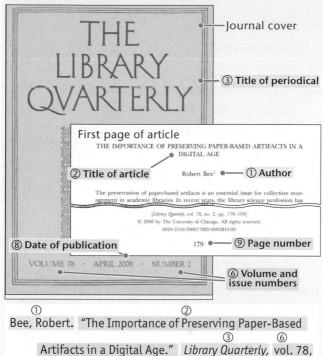

Journal cover

③ **Title of periodical**

First page of article

THE IMPORTANCE OF PRESERVING PAPER-BASED ARTIFACTS IN A
DIGITAL AGE

② **Title of article**

Robert Bee[1] ① **Author**

The preservation of paper-based artifacts is an essential issue for collection management in academic libraries. In recent years, the library science profession has

[*Library Quarterly*, vol. 78, no. 2, pp. 179–194]
© 2008 by The University of Chicago. All rights reserved.
0024-2519/2008/7802-0002$10.00

⑧ **Date of publication**

179 ⑨ **Page number**

VOLUME 78 · APRIL 2008 · NUMBER 2

⑥ **Volume and issue numbers**

①   ②
Bee, Robert. "The Importance of Preserving Paper-Based

③   ⑥
Artifacts in a Digital Age." *Library Quarterly,* vol. 78,

⑧   ⑨
no. 2, Apr. 2008, pp.179-94.

① **Author.** This may be a writer, editor, translator, or group author. Give the last name first, a comma, first name, and any middle name or initial. Omit *Dr., PhD,* or other title. End with a period.

② **Title of source.** Place a title in quotation marks if the source is an article or any work that is part of a larger work. Give the full title of the article, including any subtitle, separating them with a colon. Capitalize all important words, and end with a period inside the final quotation mark.

③ **Title of container,** in italics. This is the journal title. A larger work that "contains" a source, and is needed to locate the source, is its container. Do not omit *A, An,* or *The* from the beginning of the title.

⑥ **Numbers,** using the abbreviations *vol.* and *no.* for the volume and issue numbers, in Arabic numerals.

⑧ **Publication date,** to be given as fully as it is given in the source. Capitalize the name of a season (e.g., *Spring*).

⑨ **Location.** Give the inclusive page numbers of the article, following the abbreviation *pp.* Provide only as many digits in the last number as needed for clarity, usually two.

MLA
42b

Give the date of publication as fully as it is given in the source—this will often be the month and the year of publication. Include volume and issue number, if the magazine uses them.

Reviews, editorials, letters to the editor, interviews

14. A review (print)

Glasswell, Kathryn, and George Kamberelis. "Drawing and Redrawing the

   Map of Writing Studies." Review of *Handbook of Writing Research*,

   by Charles A. MacArthur et al., *Reading Research Quarterly*, vol. 42,

   no. 2, 2007, pp. 304-23.

The names of the authors of the work being reviewed follow the title of the work, a comma, and by. (The names of the authors of your source—the review itself—go into the first citation element.) If the review has no title of its own, then Review of and the title of the reviewed work immediately follow the name of the reviewer.

15. An editorial (print)

"A Global AIDS Campaign Stalled." Editorial. *The New York Times*, 21 June

   2008, national ed., p. A18.

For an editorial with no named author, begin with the title and add the word Editorial after the title, as in the example. For an editorial with a named author, give his or her name at the start.

16. A letter to the editor (print)

Rhodes, Paul. Letter. *The Vancouver Sun*, 30 Apr. 2012, p. A15.

Add the descriptive term Letter after the title, if there is one, or after the author's name. Enclose a title in quotation marks.

17. An interview (print)

Aloni, Shulamit. Interview. *Palestine-Israel Journal of Politics, Economics,*

   and Culture, vol. 14, no. 4, 2007, pp. 63-68.

Begin with the name of the person interviewed. If the interview does not have a title (as in the example), add Interview after the name. (Replace this description with the title if there is one.) You may also add the name of the interviewer if you know it—for example, Interview by Benson Wright.

Articles in series or in special issues

18. An article in a series (print)

Kleinfeld, N. R. "Living at an Epicenter of Diabetes, Defiance, and

> Despair." *The New York Times,* 10 Jan. 2006, national ed., pp. A1+.

> Part 2 of a series, Bad Brood, begun 9 Jan. 2006.

Cite an article in a series following the appropriate model for a scholarly journal, newspaper, or magazine. If you wish, end the entry with an optional description of the series.

19. An article in a special issue (print)

Rubini, Monica, and Michela Menegatti. "Linguistic Bias in Personnel

> Selection." *Celebrating Two Decades of Linguistic Bias Research,*

> edited by Robbie M. Sutton and Karen M. Douglas. Special issue

> of *Journal of Language and Social Psychology,* vol. 27, no. 2, 2008,

> pp. 168-81.

Follow the title of the article with the title of the special issue (its container), edited by, and the name(s) of the issue's editor(s). Add information on the second container: Special issue of and the title of the periodical that "contains" the special issue. Conclude with publication information.

Nonperiodical print sources

Nonperiodical print sources are works that are not published at regular intervals, such as books, government publications, and pamphlets.

Books

20. Basic format for a book (print)

Shteir, Rachel. *The Steal: A Cultural History of Shoplifting*. Penguin Press, 2011.

Page 180 shows the basic format for a print book and the location of the required information in the book.

**MLA
42b**

21. A second or subsequent edition (print)

Bolinger, Dwight L. *Aspects of Language*. 3rd ed., Harcourt Brace

> Jovanovich, 1981.

Information on the version (the fifth citation element— e.g., 3rd ed., revised ed.) follows the title and the fourth element—any other contributors, such as editor(s).

22. A book with an editor (print)

Sabor, Peter, and Lars E. Troide, editors. *Frances Burney: Journals and*

> *Letters*. Penguin Books, 2001.

Format for a print book

Title page

THE STEAL

A Cultural History of Shoplifting

RACHEL SHTEIR

THE PENGUIN PRESS   *New York*   2011

② Title and subtitle

① Author

⑦ Publisher's name

⑧ Date of publication

①   ②
Shteir, Rachel. *The Steal: A Cultural History of Shoplifting*.
      ⑦   ⑧
   Penguin Press, 2011.

MLA
42b

① **Author.** The author is the person or persons responsible for the aspect of the source you are interested in: writer, editor, translator, etc. Give the last name first, a comma, first name, and any middle name or initial. Omit *Dr.*, *PhD*, or other title. End the name with a period.

② **Title of source.** Italicize the title of a book or any work that is "independent" or "self-contained" (not part of a larger work). Give the full title, including any subtitle, separating them with a colon. Capitalize all important words, and end with a period.

⑦ **Publisher,** meaning the complete publisher's name, omitting business terms like *Company* (*Co.*). With academic presses, use the abbreviations *U*, *P*, and *UP*. When two publishers are responsible for a work, a slash goes between their names, with a space on each side.

⑧ **Publication date.** Follow this element with a period if it ends the citation entry. Give the year as it appears on the copyright page; if you need to cite the original date as well, put it after the title. Show an uncertain date with a question mark: *1935?* Use square brackets to provide a missing date: *[1935]*.

Handle editors' names like authors' names, but add a comma and editor(s) after the last editor's name.

23. A book with an author and an editor (print)

Austen, Jane. *Emma*. Edited by Kristen Flieger Samuelian, Broadview

Press, 2004.

When citing the work of the author, give his or her name first, and give the editor's name after the title as the fourth MLA element (other contributors), preceded by Edited by. When citing the work of the editor, use model 22 for a book with an editor, adding By and the author's name after the title:

Samuelian, Kristen Flieger, editor. *Emma*. By Jane Austen, Broadview

Press, 2004.

24. A book with a translator (print)

Marchessault, Jovette. *Mother of the Grass*. Translated by Yvonne M. Klein,

Talon Books, 1989.

When citing the work of the author, give his or her name first, and give the translator's name after the title as the other contributor (element 4), preceded by Translated by. When citing the work of the translator, give his or her name first, followed by a comma and translator. Follow the title with By and the author's name as other contributor:

Klein, Yvonne M., translator. *Mother of the Grass*. By Jovette

Marchessault, Talon Books, 1989.

25. An anthology (print)

Nischik, Reingard M., editor. *Margaret Atwood: Works and Impact*. Revised

ed., Camden House, 2002.

Cite an entire anthology only when citing the work of the editor(s) or when cross-referencing, as in model 27.

26. A selection from an anthology (print)

Palumbo, Alice M. "On the Border: Margaret Atwood's Novels." *Margaret*

Atwood: Works and Impact, edited by Reingard M. Nischik, revised

ed., Camden House, 2002, pp. 73-85.

This entry demonstrates all MLA citation elements 1 through 9, with the exception of element 6, number. Treat a selection like any other source contained within another work; the anthology is its container.

If the work you cite comes from a collection of works by one author that has no editor, use the following form:

Auden, W. H. "Family Ghosts." *The Collected Poetry of W. H. Auden,* Random

House, 1945, pp. 132-33.

If the work you cite is a scholarly article that was previously printed elsewhere, cite the version you used, followed by information for the earlier publication as an optional element at the end of the entry:

Molloy, Francis C. "The Suburban Vision in John O'Hara's Short Stories."

> *Short Story Criticism: Excerpts from Criticism of the Works of Short*
>
> *Fiction Writers,* edited by David Segal, vol. 15, Gale Publishing,
>
> 1989, pp. 287-92. Originally published in *Critique: Studies in*
>
> *Modern Fiction,* vol. 25, no. 2, 1984, pp. 101-13.

27. Two or more selections from the same anthology (print)

Nischik, Reingard M., ed. *Margaret Atwood: Works and Impact.* Revised

> ed., Camden House, 2002.

Palumbo, Alice M. "On the Border: Margaret Atwood's Novels." *Nischik,*

> pp. 73-85.

Rigney, Barbara Hill. "Alias Atwood: Narrative Games and Gender

> Politics." *Nischik,* pp. 157-65.

When you are citing more than one selection from the same anthology, you can avoid repetition by giving the anthology information in full (as in the Nischik entry) and then cross-referencing it as the container in entries for the works you used (Nischik plus page numbers).

28. An article in a reference work (print)

"Cottage." *Oxford Canadian Dictionary.* 2nd ed., 2004, p. 343.

List an article in a reference work by its title, unless the article is signed. Include volume and page numbers even for works with entries arranged alphabetically.

See also models 47 and 67, respectively, to cite reference works appearing on the Web or on a CD-ROM or DVD-ROM.

MLA 42b

29. An illustrated book or graphic narrative (print)

Chantler, Scott. *Two Generals.* Illustrated by Chantler, McClelland and

> Stewart, 2011.

When citing the work of the writer of a graphic narrative or illustrated book, include the illustrator's name as the other contributor. Use only the last name the second time a person is named in an entry.

When citing the illustrator's work, list his or her name and role first (author position: MLA element 1). After the title and By, list the author's name as the other contributor.

If you give the original publication date, put it after the title (see also model 32).

Williams, Garth, illustrator. *Charlotte's Web.* 1952. By E. B. White, Harper
    and Row, 1999.

30. A multivolume work (print)

Lincoln, Abraham. *The Collected Works of Abraham Lincoln.* Edited by Roy
    P. Basler, vol. 5, Rutgers UP, 1953. 8 vols.

Give the number(s) of the volume(s) you used before the publication information. You may add the total number of volumes at the end of the entry as an optional element.

31. A series (print)

Bergman, Ingmar. *The Seventh Seal.* Simon and Schuster, 1995. Modern
    Film Scripts Series 12.

Place the name of the series at the end of the entry as optional element.

32. A republished book (print)

James, Henry. *The Bostonians.* 1886. Penguin Books Canada, 2001.

Insert the original publication date after the title. Cite the full publication information for the version you are using.

33. The Bible (print)

New King James Version Bible. Nelson Publishing, 2006.

The Holy Bible. New International Version. Translated by Ronald
    Youngblood et al., Zondervan, 1984.

34. A book with a title in its title (print)

Eco, Umberto. *Postscript to The Name of the Rose.* Translated by William
    Weaver, Harcourt Brace Jovanovich, 1983.

This reference is to an entire book that Eco published independently, not to a postscript in Eco's novel *The Name of the Rose*. When a book's title contains another book title, do not italicize the second title. When it contains a quotation or the title of a work normally placed in quotation marks, keep the quotation marks and italicize both titles: *Critical Response to Henry James's "The Beast in the Jungle."*

MLA
42b

35. Published proceedings of a conference (print)

Stimpson, Bill, editor. *AWEA Annual Conference and Exhibition.* Curran

   Associates, 2008. Proceedings of the American Wind Energy

   Association Conference, New York, 3-6 June 2007.

Information about the conference, including its sponsor, location, and date, comes at the end, in the optional elements position. Treat a particular presentation at the conference like a selection from an anthology.

36. An introduction, preface, foreword, or afterword (print)

Samuelian, Kristin Flieger. Introduction. *Emma,* by Jane Austen,

   Broadview Press, 2004, pp. 9-46.

When your source is an introduction, foreword, or afterword, give its author followed by its descriptive title (e.g., Introduction). A descriptive title is not italicized and is not set inside quotation marks. If the source has a title of its own, provide this title, followed by a period, in quotation marks, and then its descriptive title and a period. Follow the title of the book with By and the book author's name. Give the inclusive page numbers of the part you cite.

   Use the same model when the author of the part you cite is the same as the author of the book, but use only the last name the second time the author's name appears.

Gould, Stephen Jay. Prologue. *The Flamingo's Smile: Reflections in Natural*

   History, by Gould, W. W. Norton, 1985, pp. 13-20.

Other nonperiodical print sources

37. A government or agency publication (print)

MLA
42b

Canada, Parliament. House of Commons. *Debates,* 38th Parliament,

   1st session, vol. 140, Queen's Printer for Canada, 2004.

Kogawa, Joy. *Writing in Canada.* Department of Canadian Heritage, 1994.

If a government publication does not list a person as author or editor, give as author the name of the government and agency. If the publication's author is the same as its publisher, omit the author information.

Department of Economic and Social Affairs. *World Youth Report 2012:*

   Youth and Climate Change. United Nations, 2013.

   See model 46 to cite a government publication you find on the Web.

38. A pamphlet or brochure (print)

Understanding Childhood Obesity. Obesity Action Coalition, 2013.

39. A dissertation (print)

McFaddin, Marie Oliver. *"Adaptive Reuse: An Architectural Solution for Poverty and Homelessness."* U of Maryland, PhD dissertation, 2007. *UMI, 2007.*

The dissertation service *UMI* is the source's container; an unpublished dissertation will lack this element.

40. A letter (print)

Buttolph, Mrs. Laura E. Letter to Rev. and Mrs. C. C. Jones, 20 June 1857. *The Children of Pride: A True Story of Georgia and the Civil War,* edited by Robert Manson Myers, Yale UP, 1972, pp. 334-35.

List a published letter under the writer's name. Specify in the descriptive title you use that the source is a letter and to whom it was addressed, and the date on which it was written.

For an unpublished letter in the collection of a library or archive, specify the writer, recipient, and date, and give the name of the archive. If there is a catalogue number, treat it as the final part of the location.

Atwood, Margaret. Letter to Hugh MacLennan. 22 June 1975. Rare Books and Special Collections, McGill University Libraries, Montreal.

For a letter you received, specify yourself as recipient, give the name of the writer, and create a generic description to stand in for the title. Provide the date on which it was written.

Wynne, Ava. Letter to the author, 6 Apr. 2015.

Nonperiodical Web sources

This section shows how to cite nonperiodical sources that you find on the Web. These sources may be published only once or occasionally, or they may be updated frequently but not regularly. (Most online magazines and newspapers fall into the latter category. See pp. 188 and 190.) Some nonperiodical Web sources are available only on the Web; others are available in other media as well. See also models 62–65 to cite a scholarly journal that you find on the Web and any periodical that you find in an online database.

MLA 42b

Nonperiodical sources available only on the Web

Many nonperiodical Web sources are available only online. The following list itemizes the possible elements for any source, in order, with a focus on Web sources. (See also p. 171.) Include only those elements for which you have information.

1. **Author.** Treat an online username (e.g., a Twitter handle) like a real name.

2. **Title of source.** Use quotation marks with a source's title if it is part of a larger work, or is an email or a tweet. Italicize the title of a source that is independent of any larger work. However, if a book appears in an archive or collection, italicize its title as usual. A descriptive title you create takes neither italics nor quotation marks.

3. **Title of container,** which may be a website, a blog, a wiki, an online television series, or another site or platform. A network like *Netflix* can be the container 2 of a television series that itself is the container for its episodes. A service like *YouTube*, which posts content but is not the publisher of the content, is another container 2.

4. **Other contributors,** who may be the editor or translator of an online book; the director, performers, and writers of a film or television episode; or narrators, choreographers, accompanists, composers, lyricists, or others, in literature and the arts.

5. **Version,** a description that specifies the version you used of a source that was released in more than one form (e.g., book, film, software, symphony). Use a description of this type: *director's cut, version 3.1, 4th ed.*

6. **Number,** which can be many things for an online source. Include any numbering system your source uses preceded by an appropriate description (e.g., *season 1, episode 6* for a television program).

7. **Publisher,** which can be, for example, a blog network that publishes the blogs it hosts; an institution (university, museum, government, business, etc.) that publishes its own website; or the organization responsible for a television series or a film. Omit the publisher if it is the same or nearly the same as the website title, or when a website does not create or produce the works it publishes (e.g., a service like *YouTube* and *WordPress.com*, or an archive like *JSTOR*, which may be the source's container).

8. **Publication date,** which is the date of the version you used, given as completely as your source gives it. Include the time of day for an online comment or article, if possible. (Optional elements at the end of the citation may be the original publication date or the date you accessed an undated source.)

9. **Location.** This is the final element unless there is a container 2 or an optional element. It is often the URL (dropping the *http://* or *https://*), the DOI (digital object identifier), or a permalink (stable URL). If page or section numbers are lacking or are device-specific (as for an e-book), cite either chapters or parts, or cite the work as a whole.

41. A work with a title (Web)

Miller, Emily. "Edge Effects on Lemur Behaviour and Ecology in Northwest

Madagascar." *Trafalgar Institute Research Association,* Trafalgar

Conservation Trust, Aug. 2015, www.tira/TCT/articles/2323

/contents.htm. Accessed 7 Sept. 2015.

The date of access is an optional element.

See page 188 for an analysis of this entry. If the work you are citing lacks an author, start the entry with the title of the work:

"Clean Energy." *Union of Concerned Scientists: Citizens and Scientists for*

Environmental Solutions, 5 Feb. 2013, www.ucsusa.org

/press/2013.

To cite a short Web source that also appears in another medium (such as print), see models 54–58. To cite an article from a Web journal or from an online database, see models 60–65.

42. A book (Web)

Herodotus. *The Histories.* Translated and edited by A. D. Godley, Harvard

UP, 1920. *The Perseus Digital Library,* 4 Apr. 2013, www.perseus

.tufts.edu/hopper/text?doc=Perseus:text:1999.01.0126.

First provide the same information you would for the original print version. After the original date, give the title of the database, archive, or website (container 2), italicized, and any elements that pertain to it. Often, only a URL or DOI (location) will follow container 2.

Format for a work contained in another on the Web
Top of page

Bottom of page

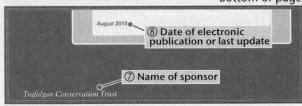

①   ②
Miller, Emily. "Edge Effects on Lemur Behaviour and Ecology

③
in Northwest Madagascar." *Trafalgar Institute Research*

⑦   ⑧
Association, Trafalgar Conservation Trust, Aug. 2015,

⑨
www.tira/TCT/articles/2323/contents.htm.

⸺ optional element ⸺
Accessed 7 Sept. 2015.

① **Author.** The author is responsible for the aspect of the source you are interested in: writer, editor, translator, etc. Give the last name first, a comma, first name, and any middle name or initial. Omit *Dr., PhD,* or other title. End the name with a period.

② **Title of source.** Use quotation marks around the title of a source that is part of a larger work, or is an email or a tweet. Italicize the title of a work that is "independent." Give the full title, including any subtitle, separated with a colon. Capitalize all important words, and end with a period.

③ **Title of container,** in italics. This is any larger work that "contains" a source and is needed to locate the source.

⑦ **Publisher,** or site sponsor. Omit it if it is the same or nearly the same as the site's name.

⑧ **Publication date,** the date of electronic publication or the latest update, given as fully as it is given in the source.

⑨ **Location.** This is the Web address. Copy it from your Web browser.

Date of access (optional element).

43. An entire site (Web)

Baillargeon, Ryan, editor. *Leadnow.ca.— people powered change,* www.leadnow.ca/. Accessed 8 Oct. 2015.

When citing an entire website, include the name of the editor, author, or compiler (if available); the title of the site, italicized; the sponsor, if it is different from the site name; the date of publication or most recent update, if available; and, as an optional element, your date of access. For ongoing Web projects, a range of years may be the most relevant publication date.

If your source lacks a named author or editor, begin with the site title:

Union of Concerned Scientists: Citizens and Scientists for Environmental Solutions. 16 Oct. 2016, www.ucsusa.org/. Accessed 18 Oct 2016.

44. An article in a newspaper (Web)

Maioni, Antonia. "Learn French, Canada, It's Good for You." *The Globe and Mail,* 22 May 2012, www.theglobeandmail.com/opinion /learn-french-canada-its-good-for-you/article4186811/.

The article's URL is its location (element 9).

Use this format to adapt the models for print periodicals if you need to cite a Web newspaper review, editorial, letter to the editor, interview, or article in a series (models 14–18). See model 64 to cite a newspaper article in an online database.

45. An article in a magazine (Web)

Webb-Campbell, Shannon. "Andrew McPhail's Quirky Band-Aid Art." *This Magazine,* 13 Apr. 2012, this.org/2012/04/13/andrew-mcphails -quirky-band-aid-art/.

46. A government publication (Web)

Canada, Canada Revenue Agency. *2010-2011 Annual Report to Parliament on the Administration of the Privacy Act.* 2 Nov. 2011, www.cra-arc .gc.ca/gncy/tp/rprts/2010-2011/rc4415-1-11eng.html.

See model 36 for examples of government publications in print.

MLA
42b

47. An article in a reference work (Web)

"Yi Dynasty." Encyclopaedia Britannica Online, 2012, www.britannica.com/.

This source does not list an author, so the entry begins with the title of the article. If a reference article has an author, place the name before the article title.

For reference works that you find in print or on CD-ROM or DVD-ROM, see models 28 and 67, respectively.

48. A visual (Web)

The following examples show formats for a range of images that are available only on the Web.

A work of visual art:

Simpson, Rick. *Overload. Museum of Computer Art,* 2008, moca.virtual
.museum/autogallery2016/autogallery_simpson/.

A photograph:

Touboul, Jean. *Desert Chronicle 01.* 2002. *Artmuse.net,* 2008,
www.artmuse.net/Stock_Photography/Desert /.

An advertisement:

FreeCreditReport.com. Facebook. Accessed 6 May 2015. Advertisement.

A map, chart, graph, or diagram:

"Greenhouse Effect." *Earthguide,* Scripps Institution of Oceanography,
2010, www.earthguide.ucsd.edu/. Diagram.

See also model 59 to cite an image that appears both on the Web and in another medium; model 75 to cite an image in a digital file; and models 80–83 to cite an image that isn't on a computer.

49. A television or radio program (Web)

Tremonti, Anna Maria, host. *The Current.* CBC Radio One, 12 Mar. 2015,
www.cbc.ca/radio/.

Cite television or radio content on the Web by its title or by the name of the person whose work you are citing. Identify the role of anyone you cite as author or contributor (host in the example). Cite other contributors after the title, as in model 51, if their contributions are important to your use of the source. *The Current* is a radio program with no individual episodes. "CBC Radio One," in the publisher position (element 7), is responsible for the source.

For a television series episode on an online service like *Netflix* (the episode's container), give both the container's date and (after the episode title) the original episode broadcast date. See also model 76 to cite a television or radio program that isn't on the Web.

50. A video recording (Web)

"The Jane Austen Book Club Trailer." YouTube, uploaded by Sony Pictures

Classics, 13 Aug. 2007, www.youtube.com/watch?v=zatP2-_NH2A.

Cite a video on the Web either by its title or by the author of the work. You may also cite other contributors (and their roles) after the title.

See also model 52 to cite a podcast; model 58 to cite a video recording or film that appears both on the Web and in another medium (such as DVD); and model 79 to cite a film, DVD, or video recording that isn't on the Web.

51. A sound recording (Web)

Beglarian, Eve. *Five Things.* Performances by Beglarian et al. *Kalvos and*

Damian New Music Bazaar, 23 Oct. 2001, www.kalvos.org.

Cite a musical sound recording by its title or by the name of the person whose work you are citing—in this example, the composer. The name of a recording that was originally distributed on its own is italicized; a track from an album is set inside quotation marks. This example also gives the performers of the work after the title. The date is that of the Web posting.

The following example shows the format for a spoken-word recording found on the Web, where the date is that of the original recording. The descriptive title takes neither quotations nor italics:

MacEwen, Gwendolyn. Poerty reading. 18 Nov. 1966. *SpokenWeb,*

spokenweb.ca/sgw-poetry-readings/gwendolyn-macewen-at

-sgwu-1966/.

See also the next model to cite a sound podcast, and model 78 to cite a sound recording that isn't on the Web.

52. A podcast (Web)

O'Reilly, Terry, writer and presenter. "The Myths of Persuasion." *The Age of*

Persuasion, CBC Radio, 5 Sept. 2009, www.cbc.ca/ageofpersuasion

/episode/2009/09/04/season-3-the-myths-of-persuasion/.

This podcast from a CBC radio broadcast lists the writer-presenter of the show, the title of the episode (in quotation marks), and the program name (the episode's container, italicized), followed by the publisher, the posting date, and the URL.

53. A blog entry (Web)

Marshall, Joshua Micah. "When Did the Dust Settle?" *Talking Points Memo,*

    TPM Media, 24 Feb. 2010, 3:39 a.m., talkingpointsmemo.com

    /edblog/when-did-the-dust-settle. Accessed 29 Mar. 2015.

This blog entry gives the title of the entry (in quotation marks) and the title of the blog or site (in italics), followed by the site's publisher. The time of the posting is given as well as the date.

54. A wiki (Web)

"Podcast." *Wikipedia,* 26 Nov. 2016, 8:58 p.m., en.wikipedia.org/wiki

    /Podcast.

Nonperiodical Web sources also available in print

Some sources you find on the Web may be books, poems, short stories, and other works that reproduce print versions. To cite such a source, begin your entry as if you were citing the print work, consulting models 20–40 for an appropriate format. Then, provide the title of the website you used as container 2, followed by any of elements 4 through 9 that apply—usually only element 9, location, which is the Web address.

55. A work contained in another with print publication information (Web)

Wheatley, Phillis. "On Virtue." *Poems on Various Subjects, Religious and*

    Moral, London, 1773. *American Verse Project,* quod.lib.umich

    .edu/a/amverse/BAP5379.0001.001/1:9?rgn=div1;view=fulltext.

The print information for this poem follows model 26 for a selection from an anthology; treat it like any other source contained within another work (the anthology is its container). You may include the city of publication for pre-1900 works. The Web collection *American Verse Project* is container 2, and its URL is the location where you found the source.

56. A book with print publication information (Web)

Sassoon, Siegfried. *Counter-Attack and Other Poems*. Dutton, 1918. *Google*

    Books, www.books.google.ca/.

The information for this electronic book follows model 20 for a print book, adding information for the Web version (container 2, which is *Google Books*). See also models 42 (a book on the Web), 66 (a book in an online database), and 73 (a book on an e-reader).

Nonperiodical Web sources also available in other media

Some visuals, films, videos, and sound recordings that you find on the Web may have been published before in other media and then digitized for the Web. To cite such a source, generally provide the information for original publication as well as that for Web publication. Begin your entry as if you were citing the original, consulting models 76–85 for an appropriate format. Then, provide the title of the website you used and its Web address.

57. A television episode with other publication information (Web)

John Franklin III et al., performers. "Most Dangerous Game." *Last Chance U,* season 1, episode 2, Condé Nast Entertainment, 2016. *Netflix,* movies.netflixable.com/Netflix-Canada/495185/last-chance-u -season-1.

This citation's focus is on the performers, whose role is given in the author position. The television episode itself is the source, and the series is its container. For a television episode, the season and episode number serve as the number (element 6); the corporation responsible for the show follows, as publisher. The date, followed here by a period, concludes container 1. The Web service *Netflix* is container 2, and its URL is the source's location.

58. A film or video recording with other publication information (Web)

Coca-Cola. Advertisement. Directed by Haskell Wexler, 1971. *American Memory,* Library of Congress, www.loc.gov/teachers /classroommaterials/connections/cocacola-ads/.

For Web films or videos with original publication information, base citations on model 79, adding the information for Web publication.

59. A visual with other publication information (Web)

Thomson, Tom. *Snow and Rocks.* 1916. *National Gallery of Canada,* www.gallery.ca/en/see/collections/artwork.php?mkey=2167.

National Gallery of Canada is cited here as the name of the website that is the image's container. For Web visuals with original publication information, base citations on models 80–83, adding the information for Web publication.

Journals on the Web and periodicals and books in online databases

This section covers scholarly journals that you reach directly on the Web and journals, newspapers, and magazines that you reach through online databases.

Web journals consulted directly

60. An article in a scholarly journal (Web)

Koerber, Duncan. "Style over Substance: Newspaper Coverage of Early

Election Campaigns in Canada, 1820-1841." *Canadian Journal of*

Communication, vol. 36, no. 3, 2011, www.cjc-online.ca/index.php

/journal/article/view/2444/2900.

For a journal article you find directly on the Web, use the format for a print journal. This Web journal does not number pages.

Use the same format to adapt the models for print periodicals if you need to cite a Web journal review, editorial, letter to the editor, or interview (models 14–17). For a journal article reached in an online database, see model 62.

61. An abstract of a journal article (Web)

Koerber, Duncan. "Style over Substance: Newspaper Coverage of Early

Election Campaigns in Canada, 1820-1841." *Canadian Journal of*

Communication, vol. 36, no. 3, 2011, www.cjc-online.ca/index

.php/journal/article/view/2444. Abstract.

Treat a Web abstract like a Web journal article. In this entry the word Abstract is needed to specify the nature of the source, so it is included at the end as an optional item. (You may omit it if the journal title clearly indicates that the cited work is an abstract.) See model 63 to cite an abstract in an online database.

Periodicals and books consulted in online databases

Citations for articles and books in online databases resemble those in print, but show the database as container 2.

62. An article in a scholarly journal (online database)

Penuel, Suzanne. "Missing Fathers: *Twelfth Night* and the Reformation of

Mourning." *Studies in Philology,* vol. 107, no. 1, Winter 2010, pp. 74-96.

JSTOR, www.jstor.org.ezproxy.torontopubliclibrary.ca/journal/studphil.

See page 196 for an analysis of the preceding entry and the location of the required information in the database.

63. An abstract of a journal article (online database)

Gorski, Paul C. "Privilege and Repression in the Digital Era: Rethinking the

Sociopolitics of the Digital Divide." *Race, Gender and Class,* vol. 10,

no. 4, 2003, pp. 145-76. *JSTOR,* www.jstor.org.ezproxy

.torontopubliclibrary.ca/stable/41675106?seq=1#page

_scan_tab_contents. Abstract.

Treat an abstract in an online database like a journal article in a database, but add *Abstract* as an optional element at the end. (You may omit it if the journal title clearly indicates that the cited work is an abstract.)

64. An article in a newspaper (online database)

Kirkey, Sharon. "'Treatment of Obesity Is a Failure,' Doctors Argue." *The*

Ottawa Citizen, 22 May 2012, pp. A1+. *WorldCat,* www.worldcat.org

/title/ottawa-citizen/oclc/.

Follow model 10 or 11 for citing a newspaper article, and add the title of the database and the Web address.

65. An article in a magazine (online database)

Ricciardi, Alessia. "Becoming Woman: From Antonioni to Anne Carson and

Cindy Sherman." *The Yearbook of Comparative Literature,* vol. 56,

2010, pp. 6-23. *Project Muse,* doi: 10.1353/cgl.2010.0003.

Follow model 12 or 13 for citing a magazine article, and add the title of the database and the Web address.

66. A book (online database)

Hazo, Samuel. *Like a Man Gone Mad: Poems in a New Century.* Syracuse UP,

2010. *Project Muse,* muse.jhu.edu/book/129595.

Follow models 20–24 for citing books, adding the name of the database and the Web address.

See also model 42 (a book on the Web), model 56 (a book on the Web with print publication information) and model 73 (a book on an e-reader).

MLA
42b

Format for a journal article in an online database

② Title of article

Missing Fathers: Twelfth Night and the Reformation of Mourning.

① Author   ⑧ Date of publication   ⑥ Volume and issue numbers

Authors: Penuel, Suzanne[1]

Source: Studies in Philology; Winter2010, Vol. 107 Issue 1, p74-96, 23p

Document Type: Literary Criticism   ③ Title of journal   ⑨ Inclusive page numbers

Subject Terms: *CRITICISM
*FATHERS & daughters
*INTERGENERATIONAL relations

Reviews & Products: TWELFTH Night (Theatrical production)

People: SHAKESPEARE, William, 1564-1616 -- Criticism & interpretation

Abstract: A literary criticism is presented of the play "Twelfth Night," by William Shakespeare, in which the absence of fathers and what that may mean is discussed. It notes that no older generation exists in the play to hover over the young and tamp down their sexuality, yet this does not result in celebration. Instead, a feeling of loss prevails. Various passages in the verse are analyzed to shed light on mourning rituals, doubling and gender changes in some of the characters.

Database: JSTOR ●————— ③ Name of database

① Penuel, Suzanne. ② "Missing Fathers: *Twelfth Night* and the Reformation of Mourning." ③ *Studies in Philology,* ⑥ vol. 107, ⑧ no. 1, Winter 2010, ⑨ pp. 74-96. ③ *JSTOR,* ⑨ www.jstor.org.ezproxy.torontopubliclibrary.ca/journal/studphil.

① **Author.** The author is responsible for the aspect of the source you are interested in: writer, editor, translator, etc. Give the last name first, a comma, first name, and any middle name or initial. Omit *Dr., PhD,* or other title. End the name with a period.

② **Title of source.** Use quotation marks around the title of a source that is part of a larger work. Italicize the title of a work that is "independent." Give the full title, including any subtitle, separated with a colon. Capitalize all important words, and end with a period.

③ **Title of container,** in italics. This is any larger work that "contains" a source and is needed to locate the source.

⑥ **Number,** using the abbreviations *vol.* and *no.* for the volume and issue numbers, in Arabic numerals.

⑧ **Publication date,** to be given as fully as it is given in the source. Capitalize the name of a season (e.g., Winter).

⑨ **Location.** Give the inclusive page numbers of the article, following the abbreviation *pp.*

Container 2:

③ **Title of container,** in italics. This is the database.

⑨ **Location.** This is the Web address of the source in the database. Copy it from your Web browser.

Other electronic sources
Publications on CD-ROM or DVD-ROM
67. A nonperiodical CD-ROM or DVD-ROM

Nunberg, Geoffrey. "Usage in the Dictionary." *The American Heritage*

> *Dictionary of the English Language,* 4th ed., CD-ROM version,

> Houghton Mifflin Harcourt, 2008.

Single-issue CD-ROMs may be encyclopedias, dictionaries, books, and other resources that are published just once, like print books. Follow models 20–36 for print books. This entry shows a work whose CD-ROM version was issued by the same publisher responsible for its print version. Including the version (element 5) clarifies that you consulted the CD-ROM version.

See also models 28 and 47 to cite reference works in print and on the Web.

68. A periodical CD-ROM or DVD-ROM

Kolata, Gina. "Gauging Body Mass Index in a Changing Body." *New York*

> *Times,* national ed., 28 June 2005, pp. D1+. *New York Times Ondisc,*

> UMI-ProQuest, Sept. 2005.

Cite an article or a periodical CD-ROM or DVD-ROM as you would a print article (pp. 175–79). Then provide the title of the CD-ROM (container 2), italicized; the name of its distributor (element 7); and the date of electronic publication (element 8). Remember that container 2 and the elements that follow it may repeat elements 3–9.

Social media
69. An email message

Bailey, Elizabeth. "On the Budget." Received by Jane E. Aaron,

> 27 Mar. 2012.

For the title of an email, use the subject heading, capitalized like any other title, in quotation marks. Name the recipient, whether yourself or someone else. As an option, you can add "Email" at the end of the entry.

70. A posting to a discussion group

buschic. "Lack of Funds Prompt Strait Area Transit Shutdown." *Canadian*

> *Public Transit Discussion Group,* 27 Mar. 2013, 3:51 a.m., cptdb.ca

> /topic/15561-lack-of-funds-prompt-strait-area-transit

> -shutdown/.

Treat online usernames like any other name. If the posting has a title, set it inside quotation marks and standardize its capitalization. The name of the group is the container, and is italicized. If there is no site sponsor or publisher, move on to the date of posting, and, as with any online comment, include the time, if available.

71. A posting to a social-networking site

Aneke, Chinwe. Comment. *Girls Inc.,* 18 Apr. 2013, 4:30 p.m., www
    .facebook.com/GirlsInc/. Facebook posting. Accessed 6 May 2015.

Give the author's name, a descriptive title, a page title (if present), and the date and time of the posting. An unexpected medium and the access date can be indicated as an option after the source's location (here, the URL) at the end of the citation.

72. A tweet

@Puglaas (Jody Wilson-Raybould). "We want to hear from you about
    #TransMountain Expansion Project contact the Ministerial Panel
    mpmo.gc.ca/measures/270 #cndpoli #VanGran." Twitter,
    26 July 2016, 8:49 a.m., twitter.com/Puglaas/status
    /757966073794662400.

Treat online usernames like any other name. The source is the text of the tweet; copy it exactly and enclose it in quotation marks. Use the name "Twitter" as the publisher. The time of a tweet is part of its publication date. As an option, you may include the date you accessed it.

Digital files

Digital files that are not on the Web include books for various e-readers (Kindle, Nook, iPad, and so on), PDF documents, JPEG images, or MP3 sound recordings that you download or access through a device. Use an appropriate model for your kind of source (for instance, model 20 for a book).

You specify an unexpected type of source or medium as an optional element at the end of the citation. That is where you can include a note like PDF file, *Microsoft Word* file, or digital file. However, if you are citing a version of a work distributed in a proprietary format (e.g., a Kindle edition), give the format as the version (element 5) of your source. If you don't know the distributor, use e-book or another appropriate designation for the version.

73. A book on an e-reader (digital)

Packer, George. *Interesting Times: Writings from a Turbulent Decade*.

Kindle ed., Farrar, Straus and Giroux, 2010.

To cite other types of electronic books, see model 42 (a book on the Web), model 56 (a book on the Web with print publication information), or model 66 (a book in an online database).

74. A text file (digital)

Blanc, Marie-Thérèse. "*Margaret Atwood's Alias Grace* and the Construction of a Trial Narrative." *ESC: English Studies in Canada,* vol. 32, no. 4, 2006, pp. 101-27. PDF file.

75. A media file (digital)

Springsteen, Bruce. "This Life." *Working on a Dream,* Columbia, 2009. MP3 file.

Masaryk, Lucy. Apple trees. Personal photograph, 2014. JPEG file.

Other print and nonprint sources

The source types covered in this section are not on a computer or, generally, in printed sources. Most of them have parallel citation formats elsewhere in this chapter. See model 17 to cite an interview in print. See models 48–51 to cite visuals, television and radio programs, video recordings, and sound recordings that are available only on the Web. See models 57–59 to cite such sources when they are available on the Web and in other media. And see model 75 to cite such sources in digital files.

76. A television or radio program

"The Time Warp." By Zoanne Clark, directed by Rob Corn. *Grey's Anatomy,* ABC, KGO, San Francisco, 18 Feb. 2015.

Start with the title unless you are citing the work of a person or persons. The source here is the episode whose title is in quotation marks, followed by the names of the episode's writer and director (in the other contributors position). The series, whose title is italicized, is the container. The network is the publisher (followed here by the call letters and city of the local station). The publication date is the date the episode was aired. If you list individuals who worked on the entire program rather than an episode, put their names after the program title.

77. A personal or broadcast interview

Paul, William. Personal interview. 6 June 2015.

Jhabvala, Ruth Prawer. Interview. By Eleanor Wachtel, *Writers and Company,*
CBC Radio One, CBHA-FM, Halifax, 27 May 2012.

Begin with the name of the person interviewed. For an
interview you conducted, specify, for example, Personal
interview, Telephone interview, or Email interview, and then give
the date. For an interview you heard or saw, provide the
title if any or Interview if there is no title. Add the name of
the interviewer if he or she is identified.

78. A sound recording

Rubenstein, Artur, performer. *Piano Concerto no. 2 in B-flat.* By Johannes
Brahms, conducted by Eugene Ormandy, performed by Philadelphia
Orchestra, RCA, 1972.

Springsteen, Bruce. "This Life." *Working on a Dream,* Columbia, 2009.

Begin with the name of the individual whose work you
are citing. If you're citing a song or song lyrics on an
album (second example), give the title in quotation
marks; then provide the title of the recording (the song's
container) in italics. The publisher is the manufacturer of
the recording.

79. A DVD or video recording

Calendar. 1993. Written and directed by Atom Egoyan, performances by
Egoyan and Arsinée Khanjian, Zeitgeist Films, 2001.

Give the date of the film's theatre release after the title.
The publisher is the organization that released the DVD
version, Zeitgeist Films, and the publication date is the
DVD's release date, 2001. If you need to specify that this is
the DVD version, include this information as an optional
element at the end of the citation, after the final period.

As with a film, with an episode of a television series
that you watched on a DVD (the episode's container), you
also give both the container's date and (after the episode
title) the original episode broadcast date.

80. A painting, photograph, or other work of visual art

Harris, Lawren. *Snow II.* 1915. National Gallery of Canada, Ottawa.

Sugimoto, Hiroshi. *Pacific Ocean, Mount Tamalpais.* 1994. Private
collection. Photograph.

To cite a work of art you saw in person, name the artist and give the title (in italics) and the date of creation. (Show an uncertain date with a question mark after the year or range of years.) The source's location (element 9) is the venue or gallery that houses it and where you saw it. Add the city name if it is not part of the venue name (an exception to this is an anonymous private collection). If you want to include the medium or other information, add it to the end of the entry as an optional element (e.g., Oil on canvas, Painting, or Photograph).

For a work you see only in a reproduction, provide the complete publication information for the source you used. Other information on the original work can appear as an optional element.

Hockney, David. *Place Furstenberg, Paris*. 1985. *David Hockney: A Retrospective,* edited by Maurice Tuchman and Stephanie Barron, Los Angeles County Museum of Art, 1988, p. 247. Original work in the collection of College Art Gallery, New Paltz.

81. A map, chart, graph, or diagram

"The Sonoran Desert." *Sonoran Desert: An American Deserts Handbook.* By Rose Houk, Western National Parks Association, 2000, p. 12. Map.

Unless the creator of an illustration is given on the source, list the illustration by its title. This map is located in a publication that is its container, so its title appears in quotation marks. If a map is published independently, italicize its title.

You may add a description (Map, Chart, and so on) as an optional element.

82. A cartoon or comic strip

Trudeau, Garry. "Doonesbury." *The Gazette* [Montreal], 28 Aug. 2015, p. E6. Comic strip.

Cite a cartoon or comic strip you saw in a publication (its container) with the artist's name, the title in quotation marks, and the container's name and publication information. You may include the description Cartoon or Comic strip as an optional element.

83. An advertisement

iPad. Advertisement. *The New Yorker,* 12 Apr. 2013, p. 3.

Cite an advertisement with the name of the product or company advertised and the descriptive title Advertisement.

84. A performance

Billy Bishop Goes to War. By John Gray, performance by Eric Peterson, directed by Sarah Rodgers, 10 Apr. 2010, Granville Island Stage, Vancouver.

Lamon, Jeanne, conductor. Concert. Performed by Lamon and Tafelmusik Baroque Orchestra, 17 Sept. 2003, Trinity-St. Paul's Centre, Toronto.

For a live performance, place the title first unless you are citing the work of an individual. (Use a descriptive title if necessary to identify the performance.) Also provide relevant information about participants as well as the performance date, venue (location—element 9), and city (if not included in the venue name). Use only the last name the second time an individual is named in a single entry.

85. A lecture, speech, address, or reading

Khouri, Katia. "Ownership Convergence." Symposium on Canadian Journalism, 16 Oct. 2002, City Hall, Cambridge.

After the speaker's name, give the title (element 2) in quotation marks or, if there is no title, a description like *Lecture* or *Address*, not in italics or quotation marks. The name of the event (which often incorporates the name of the sponsoring organization) is the container (element 3). The date follows. The location concludes the citation. However, if the type of source has not been made clear in element 2 or 3, you may add a final optional element such as *Reading, Speech, Address,* or *Lecture*.

You can adapt the preceding format to document a classroom lecture:

MLA 42b

Cavanaugh, Carol. Class lecture on teaching mentors. 4 Apr. 2014, Centennial College. Toronto.

42c MLA paper format

The document format recommended by the *MLA Handbook* is fairly simple, with just a few elements. See pages 204–05 for illustrations of the elements. See also pages 25–32 for guidelines on type fonts, headings, lists, illustrations, and other features that are not specified in MLA style.

Margins Use minimum one-inch (2.5 cm) margins on all sides of every page.

Spacing and indentions Double-space throughout. Indent the first lines of paragraphs one-half inch (1.25 cm). (See below for indention of poetry and long prose quotations.)

Paging Begin numbering on the first page, and number consecutively through the end (including the list of works cited). Type Arabic numerals (1, 2, 3) in the upper right about one-half inch (1.25 cm) from the top. Place your last name one space before the page number in case the pages later become separated.

Identification and title In the upper left of the first page, give your name, your instructor's name, the course title, and the date—all double-spaced. Centre the title. Do not type it in all-capitals or italics or place it between quotation marks.

Poetry and long prose quotations Treat a single line of poetry like any other quotation, running it into your text and enclosing it in quotation marks. You may run in two or three lines of poetry as well, separating the lines with a slash:

> In "Subject/Object," Al Purdy asks: " What shall we say of these lovers / that has not been said of others? " (1-2).

Always set aside (double indent) quotations of more than three lines of poetry from your text. Use double spacing and a one-inch (2.5 cm) indention. *Do not add quotation marks.*

> In "Separation," Al Purdy imagines how, years after they have separated, one lover will learn of the other's death:
>
> > It will happen some place else
> > One of us will know later
> > Among the crises of blurred eyesight
> > Constipation and insomnia
> > A sick old woman a sick old man
> > Spared something (5-10)

Also separate prose quotations of five or more typed lines. *Do not add quotation marks.*

In his 1967 study of the lives of unemployed black men, Elliot Liebow observes that "unskilled" construction work requires more experience and skill than is generally assumed:

> A healthy, sturdy, active man of good intelligence requires from two to four weeks to break in on a construction job. . . . It frequently happens that his foreman or the craftsman he services is not willing to wait that long for him to get into condition or to learn at a glance the difference in size between a rough 2 × 8 and a finished 2 × 10. (62)

42d Sample pages in MLA style

First page

Second page

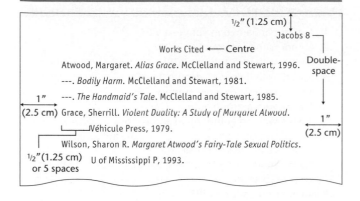

43 APA Documentation and Format

The documentation style of the American Psychological Association is used in psychology and some other social sciences and is very similar to the styles in sociology, economics, and other disciplines. The following adapts the APA style from the *Publication Manual of the American Psychological Association*, 6th ed. (2010).

Note The APA provides answers to frequently asked questions at *www.apastyle.org*.

43a APA parenthetical text citations

Citation formats

In APA style, parenthetical citations in the text refer to a list of sources at the end of the text. The basic parenthetical citation contains the author's last name and the date of publication. If you name the author in your text, then the citation includes just the date. Unless none is available, the APA also requires a page or other identifying number for a direct quotation and recommends an identifying number for a paraphrase.

APA
43a

1. Author not named in your text

One critic of Milgram's experiments insisted that the subjects "should have been fully informed of the possible effects on them" (Baumrind, 1988, p. 34).

MyWritingLab

Visit **MyWritingLab** for more help with APA documentation and format.

APA parenthetical text citations

2. Author named in your text

Baumrind (1988) insisted that the subjects in Milgram's study "should have been fully informed of the possible effects on them" (p. 34).

3. A work with two authors

Bunning and Ellis (2010) revealed significant communication differences between teachers and students.

One study (Bunning & Ellis, 2010) revealed significant communication differences between teachers and students.

4. A work with three to five authors

First references:
Pepinsky, Dunn, Rentl, and Corson (1999) further demonstrated the biases evident in gestures.
Another study further demonstrated the biases evident in gestures (Pepinsky, Dunn, Rentl, & Corson, 1999).

Later references:
In the work of Pepinsky et al. (1999), the loaded gestures included head shakes and eye contact.

5. A work with six or more authors

One study (Rutter et al., 2013) attempted to explain these geographical differences in adolescent experience.

6. A work with a group author

The students' later work improved significantly (Lenschow Research, 2015).

APA
43a

Use this model for works that list an agency, institution, corporation, or other group as the author.

7. A work with no author or an anonymous work

One article ("Leaping the Wall," 2011) examines Internet freedom and censorship in China.

For a work that lists "Anonymous" as the author, use that word in the citation: (Anonymous, 2015).

8. One of two or more works by the same author(s) published in the same year

At about age seven, most children begin to use appropriate gestures to reinforce their stories (Gardner, 1973a).

(See the reference for this source on p. 211.)

9. Two or more works by different authors

Two studies (Marconi & Hamblen, 1999; Torrence, 2014) found that monthly safety meetings can dramatically reduce workplace injuries.

10. An indirect source

Supporting data appeared in a study by Chang (as cited in Torrence, 2014).

11. An electronic source

Ferguson and Hawkins (2014) did not anticipate the "evident hostility" of participants (para. 6).

Electronic sources can be cited like printed sources, usually with the author's last name and the publication date. When quoting or paraphrasing electronic sources that number paragraphs instead of pages, provide the paragraph number preceded by para.

43b APA reference list

In APA style, the in-text parenthetical citations refer to the list of sources at the end of the text. Title this list References, and include in it the full publication information for every source you cited in your paper. Place the list at the end of the paper, and number its page(s) in sequence with the preceding pages. For an illustration of the following elements and their spacing, see page 223.

Arrangement Arrange sources alphabetically by the author's last name. If there is no author, alphabetize by the first main word of the title.

Spacing Double-space everything in the references unless your instructor requests single spacing. (If you do single-space the entries themselves, always double-space *between* them.)

Indention Begin each entry at the left margin, and indent the second and subsequent lines five to seven spaces or one-half inch (1.25 cm).

Punctuation Separate the parts of the reference (author, date, title, and publication information) with a period and one space. Do not use a final period in references that conclude with a DOI or URL. (See p. 214.)

Authors For works with up to seven authors, list all authors with last name first, separating names and parts of names with commas. Use initials for first and middle names even when names are listed fully on the source itself. Use an ampersand (&) before the last author's name. See model 3 for the treatment of eight or more authors.

Publication date Place the publication date in parentheses after the author's or authors' names, followed by a period. Generally, this date is the year only, though for some sources (such as magazine and newspaper articles) it includes the month and sometimes the day as well.

Titles In titles of books and articles, capitalize only the first word of the title, the first word of the subtitle, and proper nouns; all other words begin with small letters. In titles of journals, capitalize all significant words. (See p. 114 for guidelines.) Italicize the titles of books and journals. Do not italicize or use quotation marks around the titles of articles.

City and province (or state) of publication For sources that are not periodicals (such as books or government publications), give the city of publication, a comma, the two-letter postal abbreviation of the province or state, if applicable, and a colon. Omit the province or state if the publisher is a university whose name includes the name of the province or state, such as University of Alberta.

Publisher's name Also for nonperiodical sources, give the publisher's name after the place of publication and a colon. Shorten names of many publishers (such as Morrow for William Morrow), and omit *Co.*, *Inc.*, and *Publishers*. However, give full names for associations, corporations, and university presses (such as University of Toronto Press), and do not omit *Books* or *Press* from a publisher's name.

Page numbers Use the abbreviation p. or pp. before page numbers in books and in newspapers. Do *not* use the abbreviation for journals and magazines. For inclusive page numbers, include all figures: 667–668.

Digital Object Identifier (DOI) Many publishers assign a DOI to journal articles and other documents. A DOI is a permanent URL that links to the text and functions as a unique identifier. When a DOI is available, include it in your citation of any print or electronic source. (See models 18 and 25.) Do not add a period at the end of a DOI.

Authors

1. One author

Pinker, Steven. (2007). *The stuff of thought: Language as a window into human nature.* New York, NY: Viking.

2. Two to seven authors

Nesselroade, J. R., & Baltes, P. B. (1999). *Longitudinal research in behavioral studies.* New York, NY: Academic Press.

Separate authors' names with commas and use an ampersand (&) before the last author's name.

3. Eight or more authors

Wimple, P. B., Van Eijk, M., Potts, C. A., Hayes, J., Obergau, W. R., Smith, H., . . . Zimmer, S. (2001). *Case studies in moral decision making among adolescents.* San Francisco, CA: Jossey-Bass.

List the first six authors' names, insert an ellipsis mark (three spaced periods), and then give the last author's name.

APA
43b

APA reference-list models

APA
43b

4. A group author

Lenschow Research. (2015). *Trends in secondary curriculum.* Baltimore, MD: Arrow Books.

5. Author not named (anonymous)

Merriam-Webster's collegiate dictionary (11th ed.). (2008). Springfield, MA: Merriam-Webster.

Heroes of the environment. (2009, October 5). *Time, 174*(13), 45-54.

For a work whose author is actually given as "Anonymous," use and alphabetize that word as if it were a name:

Anonymous. (2014). *Teaching research.* Edmonton, AB: Alpine Press.

6. Two or more works by the same author(s) published in the same year

Gardner, H. (1973a). *The arts and human development.* New York, NY: Wiley.

Gardner, H. (1973b). *The quest for mind: Piaget, Lévi-Strauss, and the structuralist movement.* New York, NY: Knopf.

Print periodicals: Journals, newspapers, magazines
7. An article in a journal (print)

Garrow, S. (2013). HIPPY Montréal: Home based instruction for parents of pre-school youngsters—Evaluation of outcomes 2008–2009. *Canadian Journal of Family Literacy, 16*, 47-63.

See page 213 for the basic format for a print journal article and the location of the required information in the journal.

Note For journals that number the pages of issues consecutively through an annual volume, give the volume number (in italics) after the title, as in the example above. For magazines and for journals that start each issue with page 1, give the issue number after the volume number, in parentheses and not italicized. See model 10.

8. An abstract of a journal article (print)

Emery, R. E. (2006). Marital turmoil: Interpersonal conflict and the children of discord and divorce. *Psychological Bulletin, 92*, 310-330. Abstract retrieved from *Psychological Abstracts*, 2007, *69*, Item 1320.

9. An article in a newspaper (print)

Lopez Pacheco, A. (2003, August 11). Health lessons start at home. *National Post*, SR6.

10. An article in a magazine (print)

Rinaldi, L. (2015, March 23). Teens v. the World. *Maclean's*, 20-24.

11. A review (print)

Dinnage, R. (1987, November 29). Against the master and his men [Review of the book *A mind of her own: The life of Karen Horney,* by S. Quinn]. *The New York Times Book Review*, 10-11.

Print books

12. Basic format for a book (print)

Levitin, D. (2007). *This is your brain on music: The science of a human obsession.* Toronto, ON: Plume–Penguin.

13. A book with an editor (print)

Dohrenwend, B. S., & Dohrenwend, B. P. (Eds.). (1999). *Stressful life events: Their nature and effects.* New York, NY: Wiley.

14. A book with a translator (print)

Trajan, P. D. (1927). *Psychology of animals* (H. Simone, Trans.). Washington, DC: Halperin.

15. A later edition (print)

Bolinger, D. L. (1981). *Aspects of language* (3rd ed.). New York, NY: Harcourt Brace Jovanovich.

16. A work in more than one volume (print)

Reference to a single volume:

Lincoln, A. (1953). *The collected works of Abraham Lincoln* (R. P. Basler, Ed.). (Vol. 5). New Brunswick, NJ: Rutgers University Press.

Reference to all volumes:

Lincoln, A. (1953). *The collected works of Abraham Lincoln* (R. P. Basler, Ed.). (Vols. 1–8). New Brunswick, NJ: Rutgers University Press.

17. An article or a chapter in an edited book (print)

Paykel, E. S. (1999). Life stress and psychiatric disorder: Applications of the clinical approach. In B. S. Dohrenwend & B. P. Dohrenwend (Eds.), *Stressful life events: Their nature and effects* (pp. 239-264). New York, NY: Wiley.

Web and other electronic sources

The APA style guide discusses print and electronic sources within the same section; we discuss electronic sources separately here to help you better understand the different elements. In APA style, most electronic

(continued on p. 214)

APA
43b

Format for a print journal article
Journal cover

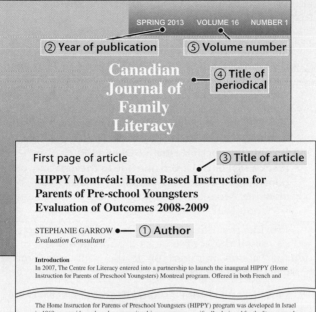

SPRING 2013   VOLUME 16   NUMBER 1

② **Year of publication**   ⑤ **Volume number**

Canadian Journal of Family Literacy   ④ **Title of periodical**

First page of article   ③ **Title of article**

HIPPY Montréal: Home Based Instruction for Parents of Pre-school Youngsters Evaluation of Outcomes 2008-2009

STEPHANIE GARROW ●— ① **Author**
Evaluation Consultant

Introduction
In 2007, The Centre for Literacy entered into a partnership to launch the inaugural HIPPY (Home Instruction for Parents of Preschool Youngsters) Montreal program. Offered in both French and

The Home Instruction for Parents of Preschool Youngsters (HIPPY) program was developed in Israel in 1969 as an evidence-based, community-driven response specifically designed for the literacy needs of families living on low incomes whose children lacked adequate school-readiness. Broadly speaking,

47 ●— ⑥ **Page number**

① ② ③
Garrow, S. (2013). HIPPY Montréal: Home based instruction

for parents of pre-school youngsters: Evaluation of
④
Outcomes 2008-2009. *Canadian Journal of Family*
⑤ ⑥
Literacy, 16, 47-63.

① **Author**. Give the last name first, a comma, the initial of the first name and any middle initial, following each initial with a period. Omit *Dr., PhD,* or any other title.

② **Year of publication**, in parentheses and followed by a period.

③ **Title of the article**. Give the full article title and any subtitle, separating them with a colon. Capitalize only the first words of the title and subtitle, and do not place the title in quotation marks.

④ **Title of the periodical,** in italics. Capitalize all significant words and end with a comma.

⑤ **Volume number**, italicized and followed by a comma. See model 7 for when to include the issue number.

⑥ **Inclusive page numbers of article**, without "pp." Do not omit any numerals.

(continued from p. 212)

references begin the same way as print references do: author, date, and title. Then you add information on how to retrieve the source.

- **Give the DOI, not the URL, when one is available.** (See models 18 and 25.)
- **Give the URL when a DOI is not available.** Provide the URL in a statement beginning Retrieved from. For most sources, use the home page URL of the website where your source can be found. (See models 19 and 23.) Use the complete URL only if the source is hard to find from the home page. (See model 32.)
- **Do not add a period after a DOI or a URL.**
- **Break a DOI or URL from one line to the next only before punctuation,** such as a period or a slash. (But break after the two slashes in http://.) Do not hyphenate a URL or a DOI.

Provide the date of your access to an electronic source only if the source lacks a publication date or edition or version number, or if the source is likely to change. (See model 29.)

18. A journal article with a Digital Object Identifier (DOI) (Web)

Kelly-Weeder, S., Phillips, K., & Rounseville, S. (2011). Effectiveness of
public health programs for decreasing alcohol consumption.
Patient Intelligence, 3, 29-38. http://dx.doi.org/10.2147/PI.S12431

See the next page for the basic format for a Web or database article with a DOI, as well as the location of the required information on the source.

19. A journal article without a DOI (Web)

Findlay, L. C., & Coplan, R. J. (2008). Come out and play: Shyness in
childhood and the benefits of organized sports participation.
Canadian Journal of Behavioural Science, 40, 153-161. Retrieved
from http://www.cpa.ca/publications/cpajournals/#cjbs

20. A periodical article without a DOI in an online database (Web)

Rosen, I. M., Maurer, D. M., & Darnall, C. R. (2008). Reducing tobacco use
in adolescents. *American Family Physician, 77*, 483-490. Retrieved
from http://www.aafp.org/online/en/home/publications
/journals/afp.html

The preceding example gives the URL of the journal's home page. If you don't find the home page of the

(continued on p. 216)

Format for a journal article on the Web

Back to Pear Press Journal: Society and Culture ●── ④ **Title of periodical**

Effectiveness of anti-bullying programs in reducing cyberbullying in Canadian secondary ●─ ③ **Title of article**
schools: insight from students

② **Year of publication** ⑤ **Volume number**

⑥ **Page numbers**

Published Date August 2015 Volume 2015: 8 Pages 22 – 35
DOI: http://dx.doi.org/10.2274/PI.S13595 ●─ ⑦ **Retrieval information**

Stacey Fraser, Charles Patterson, Kendra Scott ●─────────── ① **Authors**

Cyberbullying can be defined as using electronic communication to harass or intimidate other individuals. The use of social media to engage in bullying behaviour is a growing problem in Canadian secondary schools. Anti-bullying programs, which include education and discussion of cyberbullying and its impacts, have recently been initiated at many Canadian schools in an attempt to reduce instances of cyberbullying. We conducted a survey study of 500 secondary students from five high schools in Ontario to assess the effectiveness of these programs. Students had mixed impressions of the anti-bullying programs in place at their schools, and it appears that some strategies and techniques employed are considered more effective than others by students. We provide a breakdown of the most effective strategies according to our survey results.

Keywords: cyberbullying, anti-bullying, secondary students, adolescents, social media

① ②
Kelly-Weeder, S., Phillips, K., & Rounseville, S. (2011).
③
Effectiveness of public health programs for decreas-
④ ⑤
ing alcohol consumption. *Patient Intelligence, 3,*
⑥ ⑦
29-38. http://dx.doi.org/10.2147/PI.S12431

① **Authors.** Give each author's last name, first initial, and any middle initial. Separate names from initials with commas, and use & before the last author's name. Omit *Dr., PhD,* or any other title. See models 1–4 to cite single and multiple authors.

② **Year of publication,** in parentheses and followed by a period.

③ **Title of article.** Give the full article title and any subtitle, separating them with a colon. Capitalize only the first words of the title and subtitle, and do not place the title in quotation marks.

④ **Title of periodical,** in italics. Capitalize all significant words and end with a comma.

⑤ **Volume number,** italicized and followed by a comma. See page 211 for when to include the issue number.

⑥ **Inclusive page numbers of article,** without "pp." Do not omit any numerals.

⑦ **Retrieval information,** either a DOI (in this example) or a URL (model 19). See model 20 for how to cite an article without a DOI that you retrieve from a database.

APA
43b

(continued from p. 214)

periodical, give the database name in your retrieval statement:

Smith, E. M. (1926, March). Equal rights—internationally! *Life and Labor Bulletin, 4*, 1-2. Retrieved from Women and Social Movements in the United States, 1600-2000, database.

21. An abstract of a journal article (Web)

Koerber, D. (2011). Style over substance: Newspaper coverage of early election campaigns in Canada, 1820-1841. *Canadian Journal of Communication, 36*(3). Abstract retrieved from http://www .cjc-online.ca/index.php/journal

22. An article in a newspaper (Web)

Gootman, E. (2008, June 19). Gifted programs in the city are less diverse. *The New York Times*. Retrieved from http://www.nytimes.com

23. An article in a magazine (Web)

Young, E. (2009, February 21). Sleep well, keep sane. *New Scientist, 201*(26), 34-37. Retrieved from http://www.newscientist.com

24. Supplemental periodical content that appears only online (Web)

Gawande, A. (2009, June 1). More is less [Supplemental material]. *The New Yorker*. Retrieved from http://www.newyorker.com

25. A review (Web)

Bond, M. (2008, December 18). Does genius breed success? [Review of the book *Outliers: The story of success,* by M. Gladwell]. *Nature, 456*, 785. doi:10.1038/456874a

26. A report or other material from the website of an organization or government (Web)

Ellerman, D., & Joskow, P. L. (2008, May). *The European Union's emissions trading system in perspective.* Retrieved from the Pew Center on Global Climate Change website: http://www.pewclimate.org

If the document you cite is difficult to locate from the organization's home page, give the complete URL in the retrieval statement:

The Centre for Literacy of Quebec. *Measures of success: Workplace literacy and essential skills*. (2012, August 3). Retrieved from http://centreforliteracy.qc.calprojects /measures-success-workplace-literacy-and-essential-skills

If the document you cite is undated, use the abbreviation n.d. in place of the publication date and give the date of your access in the retrieval statement:

U.S. Department of Education. (n.d.). *Why teach*. Retrieved April 23, 2015, from https://www.teach.org/why-teach

27. A book (Web)

Reuter, P. (Ed.). (2010). *Understanding the demand for illegal drugs*. Retrieved from http://books.nap.edu/catelog.php?record_id=12976

For an electronic book on the Web or in an online database, replace the publisher's city, province, or state, and name with a DOI (see models 18 and 25) or with a retrieval statement, as above.

To cite a book on an e-reader, add the format in brackets:

Freud, S. (1920). *Dream psychology: Psychoanalysis for beginners* (M. D. Eder, Trans.). [iPad version]. Retrieved from http://www.apple .com/itunes

28. An article in a reference work (Web)

Perception. (2008). In *Encyclopaedia Britannica Online*. Retrieved from http://www.britannica.com/EBchecked/topic/451015/perception

29. An article in a wiki (Web)

Inuktitut. (n.d.). In *Wikipedia*. Retrieved August 3, 2015, from http://en.wikipedia.org/wiki/Inuktitut

30. A dissertation (Web)

A dissertation in a commercial database:

McFaddin, M. O. (2007). *Adaptive reuse: An architectural solution for pov-erty and homelessness* (Doctoral dissertation). Available from Pro-Quest Dissertations and Theses database. (ATT 1378764)

A dissertation in an institutional database:

Chang, J. K. (2003). *Therapeutic intervention in treatment of injuries to the hand and wrist* (Doctoral dissertation). Retrieved from http://medsci.archive.liasu.edu/61724

31. A podcast (Web)

O'Reilly, Terry. (Producer). (2009, May 4). The myths of persuasion. [Audio podcast]. *The Age of Persuasion*. Retrieved from http://www.cbc.ca/ageofpersuasion/episode/

APA 43b

32. A film or video recording (Web)

Green Children Foundation (Producer). (2008, January 7). *The green children visit China* [Video file]. Retrieved from http://youtube.com
/watch?v=uD4xfLTxCsY

33. A visual (Web)

United Nations Population Fund (Cartographer). (2005). Percent of population living on less than $1/day [Demographic map]. Retrieved
from http://www.unfpa.org

34. A message posted to a blog or discussion group (Web)

Munger, D. (2010, May 9). Does recess really improve classroom behav-
ior? [Web log post]. Retrieved from http://scienceblogs.com
/cognitivedaily

35. A posting on a social-networking site

Environmental Defense Fund. (2013, June 4). Extreme weather = extreme
consequences [Facebook status update]. Retrieved from
https://www.facebook.coom/EnvDefenseFund?fref=ts

Give the type of posting in brackets, such as [Facebook
note] or [Facebook status update]. If you are citing an
entire page, give the title of the site and then page in
brackets.

36. A tweet

Bittman, M. [bittmall]. (2013, March 19). Banning the big gulp ban:
http://nyti.ms/15ZcyKa [Tweet]. Retrieved from http://twitter
.com/bittman

37. A personal communication (text citation)

At least one member of the research team has expressed reservations
about the design of the study (L. Kogod, personal communication,
February 6, 2015).

Personal email and other online postings that are not
retrievable by others should be cited only in the text, as
here, not in the list of references.

Other sources
38. A report (print)

Gerald, K. (2003). *Medico-moral problems in obstetric care* (Report No.
NP-71). St. Louis, MO: Catholic Hospital Association.

Jolson, M. K. (2001). *Music education for preschoolers* (Report No. TC-622). New York, NY: Teachers College, Columbia University. (ERIC Document Reproduction Service No. ED264488)

39. A government publication (print)

Canada. Library of Parliament. (2002). *The war paintings in the Senate Chamber.* Ottawa, ON: Author.

In the above model, "Author" signifies that the author (Canada) is also the publisher.

Medicare payment for outpatient physical and occupational therapy services: Hearing before the Committee on Ways and Means, House of Representatives, 110th Cong. 3 (2007).

40. A dissertation (print)

A dissertation abstracted in DAI:

Steciw, S. K. (1986). Alterations to the Pessac project of Le Corbusier. *Dissertation Abstracts International, 46*(6), 565C.

An unpublished dissertation:

Holcomb, C. M. (2008). *Dance as therapy for reducing anxiety in elementary-age children: Case studies in grades 1 through 6* (Unpublished doctoral dissertation). University of Washington.

41. An interview (print)

Schenker, H. (2007). No peace without third-party intervention [Interview with Shulamit Aloni]. *Palestine-Israel Journal of Politics, Economics, and Culture, 14*(4), 63-68.

For an interview you conduct yourself, use an in-text parenthetical citation, as shown in model 37 for a personal communication.

APA
43b

42. A motion picture

American Psychological Association (Producer). (2001). *Ethnocultural psychotherapy* [DVD]. Available from http://www.apa.org/videos

Tyrrell, C. (Director). (2010). *The Joneses* [Motion picture]. United States: Bjort Productions.

43. A musical recording

Mitchell, J. (1970). Big yellow taxi. On *Ladies of the Canyon* [Vinyl record]. Los Angeles, CA: A & M.

44. A television series or episode

Rhimes, S. (Executive Producer). (2015). *Grey's anatomy* [Television
series]. New York, NY: CBS.

Clark, Z. (Writer), & Corn, R. (Director). (2010). The time warp [Television
series episode]. In S. Rhimes (Executive Producer), *Grey's anatomy*.
New York, NY: CBS.

43c APA paper format

The following guidelines for document format reflect
the second printing of the APA *Publication Manual*, 6th
edition. Your instructor may modify this format.

For illustrations of the following elements, see
pages 222–23. And see pages 25–32 for guidelines on type
fonts, lists, tables and figures, and other elements of
document design.

Margins Use one-inch (2.5 cm) margins on the top,
bottom, and both sides.

Spacing and indentions Double-space everywhere.
Indent paragraphs and displayed quotations one-half
inch (1.25 cm) or five to seven spaces.

Paging Begin numbering on the title page, and number consecutively through the end (including the reference list). Provide a header about one-half inch (1.25 cm)
from the top of every page, as shown in the samples on
the next two pages. The header consists of the page number on the far right and your full or shortened title on the
far left. Type the title in all-capital letters. On the title
page only, precede the title with the label Running head and
a colon. Omit this label on all other pages.

APA
43c

Title page Include the full title of the paper, your
name, the course title, the instructor's name, and the
date. Type the title on the top half of the page, followed
by the identifying in formation, all centred horizontally
and double-spaced.

Abstract Summarize (in a maximum of 120 words)
your subject, research method, findings, and conclusions.
Put the abstract on a page by itself.

Body Begin with a restatement of the paper's title and
then an introduction (not labelled). The introduction concisely presents the problem you researched, your research

method, the relevant background (such as related studies), and the purpose of your research.

The **Method** section provides a detailed discussion of how you conducted your research, including a description of the research subjects, any materials or tools you used (such as questionnaires or lab equipment), and the procedure you followed.

The **Results** section summarizes the data you collected, explains how you analyzed them, and presents them in detail, often in tables, graphs, or charts.

The **Discussion** section interprets the data and presents your conclusions. (When the discussion is brief, you may combine it with the previous section under the heading **Results and Discussion**.)

Headings Label the **Method, Results,** and **Discussion** sections with centred first-level headings, and use second- and third-level headings as needed. Double-space all headings.

First-Level Heading

Second-Level Heading

Third-level heading. Run this heading into the text paragraph.

Long quotations Run into your text all quotations of forty words or less and enclose them in quotation marks. For quotations of more than forty words, set them off from your text by indenting all lines one-half inch (1.25 cm) or five to seven spaces, double-spacing above and below.

Echoing the opinions of other Europeans at the time, Freud (1961) had a poor view of Americans:

> The Americans are really too bad. . . . Competition is much more pungent with them, not succeeding means civil death to every one, and they have no private resources apart from their profession, no hobby, games, love or other interests of a cultured person. And success means money. (p. 86)

APA 43c

Do not use quotation marks around a quotation displayed in this way.

43d Sample pages in APA style

Title page

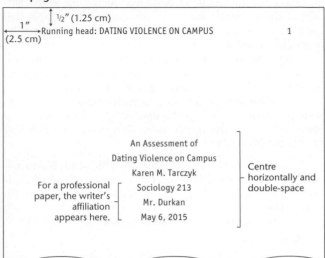

½″ (1.25 cm)
1″ (2.5 cm) →Running head: DATING VIOLENCE ON CAMPUS 1

An Assessment of
Dating Violence on Campus
Karen M. Tarczyk
Sociology 213
Mr. Durkan
May 6, 2015

For a professional paper, the writer's affiliation appears here.

Centre horizontally and double-space

Abstract

½″ (1.25 cm)
DATING VIOLENCE ON CAMPUS 2

No indention

Abstract ← Centre

Little research has examined the patterns of abuse and violence occurring within couples during courtship. With a questionnaire administered to a sample of college students, the extent and nature of such abuse and violence were investigated. The results, interpretations, and implications for

1″ (2.5 cm) ... 1″ (2.5 cm)

Double-space

APA 43d

First page of body

½″ (1.25 cm)
DATING VIOLENCE ON CAMPUS 3

An Assessment of
Dating Violence on Campus

Centre

½″(1.25 cm) or 5–7 spaces
In recent years, a great deal of attention has been devoted to family violence. Numerous studies have been done on spouse and child abuse. However, violent behaviour occurs

1″ (2.5 cm) ... 1″ (2.5 cm)

Double-space

premarital violence was a problem of "abusive relationships" as well as "abusive individuals" (p. 90).

1″ (2.5 cm)

Later page of body

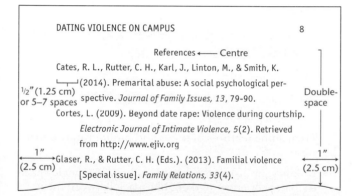

DATING VIOLENCE ON CAMPUS   4

    All the studies indicate a problem that is being neglected.
My objective was to gather data on the extent and nature of premarital violence and to discuss possible interpretations.

                                    Method ⟩⟩Double-space
Sample

    I conducted a survey of 200 students (134 females, 66
males) at a large university in southern Ontario. The sample con-
sisted of students enrolled in an introductory sociology course.

References

DATING VIOLENCE ON CAMPUS   8

                    References ⟵ Centre

Cates, R. L., Rutter, C. H., Karl, J., Linton, M., & Smith, K.

½"(1.25 cm) ⌐⌐(2014). Premarital abuse: A social psychological per-   Double-
or 5–7 spaces spective. *Journal of Family Issues, 13,* 79-90.   space

    Cortes, L. (2009). Beyond date rape: Violence during courtship.

        Electronic Journal of Intimate Violence, 5(2). Retrieved

        from http://www.ejiv.org

1" ⟶Glaser, R., & Rutter, C. H. (Eds.). (2013). Familial violence   1"
(2.5 cm)   [Special issue]. *Family Relations, 33*(4).   (2.5 cm)

---

44 Chicago Documentation and Format

Writers in history, art history, philosophy, religion, and
other humanities use the note style of documentation
from *The Chicago Manual of Style*, 16th ed. (2010), or the
student reference adapted from it, *A Manual for Writers of
Research Papers, Theses, and Dissertations*, by Kate L.
Turabian, 8th ed., revised by Wayne C. Booth, Gregory G.
Colomb, and Joseph M. Williams (2013). *The Chicago
Manual* has a website that answers frequently asked questions about its style: *www.chicagomanualofstyle.org*.

> **My**WritingLab
>
> Visit **My**WritingLab for more help
> with Chicago documentation and
> format.

This chapter explains the Chicago note style (below) and Chicago paper format (p. 235).

44a Chicago notes and bibliography

In the Chicago note style, a superscripted number in the text refers the reader to source information in endnotes (at the end of the paper) or footnotes (at the bottom of pages). In these notes, the first citation of each source contains all the information readers need to find the source. Thus your instructor may consider a bibliography optional because it provides much the same information. Ask your instructor whether you should use footnotes or endnotes and whether you should include a bibliography along with the notes.

The examples below show the essentials of a note and a bibliography entry. (See pp. 236–37 for more illustrations.)

Note

    6. Martin Gilbert. *Pictorial Atlas of British History* (New York: Dorset Press, 2006), 96.

Bibliography entry

Gilbert, Martin. *Pictorial Atlas of British History*. New York: Dorset Press, 2006.

Treat some features of notes and bibliography entries the same:

- Unless your instructor requests otherwise, single-space each note or entry, and double-space between them.
- Italicize the titles of books and periodicals.
- Enclose in quotation marks the titles of parts of books or articles in periodicals.
- Do not abbreviate publishers' names, but omit "Inc.," "Co.," and similar abbreviations.
- Do not use "p." or "pp." before page numbers.

Treat other features of notes and bibliography entries differently:

Note	Bibliography entry
Start with a number that corresponds to the note number in the text.	Do not begin with a number.
Indent the first line five spaces.	Indent the second and subsequent lines five spaces.
Give the author's name in normal order.	Begin with the author's last name.

Use commas between elements such as author's name and title.	Use periods between elements.
Enclose publication information in parentheses, with no preceding punctuation.	Precede a book's publication information with a period, and don't use parentheses.
Include the specific page number(s) you borrowed from, omitting "p." or "pp."	Omit page numbers except for parts of books or articles in periodicals.

You can instruct your computer to position footnotes at the bottoms of appropriate pages. It will also automatically number notes and renumber them if you add or delete one or more.

44b Chicago models

The Chicago models for common sources are indexed below. The models show notes and bibliography entries together for easy reference. Be sure to use the correct form—numbered note or unnumbered bibliography entry. Note that the *Chicago Manual of Style* does not separate out electronic sources, as we do here.

Chicago note and bibliography models

(continued)

Chic
44b

Authors

1. One, two, or three authors

    1. Joseph Boyden, *Three Day Road* (Toronto: Viking Canada, 2005), 134.

Boyden, Joseph. *Three Day Road*. Toronto: Viking Canada, 2005.

    1. Dennis L. Wilcox, Phillip H. Ault, and Warren K. Agee, *Public Relations: Strategies and Tactics,* 6th ed. (New York: Irwin, 2005), 182.

Wilcox, Dennis L., Phillip H. Ault, and Warren K. Agee. *Public Relations: Strategies and Tactics*. 6th ed. New York: Irwin, 2005.

2. More than three authors

    2. Geraldo Lopez et al., *China and the West* (Boston: Little, Brown, 2004), 461.

Lopez, Geraldo, Judith P. Salt, Anne Ming, and Henry Reisen. *China and the West*. Boston: Little, Brown, 2004.

The Latin abbreviation et al. means "and others."

3. Author not named (anonymous)

3. *The Dorling Kindersley World Reference Atlas*, 8th ed. (London: Dorling Kindersley, 2013), 150-51.

The Dorling Kindersley World Reference Atlas, 8th ed. London: Dorling
      Kindersley, 2013.

Print books

4. Basic format for a book (print)

4. Barbara Ehrenreich, *Dancing in the Streets: A History of Collective Joy* (New York: Henry Holt, 2006), 97-117.

Ehrenreich, Barbara. *Dancing in the Streets: A History of Collective Joy.*
      New York: Henry Holt, 2006.

5. A book with an editor (print)

5. Hendrick Ruitenbeek, ed., *Freud as We Knew Him* (Detroit: Wayne State University Press, 1973), 64.

Ruitenbeek, Hendrick, ed. *Freud as We Knew Him.* Detroit: Wayne State
      University Press, 1973.

6. A book with an author and an editor (print)

6. Frances Burney, *Evelina, or, The History of a Young Woman's Entrance into the World*, Norton Critical Edition, ed. Stewart J. Cooke (New York: Norton, 1998), 214-16.

Burney, Frances. *Evelina, or, The History of a Young Woman's Entrance into
      the World.* Norton Critical Edition. Edited by Stewart J. Cooke. New
      York: Norton, 1998.

7. A translation (print)

7. Jovette Marchessault, *Mother of the Grass*, trans. Yvonne M. Klein (Vancouver: Talon, 1989), 112.

Marchessault, Jovette. *Mother of the Grass.* Translated by Yvonne M. Klein.
      Vancouver: Talon, 1989.

8. A later edition (print)

8. Dwight L. Bolinger, *Aspects of Language,* 3rd ed. (New York: Harcourt Brace Jovanovich, 1981), 20.

Bolinger, Dwight L. *Aspects of Language.* 3rd ed. New York: Harcourt
      Brace Jovanovich, 1981.

**Chic
44b**

9. A work in more than one volume (print)

Citation of one volume without a title:

9. Abraham Lincoln, *The Collected Works of Abraham Lincoln,* ed. Roy P. Basler (New Brunswick: Rutgers University Press, 1953), 5:426-28.

Lincoln, Abraham. *The Collected Works of Abraham Lincoln.* Edited by Roy
P. Basler. Vol. 5. New Brunswick: Rutgers University Press, 1953.

Citation of one volume with a title:

9. Linda B. Welkin, *The Age of Balanchine,* vol. 3 of *The History of Ballet* (New York: Columbia University Press, 1999), 56.

Welkin, Linda B. *The Age of Balanchine.* Vol. 3 of *The History of Ballet.* New
York: Columbia University Press, 1999.

10. A selection from an anthology (print)

10. Leslie Duer, "Portraits, Effigies, and the Narrative Impulse," in *Literature and Ethics: Essays Presented to A. E. Malloch,* ed. Gary Wihl and David Williams (Kingston: McGill-Queen's University Press, 1998), 38-39.

Duer, Leslie. "Portraits, Effigies, and the Narrative Impulse." In *Literature
and Ethics: Essays Presented to A. E. Malloch,* edited by Gary Wihl
and David Williams, 32-45. Kingston: McGill-Queen's University
Press, 1988.

11. A work in a series (print)

11. Ingmar Bergman, *The Seventh Seal,* Modern Film Scripts 12 (New York: Simon and Schuster, 1995), 27.

Bergman, Ingmar. *The Seventh Seal.* Modern Film Scripts 12. New York:
Simon and Schuster, 1995.

12. An article in a reference work (print)

12. *Merriam-Webster's Collegiate Dictionary,* 11th ed., s.v. "reckon."
Merriam-Webster's Collegiate Dictionary. 11th ed. S.v. "reckon."

Use the abbreviation s.v. (Latin *sub verbo,* "under the word") for reference works that are alphabetically arranged. Well-known works like the one listed here do not need publication information except for edition number.

Print periodicals: Journals, newspapers, magazines

13. An article in a journal (print)

13. Janet Lever, "Sex Differences in the Games Children Play," *Social Problems* 23 (Spring 1996): 482.

Lever, Janet. "Sex Differences in the Games Children Play." *Social Problems* 23 (Spring 1996): 478-87.

Provide the issue number if the journal numbers issues:

13. Robert Bee, "The Importance of Preserving Paper-Based Artifacts in a Digital Age," *Library Quarterly* 78, no. 2 (April 2008): 176.

Bee, Robert. "The Importance of Preserving Paper-Based Artifacts in a Digital Age." *Library Quarterly* 78, no. 2 (April 2008): 174-94.

14. An article in a newspaper (print)

14. Alexandra Lopez Pacheco, "Health Lessons Start at Home," *National Post*, August 11, 2003, SR6.

Lopez Pacheco, Alexandra. "Health Lessons Start at Home." *National Post*, August 11, 2003, SR6.

15. An article in a magazine (print)

15. Adam Gopnik, "In the Memory Ward," *New Yorker,* March 16, 2015, 35.

Gopnik, Adam. "In the Memory Ward." *New Yorker,* March 16, 2015, 34-41.

16. A review (print)

16. John Gregory Dunne, "The Secret of Danny Santiago," review of *Famous All over Town,* by Danny Santiago, *New York Review of Books,* August 16, 1994, 25.

Dunne, John Gregory. "The Secret of Danny Santiago." Review of *Famous All over Town,* by Danny Santiago. *New York Review of Books,* August 16, 1994, 17-27.

Web and other electronic sources

The *Chicago Manual*'s models for documenting electronic sources mostly begin as those for print sources do. Then you add electronic publication information that will help readers locate the source. If one is available, give the Digital Object Identifier (DOI) for the source—a unique identifier that many publishers assign to periodical articles and other documents. (See model 17.) If no DOI is available, give the URL, as shown in models 18 and 19. If you retrieve an article from an online database, see model 20.

For webpages and other electronic sources that are likely to change, the *Chicago Manual* suggests including the date of the most recent update in a statement beginning last modified (see model 22). If no date is available, give the date of your access (see model 23).

Note Chicago style allows many ways to break URLs between the end of one line and the beginning of the next: after a colon or double slash and before a single slash, period, comma, and most other marks. *Do not* break after a hyphen or add any hyphens.

17. An article in a journal (Web)

17. Joseph J. Campos et al., "Reconceptualizing Emotion Regulation," *Emotion Review* 3, no. 1 (2011): 32, doi:l0.1177 /1754073910380975.

Campos, Joseph J., Eric A. Walle, Audun Dahl, and Alexandra Main. "Reconceptualizing Emotion Regulation." *Emotion Review* 3, no. 1 (2011): 26-35. doi:l0.11//1754073910380975.

18. An article in a magazine (Web)

18. Nouriel Roubini, "A Rose among Thorns," *Slate,* April 7, 2013, http://www.slate.com/id/2192272.

Roubini, Nouriel. "A Rose among Thorns." *Slate,* April 7, 2013. http://www.slate.com/id/2192272.

19. An article in a newspaper (Web)

19. Sindya N. Bhanoo, "With Incentive, Monkeys Can Coordinate," *New York Times,* April 8, 2013, http://www.nytimes.com/2013/04/09 /science/monkeys-show-ability-to-coordinate.html?ref.=science.

Bhanoo, Sindya N. "With Incentive, Monkeys Can Coordinate." *New York Times,* April 8, 2013. http://www.pytimes.com/2013/04/09 /science/monkeys-show-ability-to-coordinate.html?ref=science.

20. An article in an online database (Web)

20. Jonathan Dickens, "Social Policy Approaches to Intercountry Adoption," *International Social Work* 52, no. 5 (September 2009): 600, doi:10.1177/0020872809337678.

Dickens, Jonathan. "Social Policy Approaches to Intercountry Adoption." *International Social Work* 52, no. 5 (September 2009): 595-607. doi:10.1177/0020872809337678.

If a database article has neither a DOI nor a stable URL, end with the name of the database.

21. A book (Web)

21. Jane Austen, *Emma*, ed. R. W. Chapman (1816; Oxford: Clarendon, 1926; Oxford Text Archive, 2004), chap. 1, http://ota.ahds .ac.uk/Austen/Emma.1519.

Austen, Jane. *Emma*. Edited by R. W. Chapman. 1816. Oxford: Clarendon, 1926. Oxford Text Archive, 2004. http://ota.ahds.ac.uk/Austen /Emma.1519.

Provide print publication information, if any.

22. An article in a reference work (Web)

22. *Wikipedia,* s.v. "Wuhan," last modified July 16, 2015, http://en.wikipedia.org/wiki/Wuhan.

Wikipedia. S.v. "Wuhan." Last modified July 16, 2015. http://en .wikipedia.org/wiki/Wuhan.

23. A webpage

23. "Toyota Safety," Toyota Motor Sales, accessed July 23, 2015, http://www.toyota.com/safety.

Toyota Motor Sales. "Toyota Safety." Accessed July 23, 2015. http://www.toyota.com/safety.

24. An audio or visual source (Web)
A work of art:

24. Jackson Pollock, *Shimmering Substance,* 1946, Museum of Modern Art, New York. http://moma.org/collection/conservation/pollock /shimmering_substance.html.

Pollock, Jackson. *Shimmering Substance*. 1946. Museum of Modern Art, New York. http://moma.org/collection/conservation/pollock /shimmering_substance.html.

A sound recording:

24. William Lyon Mackenzie King, "Why Is Canada Entering the War in 1939?" October 27, 1939, Canadian Broadcasting Corporation, CBC Digital Archives. http://www.cbc.ca/player/Digital+Archives /War+and+Conflict/Second+World+War/ID/2203192964/.

King, William Lyon Mackenzie. "Why Is Canada Entering the War in 1939?" October 27, 1939. Canadian Broadcasting Corporation. CBC Digital Archives. http://www.cbc.ca/player/Digital+Archives /War+and+Conflict/Second+World+War/ID/2203192964/.

A film or film clip:

24. Leslie J. Stewart, *96 Ranch Rodeo and Barbecue* (1951), 16mm, from Library of Congress, *Buckaroos in Paradise: Ranching Culture in Northern Nevada, 1945-1982*, MPEG. http://memory.loc.gov/cgi-bin /query.

Stewart, Leslie J. 96 *Ranch Rodeo and Barbecue.* 1951; 16 mm. From Library of Congress, *Buckaroos in Paradise: Ranching Culture in Northern Nevada, 1945-1982.* MPEG. http://memory.loc.gov /cgi-bin/query.

25. A message posted to a blog or discussion group (Web)

25. Steve Kux, "G7 Nations Commit to End Carbon Pollution," *Climate & Clean Energy* (blog) June 9, 2015, http://www.davidsuzuki.org/blogs /climate-blog/2015/06/g7-nations-commit-to-end-carbon-pollution/

Kux, Steve. "G7 Nations Commit to End Carbon Pollution." *Climate & Clean Energy* (blog). June 9, 2015. http://www.davidsuzuki.org/blogs /climate-blog/2015/06/g7-nations-commit-to-end-carbon-pollution/.

25. Michael Tourville, "European Currency Reform," email to International Finance discussion list, January 6, 2015, http://www.weg.isu .edu/finance-dl/archive/46732.

Tourville, Michael. "European Currency Reform." Email to International Finance discussion list. January 6, 2015. http://www.weg.isu.edu /finance-dl/archive/46732.

26. Email

26. Elizabeth Bailey, "Re: London," email message to author, May 4, 2015.

Bailey, Elizabeth. "Re: London." Email message to author. May 4, 2015.

27. A work on CD-ROM or DVD-ROM

27. *The American Heritage Dictionary of the English Language,* 5th ed. (Boston: Houghton Mifflin, 2011), CD-ROM.

The American Heritage Dictionary of the English Language. 5th ed. Boston: Houghton Mifflin, 2011. CD-ROM.

Other sources
28. A government publication (print)

28. House Comm. on Ways and Means, *Medicare Payment for Outpatient Physical and Occupational Therapy Services,* 112th Cong., 1st sess., H.R. Doc. 778, 16-19 (2011).

House Comm. on Ways and Means. *Medicare Payment for Outpatient Physical and Occupational Therapy Services.* 112th Cong. 1st sess. H.R. Doc. 778 *(2011).*

28. Library of Parliament, *The War Paintings in the Senate Chamber* (Ottawa, 2002), 3.

Canada. Library of Parliament. *The War Paintings in the Senate Chamber.* Ottawa, 2002.

29. A published letter (print)

29. Mrs. Laura E. Buttolph to Rev. and Mrs. C. C. Jones, June 20, 1857, in *The Children of Pride: A True Story of Georgia and the Civil War,* ed. Robert Manson Myers (New Haven, CT: Yale University Press, 1972), 334.

Buttolph, Laura E. Mrs. Laura E. Buttolph to Rev. and Mrs. C. C. Jones, June 20, 1857. In *The Children of Pride: A True Story of Georgia and the Civil War,* edited by Robert Manson Myers. New Haven, CT: Yale University Press, 1972.

30. A published or broadcast interview

30. Carey Mulligan, interview by Terry Gross, *Fresh Air,* NPR, June 5, 2015.

Mulligan, Carey. Interview by Terry Gross. *Fresh Air.* NPR. June 5, 2015.

31. A personal letter or interview

31. Ann E. Packer, letter to author. June 15, 2015.

Packer, Ann E. Letter to author. June 15, 2015.

31. Andrew Stern, interview by author, December 19, 2014.

Stern, Andrew. Interview by author. December 19, 2014.

32. A work of art

32. John Singer Sargent, *In Switzerland,* 1908, Metropolitan Museum of Art, New York.

Sargent, John Singer. *In Switzerland.* 1908. Metropolitan Museum of Art, New York.

33. A film, DVD, or video recording

33. George Balanchine, *Serenade,* San Francisco Ballet, performed February 2, 2000 (New York: PBS Video, 2006), DVD.

Balanchine, George. *Serenade.* San Francisco Ballet. Performed February 2, 2000. New York: PBS Video, 2006. DVD.

34. A sound recording

34. Philip Glass, *String Quartet no. 5,* with Kronos Quartet, recorded 1991, Nonesuch 79356-2, 1995, compact disc.

Glass, Philip. *String Quartet no. 5*. Kronos Quartet. Recorded 1991. Nonesuch 79356-2, 1995, compact disc.

Shortened notes

To streamline documentation, Chicago style recommends shortened notes for sources that are fully cited elsewhere, either in a complete bibliography or in previous notes. Ask your instructor whether your paper should include a bibliography and, if so, whether you may use shortened notes for first references to sources as well as for subsequent references.

A shortened note appears on the next page. It includes the author's last name, the work's title (minus any initial *A, An,* or *The*), and the page number. Reduce long titles to four or fewer key words.

Complete note

4. Janet Lever, "Sex Differences in the Games Children Play," *Social Problems* 23 (Spring 1996): 482.

Complete bibliography entry

Lever, Janet. "Sex Differences in the Games Children Play." *Social Problems* 23 (Spring 1996): 478-87.

Shortened note

12. Lever, "Sex Differences," 483.

You may use the Latin abbreviation ibid. (meaning "in the same place") to refer to the same source cited in the preceding note. Give a page number if it differs from that in the preceding note.

12. Lever, "Sex Differences," 483.

13. Gilligan, *In a Different Voice*, 92.

14. Ibid., 93.

15. Lever, "Sex Differences," 483.

Chicago style allows for in-text parenthetical citations when you cite one or more works repeatedly. In the following example, the raised number 2 refers to the source information in a note; the number in parentheses is a page number in the same source.

British rule, observes Stuart Cary Welch, "seemed as permanent as Mount Everest:"[2] Most Indians submitted, willingly or not, to British influence in every facet of life (42).

**Chic
44b**

44c Chicago paper format

The following guidelines come mainly from Turabian's *Manual for Writers*, which offers more specific advice than *The Chicago Manual* on the format of students' papers. See the next two pages for illustrations of the following elements. And see pages 25–32 for advice on type fonts, lists, illustrations, and other elements of document design.

Margins and spacing Use minimum one-inch (2.5 cm) margins on all pages of the body. (The first page of endnotes or the bibliography begins two inches [5 cm] from the top; see p. 237.) Double-space your own text and between notes and bibliography entries; single-space displayed quotations (see below) and each note and bibliography entry.

Paging Number pages consecutively from the first text page through the end (endnotes or bibliography). Use Arabic numerals (1, 2, 3) in the upper right corner.

Title page On an unnumbered title page provide the title of the paper (typed in capitals), your name, the course title, your instructor's name, and the date (all centred). Double-space between adjacent lines, and add extra space below the title as shown on the next page.

Poetry and long prose quotations Display certain quotations separately from your text: three or more lines of poetry and two or more sentences of prose. Indent a displayed quotation a half inch (1.25 cm) from the left, single-space the quotation, and double-space above and below it. *Do not add quotation marks.*

Gandhi articulated the principles of his movement in 1922:

> I discovered that pursuit of truth did not permit violence being inflicted on one's opponent, but that he must be weaned from error by patience and sympathy. For what appears to be truth to one may appear to be error to the other.[6]

44d Sample pages in Chicago style

Title page

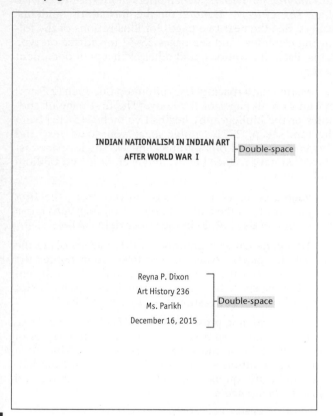

INDIAN NATIONALISM IN INDIAN ART
AFTER WORLD WAR I ⎤ -Double-space

Reyna P. Dixon
Art History 236
Ms. Parikh
December 16, 2015 ⎤ -Double-space

First page of paper with footnotes

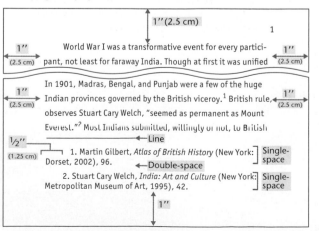

1'' (2.5 cm)

1

1''
(2.5 cm) ⟶ World War I was a transformative event for every partici- ⟵ 1''
(2.5 cm)
pant, not least for faraway India. Though at first it was unified

1''
(2.5 cm) ⟶ In 1901, Madras, Bengal, and Punjab were a few of the huge
Indian provinces governed by the British viceroy.¹ British rule, ⟵ 1''
(2.5 cm)
observes Stuart Cary Welch, "seemed as permanent as Mount
Everest."² Most Indians submitted, willingly or not, to British

½''
(1.25 cm) ⟵ Line
⎤ 1. Martin Gilbert, *Atlas of British History* (New York: ⎤ Single-
Dorset, 2002), 96. ⟵ Double-space space

2. Stuart Cary Welch, *India: Art and Culture* (New York: ⎤ Single-
Metropolitan Museum of Art, 1995), 42. space

1''

Endnotes

Bibliography

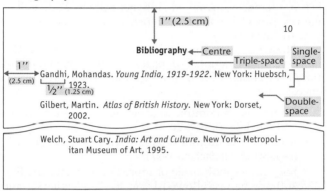

45 CSE and IEEE Documentation

Writers in the life sciences, physical sciences, and mathematics rely for documentation style on *Scientific Style and Format: The CSE Manual for Authors, Editors, and Publishers*, 8th ed. (2014), published by the Council of Science Editors.

Scientific Style and Format describes three styles of scientific documentation: one uses the source's author and date (name-year) while another numbers the sources in the order that they are used (citation-sequence). A third style (introduced in the 8th edition) uses a

---

MyWritingLab

Visit **MyWritingLab** for more help
with CSE and IEEE documentation.

numbered source list in which sources are listed alphabetically by author's name (citation-name) and in-text citations are by source number. Each method requires a list of references at the end of the paper, but each reference list is formatted differently. (See pp. 239–245.) Ask your instructor which style to use. This chapter gives models for both name-year and citation-sequence.

Electrical engineers can follow the documentation style of the IEEE (formerly Institute of Electrical and Electronics Engineers) (p. 245), based on the CSE style.

45a CSE name-year text citations

In the CSE name-year style, parenthetical text citations provide the last name of the author being cited and the source's year of publication. At the end of the paper, a list of references, arranged alphabetically by authors' last names, provides complete information on each source. (See the next page.)

The CSE name-year style closely resembles the APA name-year style detailed on pages 205–07. You can follow the APA examples for in-text citations, with three differences:

- Do not use a comma to separate the author's name and the date: (Lensky 2010).
- Separate two authors' names with "and" (not "&"): (Pepinsky and DeStefano 1997).
- For sources with three or more authors, give the first author's name followed by et al. ("and others") and the date of publication.

45b CSE citation sequence (numbered text citations)

In the CSE number style, superscript (raised) numbers in the text refer to a numbered list of references at the end of the paper.

Two standard references[1,2] use this term.

These forms of immunity have been extensively researched.[3]

Assignment of numbers The number for each source is based on the order in which you cite the source in the text. the first cited source is 1, the second is 2, and so on.

Reuse of numbers When you cite a source you have already cited and numbered, use the original number again. This reuse is the key difference between the CSE numbered citations and numbered references to footnotes or endnotes.

Citation of two or more sources When you cite two or more sources at once, arrange their numbers in sequence and separate them with a comma and no space, as in the first of the preceding examples. When you cite three or more sources whose numbers are in sequence, use the first and last numbers in the sequence, separated by a hyphen: [3-6].

45c CSE reference list

For both the name-year and the number styles of in-text citation, provide a list (titled References, Cited References, Literature Cited, or Bibliography), of all sources you have cited. Centre this heading about an inch (2.5 cm) from the top of the page, and double-space beneath it.

Spacing Single-space throughout.

Arrangement In the name-year style, arrange entries alphabetically by authors' last names. In the number style, arrange entries in numerical order—that is, in order of their citation in the text.

Format In the name-year style, type all lines of entries at the left margin—do not indent. In the number style, begin the first line of each entry at the left margin and indent subsequent lines.

Authors List each author's name with the last name first, followed by initials for first and middle names. Do not use a comma between an author's last name and initials, and do not use periods or space with the initials. Do use a comma to separate authors' names.

Placement of dates In the name-year style, the date follows the author's or authors' names. In the number style, the date follows the publication information (for a book) or the periodical title (for a journal, magazine, or newspaper).

Journal titles Do not italicize or underline journal titles. For titles of two or more words, abbreviate words of six or more letters (without periods) and omit most **prepositions**°, **articles**° and **conjunctions**°. Capitalize each word. For example, *Journal of Chemical and Biochemical Studies* becomes J Chem Biochem Stud.

Book and article titles Do not italicize, underline, or use quotation marks around a book or an article title. Capitalize only the first word and any proper nouns. See model 1.

Publication information for journal articles The name-year and number styles differ in the placement of the publication date (see above). However, both styles end

° See "Grammar Terms," page 272.

with the journal's volume number, any issue number in parentheses, a colon, and the inclusive page numbers of the article, run together without space: 28:329–30 or 62(2):26–40.

The following examples show both a name-year reference and a number reference for each type of source.

Authors

1. One author

Gould SJ. 1987. Time's arrow, time's cycle. Cambridge (MA): Harvard University Press.

1. Gould SJ. Time's arrow, time's cycle. Cambridge (MA): Harvard University Press; 1987.

2. Two to ten authors

Hepburn PX, Tatin JM, Tatin JP. 2008. Human physiology. New York (NY): Columbia University Press.

2. Hepburn PX, Tatin JM, Tatin JP. Human physiology. New York (NY): Columbia University Press; 2008.

3. More than ten authors

Evans RW, Bowditch L, Dana KL, Drummond A, Wildovitch WP, Young SL,
    Mills P, Mills RR, Livak SR, Lisi OL, et al. 2004. Organ transplants:
    ethical issues. Ann Arbor (MI): University of Michigan Press.

3. Evans RW, Bowditch L, Dana KL, Drummond A, Wildovitch WP, Young
    SL, Mills P, Mills RR, Livak SR, Lisi OL, et al. Organ transplants: ethical
    issues. Ann Arbor (MI): University of Michigan Press; 2004.

4. Author not named

Health care for children with diabetes. 2008. New York (NY): US Health
    Care.

4. Health care for children with diabetes. New York (NY): US Health Care;
    2008.

5. Two or more cited works by the same author(s) published in the same year

Gardner H. 1973a. The arts and human development. New York (NY):
    Wiley.

5. Gardner H. 1973b. The quest for mind: Piaget, Lévi-Strauss, and the
    structuralist movement. New York (NY): Knopf.

(The number style does not require such forms.)

Print periodicals: Journals, newspapers, magazines
6. An article in a journal (print)

Campos JJ, Walle EA, Dahl A, Main A. 2011. Reconceptualizing emotion reg-
    ulation. Emotion Rev. 3(1):26–35. doi:10.1177/1754073910380975.

6. Campos JJ, Walle EA, Dahl A, Main A. Reconceptualizing emotion
    regulation. Emotion Rev. 2011;3(1):26–35. doi:10.1177
    /1754073910380975.

CSE
45c

If a journal article has a Digital Object Identifier (DOI), you may include the number at the end of the entry for readers' convenience. (See p. 209 for more on DOIs.)

7. An article in a newspaper (print)

Stout D. 2008 May 28. Blind win court ruling on US currency. New York Times (National Ed.). Sect. A:23 (col. 3).

7. Stout D. Blind win court ruling on US currency. New York Times (National Ed.). 2008 May 28; Sect. A:23 (col. 3).

8. An article in a magazine (print)

Wilkinson A. 2008 June 2. Crime fighting of the future. New Yorker. 26–33.

8. Wilkinson A. Crime fighting of the future. New Yorker. 2008 June 2:26–33.

Print books

9. Basic format for a book (print)

Wilson EO. 2004. On human nature. Cambridge (MA): Harvard University Press.

9. Wilson EO. On human nature. Cambridge (MA): Harvard University Press; 2004.

10. A book with an editor (print)

Jonson P, editor. 2008. Anatomy yearbook 2008. Los Angeles (CA): Anatco.

10. Jonson P, editor. Anatomy yearbook 2008. Los Angeles (CA): Anatco; 2008.

CSE 45c

11. A selection from a book (print)

Kriegel R, Laubenstein L, Muggia F. 2005. Kaposi's sarcoma. In: Ebbeson P, Biggar RS, Melbye M, editors. AIDS: a basic guide for clinicians. 2nd ed. Philadelphia (PA): Saunders. p. 100–126.

11. Kriegel R, Laubenstein L, Muggia F. Kaposi's sarcoma. In: Ebbeson P, Biggar RS, Melbye M, editors. AIDS: a basic guide for clinicians. 2nd ed. Philadelphia (PA): Saunders; 2005. p. 100–126.

Web and other electronic sources

CSE references to electronic sources require additions to the basic print formats:

- Give the date you accessed an online source preceded by accessed, in brackets: [accessed 2015 Dec 7].
- Give the URL of an Internet source. End the source with the URL and a period. If you must break a URL from one line to the next, do so only before punctuation such as a period or a slash and do not hyphenate. If an article has a Digital Object Identifier (DOI), you may include the number at the end of the entry for readers' convenience. (See p. 209 for more on DOIs.)
- For non-Internet electronic sources, give the medium you used to find the source, in brackets: [DVD], [CD], and so on.

12. An article in a journal (Web)

Grady GF. 2007. The here and now of hepatitis B immunization. Today's Med. [accessed 2015 Dec 7] 6(2):39–41. http://www.fmrt.org /todaysmedicine/Grady050293.pdf6.

12. Grady GF. The here and now of hepatitis B immunization. Today's Med. [accessed 2015 Dec 7];6(2):39–41. http://www.fmrt.org /todaysmedicine/Grady050293.pdf6.

13. An article in a database (Web)

McAskill MR, Anderson TJ, Jones RD. 2005. Saccadic adaptation in neurological disorders. Prog Brain Res. 140:417–431. PubMed. Bethesda (MD): National Library of Medicine. 2014 [accessed 2015 Mar 6]. http://www.ncbi.nlm.nih.gov/PubMed.

13. McAskill MR, Anderson TJ, Jones RD. Saccadic adaptation in neurological disorders. Prog Brain Res. 2005;140:417–431. PubMed. Bethesda (MD): National Library of Medicine. [accessed 2015 Mar 6]. http://www.ncbi.nlm.nih.gov/PubMed.

CSE 45c

Provide information on the database: title, place of publication, and publisher. (If the database author is different from the publisher, give the author's name before the title.) If you see a date of publication or a copyright date for the database, give it after the publisher's name.

14. A book (Web)

Ruch BJ, Ruch DB. 2012. Homeopathy and medicine: resolving the conflict. New York (NY): Albert Einstein College of Medicine [accessed 2015 Jan 28]. http://www.einstein.edu/medicine/books /ruch.html.

14. Ruch BJ, Ruch DB. Homeopathy and medicine: resolving the conflict. New York (NY): Albert Einstein College of Medicine; 2012 [accessed 2015 Jan 28]. http://www.einstein.edu/medicine/books/ruch.html.

15. A website

Canadian Medical Association. c1994–2015 Ottawa (ON): Canadian Medical Association; [accessed 2015 Jan 2]. http://www.cma.ca.

15. Canadian Medical Association Ottawa (ON): Canadian Medical Association; c1994–2015 [accessed 2015 Jan 2]. http://www.cma.ca.

If you can't determine the year of publication of a website, use the site's year of copyright, preceded by "c": "c2015."

16. A message posted to a discussion list

Stalinsky Q. 2015 Aug 16. Reconsidering the hormone-replacement study. [discussion list]. Woman Physicians Association listserv. [accessed 2015 Aug 17]. http://wpa.com/1666930.

16. Stalinsky Q. Reconsidering the hormone-replacement study. [discussion list]. Woman Physicians Association listserv. 2015 Aug 16. [accessed 2015 Aug 17]. http://wpa.com/1666930.

17. A personal online communication (text citation)

One member of the research team has expressed reservation about the study design (2015 Feb 6 email from L. Kogod, to me; unreferenced).

A personal letter or email message should be cited in your text, not in your reference list. The format is the same for both the name-year and the number styles.

CSE
45c

18. A document on CD-ROM or DVD-ROM

Reich WT, editor. 2012. Encyclopedia of bioethics [DVD-ROM]. New York (NY): Co-Health.

18. Reich WT, editor. Encyclopedia of bioethics [DVD-ROM]. New York (NY): Co-Health; 2012.

Other sources
19. A report written and published by the same organization

Olkowski AA. 2009. Livestock water quality. Ottawa (ON): Agriculture and Agri-Food Canada.

19. Olkowski AA. Livestock water quality. Ottawa (ON): Agriculture and Agri-Food Canada; 2009.

20. A report written and published by different organizations

Hackney, JD (Rancho Los Amigos Hospital, Downey, CA). 2007. Effect of atmospheric pollutants on human physiologic function. Washington (DC): Environmental Protection Agency (US). Report No.: R-801396.

20. Hackney, JD (Rancho Los Amigos Hospital, Downey, CA). Effect of atmospheric pollutants on human physiologic function. Washington (DC): Environmental Protection Agency (US); 2007. Report No.: R-801396.

21. An audio or visual recording

Cell mitosis [DVD-ROM]. 2014. White Plains (NY): Teaching Media.

21. Cell mitosis [DVD-ROM]. White Plains (NY): Teaching Media; 2014.

45d IEEE numbered text citations

IEEE (formerly the Institute of Electrical and Electronics Engineers) recommends a documentation style based on the CSE number style, but using square brackets instead of superscripted numbers in the text. Cite multiple source numbers within the same brackets, separated by a comma but without a space. If three or more source numbers occur in a sequence, cite the first and last number separated by a hyphen.

These forms of immunity have been extensively researched [1].

Two standard references [2,3] use this term.

Four studies disagree with these findings [2–5].

CSE
45d

As with the CSE style, these numbers refer readers to a reference list numbered in the order you refer to the sources (not listed alphabetically by author), as described in 45b. Reuse numbers each time you refer to the source. For more detailed examples, see *www.ieee.org*.

PART 7

Other Forms of Communication

46 Writing Online

The main forms of online writing—email and Web compositions—dramatically expand your options as a writer. This chapter addresses some special concerns of writing online.

46a Email

The guidelines below apply to various email functions, from conversing with friends to conducting serious research.

Sending messages

- **Give your message a subject heading that describes its content.** Then your reader knows what priority to assign the message—a particular help for readers who receive many messages a day. A clear subject heading distinguishes your message from spam (junk email). Make your subject line work: not "Notice of meeting" but "Budget meeting Tuesday."
- **Compose a message that is concise and relevant to your recipients' concerns.** Adjust the formality of your message to your writing situation.
- **Use short paragraphs with blank lines between them.** For long messages, a tight structure, a clear forecast of the content, and a clear division into parts (using headings if necessary) not only improve effectiveness but also show courtesy.
- **Proofread** all but the most informal messages for errors in grammar, punctuation, and spelling.

Responding to messages

- **Check that your reply has an appropriate subject heading.** Most email programs label a response with the same subject heading as the original, preceded by *Re:* (from Latin, meaning "in reference to"). If your response does continue on the same subject, then *Re:* indicates as much. If, however, you raise a new issue, you should revise the subject heading accordingly.
- **Use quoted material from earlier messages critically.** By weaving your replies into the material quoted from someone else's message, you can respond to the

46a

MyWritingLab

Visit **MyWritingLab** for more help with writing online.

author point by point, as you would in conversation.
However, delete from the original anything you are
not responding to so that your recipient can focus on
what you have to say without wading through his or
her own words.

Observing netiquette

You won't always see others observing **netiquette**, or
Internet etiquette, but you will see that those who do
observe it receive more thoughtful and considerate
replies.

- **Pay careful attention to tone.** Refrain from **flaming**, or
  attacking, correspondents. Don't use all-capital letters, which SHOUT. And use irony or sarcasm with
  caution, perhaps clarifying your intended tone by
  adding emoticons to avoid misunderstandings.

- **Avoid participating in flame "wars,"** overheated dia-
  logues that contribute little or no information or
  understanding. If a war breaks out in a discussion,
  ignore it: don't rush to defend someone who is being
  attacked, and don't respond even if you are under
  attack yourself.

- **Be a forgiving reader.** Avoid nitpicking over spelling or
  other surface errors. And because attitudes are sometimes difficult to convey, give authors an initial bene-
  fit of the doubt: a writer who at first seems hostile
  may simply have tried too hard to be concise; a writer
  who at first seems unserious may simply have failed
  at injecting humour into a worthwhile message.

- **Forward a message only with the permission of the
  author.** Always delete third-party addresses when for-
  warding messages to preserve the privacy of others
  and protect them from spam. Similarly, use "bcc"
  when sending a mass email.

- **Avoid spamming.** With a few keystrokes, you can
  broadcast a message to many recipients at once.
  Occasionally you may have important information
  that everyone on a list will want to know. But flood-
  ing whole lists with irrelevant messages—called
  spamming—is rude and irritating.

46b Web composition

Unlike traditional documents, which are meant to be
read in sequence from start to finish, most websites are
intended to be examined in whatever order readers
choose as they follow links within the site and to other

46b

sites. A website thus requires careful planning of the links and thoughtful cues to orient readers:

- **Sketch possible site plans before getting started,** using a branching diagram to show major divisions and connections.
- **Plan a menu for each of the site's pages** that overviews the organization and links directly to other pages.
- **Distill your text** to include only essential information, and use headings to break the text into accessible chunks. Readers have difficulty following long, uninterrupted text passages onscreen.
- **Standardize elements of the design** so that readers know what to expect and can scan your pages easily.
- **Use icons, photographs, artwork, and other visual elements for a purpose, not merely for decoration.** Use captions to relate the visuals to your text.

47 Making Oral Presentations

Oral communication is researched and organized much like written communication, but this chapter explains how to adapt your message for oral delivery.

47a Written vs. oral communication

Since listeners cannot skim or review a speech as they can an essay, oral presentations require a more explicit structure and a greater use of repetition to compensate.

Organization: Introduction, conclusion, transitions

Like an essay or a report, a speech has an introduction, a body, and a conclusion. (See Chapter 1.)

The introduction of a speech, however, provides a more explicit statement of the thesis (the idea or message conveyed by the speech). It also features a preview of the organization of the speech (the division of the topic).

Use the introduction to set an appropriate tone and to persuade your audience to hear your message. Use more frequent and explicit **transitional expressions°** as well as more repetition in the form of summaries and

47a

MyWritingLab

Visit MyWritingLab for more help with making oral presentations.

°See "Grammar Terms," page 272.

previews. Use more signposting than you would when writing:

Written	Louis Riel was found guilty of high treason and hanged on November 16, 1885. Today many Canadians look upon him as a hero, a patriot, a founding father of the nation. Thus, a traitor for one age becomes a hero for another. Clearly, the way we interpret history depends on who we are, where we live, and what we believe.
Oral	On November 16, 1885, Louis Riel was found guilty of high treason and hanged, yet today many Canadians look upon him as a hero, a patriot, and a founding father of the nation. I want to talk to you about how we interpret history. Specifically, I'll discuss how our view of history depends on who we are, where we live, and what we believe. I'll look at the case of Louis Riel, show how opinions about him have evolved over the last century, and, finally, suggest some contemporary figures whose reputations may go through surprising changes by the next century.
Transition	I'll begin by reminding you of the historical record of Riel and the North-West Rebellion.

Signal the approach of your conclusion:

"Before concluding, I will add one further example . . ."
"To sum up . . ."

Visualization

Use vivid language and concrete examples to help your audience visualize what you are describing.

Not	Among the schoolchildren in this city, 34.5 percent do not receive sufficient nourishment at breakfast and lunch.
But	Right now Alice is sitting in her Grade 3 classroom with a rumbling stomach. She'll go hungry at recess and lunch hour because her mum had an empty fridge this morning. In our city's schools, every third child, like Alice, comes to school hungry.

47a

Audiovisual presentation aids are also useful, but they are no substitute for vivid language, and they can distract from the speaker's words.

Diction

Use vocabulary appropriate to your audience. Since listeners cannot consult a dictionary or glossary, avoid technical language unless you are addressing experts. If you can't avoid terms that your audience may not know, define the words as you use them (see Chapter 9). Avoid slang, blasphemy, profanity, or offensive terms.

Statistics

In oral delivery, round off statistics.

Not   48.73 percent of votes
But   nearly half the votes

Documentation

Provide oral footnotes:

According to a recent Statistics Canada study, the population of our town is expanding.

The newly elected head of the CMA told *The Globe and Mail* last week that Canadian medicare is in crisis.

Note Be prepared to provide detailed citations if someone questions your sources.

47b Oral delivery

Methods of oral delivery

Reading

Reading prevents effective eye contact and encourages a monotonous delivery. Avoid reading a prepared speech to an audience.

If you *must* read a speech, print it out in a large font, double-spaced, and add cues to remind yourself to look at the audience, tell a joke, pause, slow down, or ask a question.

Memorization

A memorized speech can be deadly to listen to and deadlier to give, especially if your memory dries up. Unless you are an accomplished actor, a memorized delivery also sounds unnatural. Avoid memorizing a text for delivery.

Extemporaneous delivery

Extemporaneous public speaking is the most difficult form to master, but with practice it is the easiest and most effective to use. An extemporaneous speech is thoroughly researched, planned, and rehearsed, but it is not memorized, nor is it written out in sentences to be read.

Instead, speak from brief notes, preferably a few key words jotted down on cue cards, or possibly displayed on *PowerPoint* (see "Presentational aids" below), to remind

you of your next point. You are thus *thinking* about your
ideas, not just *reciting* them. You are looking at your *audience*, not your *script*. Your sentences may not be as perfectly crafted as if you were reading—although with
practice you will gain confidence and fluency—but what
you lose in correctness you gain in communication with
your audience. It's a worthwhile trade.

Techniques of oral delivery

Eye contact

Look at your audience. Sweep the room with your
eyes. Glance briefly at your notes when necessary, but
maintain regular eye contact.

Posture and body language

Stand comfortably without slouching. Avoid leaning
on a lectern, random arm waving, constant weight shifting, restless pacing. Do not chew gum, twirl hair, jangle
bracelets, rustle notes, or click pens. Adjust your facial
expression to the tone and content of your speech.

Voice

Speak loudly enough to be heard without shouting.
Vary your pitch and pace to avoid boredom. Avoid a sing-
song or repetitive inflection. Drop your voice, slow down,
or pause occasionally for emphasis, but do not speak so
slowly that listeners lose the thread of what you are say-
ing. (Our minds process words faster than most speakers
can say them.) Enunciate clearly, especially consonants.
If necessary, exaggerate slightly for clarity.

Presentational aids

Practise using props, projectors, computer displays,
or other presentational aids you intend to use in your
speech. Cue recorded material, and check equipment
before your speech begins. Introduce aids only when
needed: explain their significance, then turn them off or
put them away to avoid distracting your audience.

PowerPoint and *Prezi* software can help you to integrate visual aids with your speaking notes, but be careful
to create readable slides that enhance rather than distract
from your presentation. Remember that when people are
reading your *PowerPoint* or *Prezi* displays, they are not
listening to your delivery. For visibility, use light text on a
dark background (e.g., white on dark blue) and large
fonts: 28–32 points for text, 36–44 points for headings.
Use motion features such as flying and zooming sparingly
(if at all), and avoid multiple font styles and text that
echoes what you are speaking. Keep graphics simple and
clear to reinforce your ideas.

47b

Confidence

Confidence comes with experience. Control stage fright in the following ways:

- **Breathing:** Breathe deeply to slow down a racing pulse.
- **Muscle relaxation:** Systematically flex and relax muscle groups to reduce tension before speaking.
- **Visualization:** Practise imagining yourself speaking eloquently to an appreciative audience.
- **Thorough preparation:** Prepare thoroughly so you will feel confident.

If you lose your train of thought or make a mistake, keep talking: chances are the audience members won't notice unless you tell them. If all else fails, summarize what you've said so far. You'll probably remember where your speech was heading, and you'll soon be back on track. Above all, remember that your listeners want you to succeed: they want to relax for the duration of your speech while you take charge.

47c Listening

We spend many more hours listening in class, at work, and in social situations than we do speaking. Learn to be an effective listener:

- *Do not* fake listening while you are really thinking about something else.
- *Do not* prejudge the speaker or dwell on his or her speech habits or bad fashion sense.
- *Do not* let yourself be distracted by physical noise (a banging door, the scene outside the window), psychological noise (your private thoughts), or semantic noise (your misunderstanding of, or emotional reaction to, the speaker's choice of words).
- *Do* motivate yourself to listen by asking yourself, "What can this speaker teach me?"
- *Do* concentrate on the sequence of ideas being presented, listening critically to the arguments and evidence.
- *Do* take notes to help focus your attention.

47c

We all perform better for a responsive audience. Good listeners encourage good speakers.

48 Writing for Business

The principles of document design covered in Chapter 4 apply to most business writing. This chapter discusses business letters, résumés, and business memos. For help with email, see pages 248–49.

The sample documents in this chapter do not accurately depict the proportions of actual business documents. Be sure to follow the instructions provided for setting up your documents on 8½" × 11" (21 cm × 28 cm) paper.

48a Job application letter

In any letter to a businessperson, you are addressing someone who wants to see quickly why you are writing and how to respond to you. For a job application, see the sample print letter on the next page.

Note that some employers demand a particular format for application letters or require job seekers to use a special online application form. Whether print or online, however, your letter will be judged for clarity, conciseness, and correctness. In the absence of specific instructions, use the following guidelines, which may be adapted for online forms.

Content

- **Interpret your résumé for the particular job.** Instead of reciting your job history, highlight and reshape only the relevant parts.
- **Announce at the outset what job you seek and how you heard about it.**
- **Include any special reason you have for applying,** such as a specific career goal.
- **Summarize your qualifications for the job,** including relevant facts about your education and employment, and emphasizing your notable accomplishments. Since many employers will search application letters electronically, use concise, appropriate keywords. Mention that additional information appears in an accompanying résumé. (See 48b.)
- **Describe your availability.** At the end of the letter, mention that you are available for an interview at the convenience of the addressee, or specify when you will be available.

48a

MyWritingLab

Visit **MyWritingLab** for more help with writing for business.

Minimum 1" (2.5 cm)

367 rue des Erables
Verdun QC H3E 1W6 — Return-address
heading
17 March 2016

Double-
space →

Charles Pelletier
Director of Human Resources
SNC-Lavalin Inc. — Inside address
1100 Blvd. René-Lévesque West
Montreal, QC H3B 4P3

Double-
space → Dear Mr. Pelletier, — Salutation

Double-
space → In response to your advertisement in the *Montreal Gazette*, I am applying for the position of surveyor.

I am completing my final year of civil engineering
studies at Dawson College and will receive my
Double-
space → Diploma of Collegial Studies in June 2016.

While at Dawson College I remained on the honour
roll for six semesters, earning a grade average of 86.4
1"
(2.5 cm) → percent. As president of the Civil Tech Club from 2014
to 2016, I was instrumental in organizing an
engineering fair for civil tech students. My work
experience at the Royal Victoria Hospital demonstrates
that I possess the discipline and personal skills that
Double-
space → your company seeks. I am also fully bilingual.

1"
(2.5 cm) ←

Double-
space → As my enclosed résumé shows, I have the education
and experience you are looking for.

I am available for an interview at your convenience.
Please call me at 514-555-4783 or email me at
adimaio@dawsoncollege.qc.ca.

Double-space →

Yours sincerely, — Close

Anna Di Maio — Signature — Quadruple-
space

Anna DiMaio

Enc: Résumé

48a

Format for a print letter

- **Use standard paper,** either unlined white paper measuring 8½ inches by 11 inches (21 cm × 28 cm) or letterhead stationery with your address printed at the top of the sheet.
- **Type the letter single-spaced.** Use double space between elements and paragraphs. Use only one side of a sheet. Align all elements with the left margin.
- **Address your letter to a specific person.** The company's website should help you identify the person to whom you should submit your application. If you can't find a person's name, then use a job title (*Dear Human Resources Manager*) or a general salutation (*Dear Smythe Shoes*).
- **Close the letter with an expression that reflects the formality of the situation.** *Respectfully, Cordially,* and *Sincerely* are more formal than *Best wishes* or *Regards*.
- **Use an envelope that will accommodate the letter once it is folded horizontally in thirds.** Show your name and address in the upper-left corner and the addressee's name, title, and address in the centre.

Note If asked to submit your application letter by email, turn it into a PDF (portable document format) and send it as an attachment or paste the content of the letter into the body of an email message, taking care to correct any formatting changes.

48b Résumé

For the résumé that accompanies your letter of application, you can use the sample on the next page and the following guidelines.

- **Provide the appropriate information in table form:** your name and address, career objective, education, employment history, any special skills or awards, and information about how to obtain your references.
- **Use headings to mark the sections of the résumé.** Space around the headings and within sections so that important information stands out.
- **Use capital letters conventionally.** Passages with many capitals can be hard to read. Do use capitals for proper nouns (pp. 113–14), but drop them for job titles, course names, department names, and the like.
- **Limit your résumé to one page so that it can be quickly reviewed.** However, if your experience and education are extensive, a two-page résumé is preferable to a single cramped, unreadable page.

48b

Anna DiMaio
367 rue des Erables
Verdun, QC H3E 1W6
Telephone: 514-555-4783
email: adimaio@dawsoncollege.qc.ca
Languages: English, French, Italian, some Spanish

Position desired
Surveyor, with possibility of career development, including
university studies in civil engineering.

Education

2013–16	**Civil Engineering Technology, Dawson College**, D.E.C. to be completed June 2016 President, Civil Tech Club 2014–16 Honour Roll
2008–13	**Centennial Regional High School**, Greenfield Park, Quebec DES completed June 2013

Technical Knowledge

Surveying:	Theodolites, Levels, Transits, Total Stations
Drafting:	manual, computer (AutoCAD LT 2015)
Estimating:	quantity take-offs
Software:	Microsoft Office 365, Sage 300 ERP, Primavera P6 (Project Management), Softdesk 8
Laboratory testing:	concrete, soils, asphalt, aggregates

Employment History

2015–16	**Assistant Laboratory Technician, Dawson College** Organized and directed laboratory affairs, monitored laboratory tests, cleaned and reorganized after laboratory tests
2014–16	**Admitting and Discharge Clerk, Royal Victoria Hospital** Admitted patients, booked surgery time for patients, booked beds for patients

References

Academic:	Mr. Howard Babcock, Chair Civil Engineering Technology Dept. Dawson College 3040 Sherbrooke Street West Westmount, QC H3Z 1A4
Employment:	Ms. Lise Dufresne Royal Victoria Hospital 687 Pine Avenue West Montreal, QC H3A 1A1
Personal:	Dr. Carole Adilman 9871 Gouin Blvd. West Pierrefonds, QC H8Y 1R9

48b

- **Keep the design simple.** Avoid images, colours, unusual or multiple fonts, and excessive use of vertical and horizontal lines or highlighting.
- **Use specific words to describe your skills and experience, especially if emailing a PDF version or completing an online form.** Prospective employers may search electronic résumés for appropriate keywords, usually nouns, so *manager* is preferable to *person with responsibility for*.

48c Business memo (print or email)

Business memos (short for "memorandums") address people within the same organization. A memo can be quite long, but more often it deals briefly with a specific topic, such as an answer to a question, a progress report, or an evaluation. Frequently it has more than one recipient. Both the content and the format of a memo aim to get to the point and dispose of it quickly, as in the sample of a print memo on the next page.

- **State your reason for writing in the first sentence as well as in the subject line.** (See p. 248).
- **Make your first paragraph work.** Concisely present your solution, recommendation, answer, or evaluation.
- **Deliver the support in the body of the memo.** The paragraphs may be numbered or bulleted so that the main divisions of your message are easy to see. In a long memo, you may need headings. (See p. 26.)
- **Suit your style and tone to your audience.** For instance, you'll want to address your boss or a large group of readers more formally than you would a co-worker who is also a friend.
- **For print memos, use a conventional memo heading.** Include the company's name, the addressee's name, the writer's name (initialled in handwriting), the date, and a subject description or title.
- **Type the body of the memo single-spaced.** Double-space between paragraphs, with no paragraph indentations.
- **For print memos that do not have a "cc" line in the heading,** list the people receiving copies of the memo two spaces below the last line.

48c

Bigelow Wax Company

TO: Aileen Rosen, Director of Sales
FROM: Patricia Phillips, Territory 12 *PP*
DATE: February 12, 2016
SUBJECT: 2015 sales of Quick Wax in Territory 12

Since it was introduced in January of 2015, Quick Wax has been unsuccessful in Territory 12 and has not affected the sales of our Easy Shine. Discussions with customers and my own analysis of Quick Wax suggest three reasons for its failure to compete with our product.

1. Quick Wax has not received the promotion necessary for a new product. Advertising— primarily on radio—has been sporadic and has not developed a clear, consistent image for the product. In addition, the Quick Wax sales representative in Territory 12 is new and inexperienced; he is not known to customers, and his sales pitch (which I once overheard) is weak. As far as I can tell, his efforts are not supported by phone calls or mailings from his home office.

2. When Quick Wax does make it to the store shelves, buyers do not choose it over our product. Though priced competitively with our product, Quick Wax is poorly packaged. The container seems smaller than ours, though in fact it holds the same 250 grams. The lettering on the Quick Wax package (red on blue) is difficult to read, in contrast to the white-on-green lettering on the Easy Shine package.

3. Our special purchase offers and my increased efforts to serve existing customers have had the intended effect of keeping customers satisfied with our product and reducing their inclination to stock something new.

Copies: L. Marchand, Director of Marketing
P. MacGregor, Customer Service Manager

48c

Commonly Misused Words

This section provides notes on words or phrases that often cause problems for writers. The recommendations for standard written English are based on current dictionaries and usage guides. Items labelled *nonstandard* should be avoided in final drafts of academic and business writing. Those labelled *colloquial* and *slang* appear in some informal writing and may occasionally be used for effect in more formal academic and career writing. (Words and phrases labelled *colloquial* include those labelled *informal* by many dictionaries.) See Chapter 9 for more on levels of language.

a, an Use *a* before words beginning with consonant sounds: *a̲ historian, a̲ one-o'clock class, a̲ university.* Use *an* before words that begin with vowel sounds, including silent *h*'s: *a̲n organism, a̲n L, a̲n honour.*

The article before an abbreviation depends on how the abbreviation is read: *She has a̲n NSRC grant.* (*NSRC* is read as one word beginning with the vowel sound "*en.*") *He is writing a̲n SAT exam tomorrow.* (*SAT* is read as three separate letters beginning with the vowel sound "*ess*").

See also pp. 77–79 on the uses of *a/an* versus *the.*

accept, except *Accept* is a **verb**° meaning "to receive." *Except* is usually a **preposition**° or **conjunction**° meaning "but for" or "other than"; when it is used as a verb, it means "to leave out." *I can a̲c̲c̲e̲p̲t̲ all your suggestions e̲x̲c̲e̲p̲t̲ the last one. I'm sorry you e̲x̲c̲e̲p̲t̲e̲d̲ my last suggestion from your list.*

advice, advise *Advice* is a **noun**,° and *advise* is a **verb**.° *Take my a̲d̲v̲i̲c̲e̲; do as I a̲d̲v̲i̲s̲e̲ you.*

affect, effect Usually *affect* is a **verb**° meaning "to influence," and *effect* is a **noun**° meaning "result": *The drug did not a̲f̲f̲e̲c̲t̲ his driving; in fact, it seemed to have no e̲f̲f̲e̲c̲t̲ at all.* (Note that *effect* occasionally is used as a verb meaning "to bring about": *Her efforts e̲f̲f̲e̲c̲t̲e̲d̲ a change.* And *affect* is used in psychology as a noun meaning "feeling or emotion": *One can infer much about a̲f̲f̲e̲c̲t̲ from behaviour.*)

aggravate *Aggravate* should not be used in its colloquial meaning of "irritate" or "exasperate" (for example, *We were a̲g̲g̲r̲a̲v̲a̲t̲e̲d̲ by her constant arguing*). *Aggravate* means "make worse": *The chief of campus security was i̲r̲r̲i̲t̲a̲t̲e̲d̲ by the student demonstration because he feared it might a̲g̲g̲r̲a̲v̲a̲t̲e̲ the unrest on campus.*

all, always, never, no one These absolute words often exaggerate a situation in which *many, often, rarely,* or *few* is more accurate.

all ready, already *All ready* means "completely prepared," and *already* means "by now" or "before now": *We were all ready to go to the movie, but it had already started.*

all right *All right* is always two words. *Alright* is an error.

all together, altogether *All together* means "in unison," or "gathered in one place." *Altogether* means "entirely." *It's not altogether true that our family never spends vacations all together.*

allusion, illusion An *allusion* is an indirect reference, and an *illusion* is a deceptive appearance: *Paul's constant allusions to Shakespeare created the illusion that he was an intellectual.*

a lot *A lot* is always two words, used informally to mean "many." *Alot* is a common misspelling.

always See *all, always, never, no one.*

among, between In general, use *between* only for relationships of two and *among* for more than two.

amount, number Use *amount* with a singular noun that names something not countable (a **noncount noun**°): *The amount of food varies.* Use *number* with a plural noun that names more than one of something countable (a **count noun**°): *The number of calories must stay the same.*

and/or *And/or* indicates three options: one or the other or both (*The decision is made by the mayor and/or the council*). If you mean all three options, *and/or* is appropriate. Otherwise, use *and* if you mean both, *or* if you mean either.

anxious, eager *Anxious* means "nervous" or "worried" and is usually followed by *about*. *Eager* means "looking forward" and is usually followed by *to*. *I've been anxious about getting blisters. I'm eager [not anxious] to get new cross-training shoes.*

anybody, any body; anyone, any one *Anybody* and *anyone* are **indefinite pronouns**;° *any body* is a **noun**° modified by *any; any one* is a **pronoun**° or **adjective**° modified by *any. How can anybody communicate with any body of government? Can anyone help Amy? She has more work than any one person can handle.*

any more, anymore *Any more* means "no more"; *anymore* means "now." Both are used in negative constructions: *He doesn't want any more. She doesn't live here anymore.*

anyways, anywheres Nonstandard for *anyway* and *anywhere.*

are, is Use *are* with a plural **subject**° (*books are*), *is* with a singular subject (*book is*). See p. 67.

as *As* may be vague or ambiguous when it substitutes for *because, since,* or *while*: *As we were stopping to rest, we decided to eat lunch.* (Does *as* mean "while" or "because"?) *As* should never be used as a substitute for *whether* or *who*. *I'm not sure _whether_ [not _as_] we can make it. That's the man _who_ [not _as_] gave me directions.*

as, like See *like, as.*

at this point in time Wordy for *now, at this point,* or *at this time.*

awful, awfully Strictly speaking, *awful* means "inspiring awe." As intensifiers meaning "very" or "extremely" (*He tried _awfully_ hard*), *awful* and *awfully* should be avoided in formal speech or writing.

a while, awhile *Awhile* is an **adverb**;° *a while* is an **article**° and a **noun.**° *I will be gone _awhile_ [not _a while_]. I will be gone for _a while_ [not _awhile_].*

bad, badly In formal speech and writing, *bad* should be used only as an **adjective**;° the **adverb**° is *badly. He felt _bad_ because his tooth ached _badly_.* In *He felt bad*, the verb *felt* is a **linking verb**° and the adjective *bad* modifies the **subject**° *he*, not the verb *felt.* See also pp. 75–76.

beg the question "Beg the question" is the name of a logical fallacy, a form of circular reasoning in which the claim to be proven ("the question") is used as evidence that the claim is true. It *does not* mean "raise the question."

being as, being that Colloquial for *because,* the preferable word in formal speech or writing: *Because [not _Being as_] the world is round, Columbus never did fall off the edge.*

beside, besides *Beside* is a **preposition**° meaning "next to." *Besides* is a preposition meaning "except" or "in addition to" as well as an **adverb**° meaning "in addition." *_Besides_, several other people _besides_ you want to sit _beside_ Dr. Christensen.*

between, among See *among, between.*

bring, take Use *bring* only for movement from a farther place to a nearer one and *take* for any other movement. *First, _take_ these books to the library for renewal, then _take_ them to Mr. Daniels. _Bring_ them back to me when he's finished.*

can, may Strictly, *can* indicates capacity or ability, and *may* indicates permission: *If I _may_ talk with you a moment, I believe I _can_ solve your problem.*

climatic, climactic *Climatic* comes from *climate* and refers to weather: *Recent droughts may indicate a _climatic_ change. Climactic* comes from *climax* and refers to a dramatic high point: *During the _climactic_ duel between Hamlet and Laertes, Gertrude drinks poisoned wine.*

complement, compliment To *complement* something is to add to, complete, or reinforce it: *Her yellow blouse _complemented_ her black hair.* To *compliment* something is to make a flattering remark about it: *He _complimented_ her on her hair. Complimentary* can also mean "free": *_complimentary_ tickets.*

Words

conscience, conscious   *Conscience* is a **noun°** meaning "a sense of right and wrong"; *conscious* is an **adjective°** meaning "aware" or "awake." *Though I was barely conscious, my conscience nagged me.*

continual, continuous   *Continual* means "constantly recurring": *Most movies on television are continually interrupted by commercials. Continuous* means "unceasing": *Many on-demand streaming services present movies continuously without commercials.*

could of   See *have, of.*

criteria   The plural of *criterion* (meaning "standard for judgment"): *Our criteria are strict. The most important criterion is a sense of humour.*

data   The plural of *datum* (meaning "fact"). Though *data* is often used with a singular verb, many readers prefer the plural verb and it is always correct: *The data fail* [not *fails*] *to support the hypothesis.*

device, devise   *Device* is the **noun,°** and *devise* is the **verb:°** *Can you devise some device for getting his attention?*

different from, different than   *Different from* is preferred: *His purpose is different from mine.* But *different than* is widely accepted when a construction using *from* would be wordy: *I'm a different person now than I used to be* is preferable to *I'm a different person now from the person I used to be.*

disinterested, uninterested   *Disinterested* means "impartial": *We chose Pete, as a disinterested third party, to decide who was right. Uninterested* means "bored" or "lacking interest": *Unfortunately, Pete was completely uninterested in the question.*

don't   *Don't* is the contraction for *do not,* not for *does not: I don't care, you don't care,* and *he doesn't* [not *don't*] *care.*

due to   *Due* is an **adjective°** or **noun;°** thus *due to* is always acceptable as a subject complement:° *His grey hairs were due to age.* Many object to *due to* as a **preposition°** meaning "because of" (*Due to the holiday, class was cancelled*). A rule of thumb is that *due to* is always correct after a form of the verb *be* but questionable otherwise.

eager, anxious   See *anxious, eager.*

effect   See *affect, effect.*

elicit, illicit   *Elicit* is a **verb°** meaning "bring out" or "call forth." *Illicit* is an **adjective°** meaning "unlawful." *The crime elicited an outcry against illicit drugs.*

emigrate, immigrate   *Emigrate* means "to leave one's own country to settle in another": *The Fahias emigrated from Somalia. Immigrate* means "to settle into a place where one was not born": *They immigrated to Canada.*

enthused Sometimes used colloquially as an **adjective**° meaning "showing enthusiasm." The preferred adjective is *enthusiastic*: *The coach was enthusiastic [not enthused] about the team's victory.*

etc. *Etc.,* the Latin abbreviation for "and other things," should be avoided in formal writing and should not be used to refer to people. When used, it should not substitute for precision, as in *The government provides health care, etc.,* and it should not end a list beginning *such as* or *for example.*

everybody, every body; everyone, every one *Everybody* and *everyone* are indefinite **pronouns**:° *Everybody [or Everyone] knows Tom steals. Every one* is a **pronoun**° modified by *every,* and *every body* is a **noun**° modified by *every.* Both refer to each thing or person of a specific group and are typically followed by *of: Every body of water in the province has been tested, so everybody can swim safely this summer.*

everyday, every day *Everyday* is an **adjective**° meaning "used daily" or "common"; *every day* is a **noun**° modified by *every*: *Everyday problems tend to arise every day.*

everywheres Nonstandard for *everywhere.*

except See *accept, except.*

explicit, implicit *Explicit* means "stated outright": *I left explicit instructions. Implicit* means "implied, unstated": *We had an implicit understanding.*

farther, further *Farther* refers to additional distance (*How much farther is it to the beach?*), and *further* refers to additional time, amount, or other abstract matters (*I don't want to discuss this any further*).

feel Avoid this word in place of *think* or *believe: She thinks [not feels] that the law should be changed.*

fewer, less *Fewer* refers to individual countable items (a plural count noun°), *less* to general amounts (a **noncount noun**,° always singular): *Skim milk has fewer calories than whole milk. We have less milk left than I thought.*

further See *farther, further.*

get *Get* is easy to overuse; watch out for it in expressions such as *it's getting better* (substitute *improving*), *we got done* (substitute *finished*), and *the mayor has got to* (substitute *must*).

good, well *Good* is an **adjective**,° and *well* is nearly always an **adverb**:° *Larry's a good dancer. He and Linda dance well together. Well* is properly used as an adjective only to refer to health: *You look well.* (*You look good,* in contrast, means "Your appearance is pleasing.") See also p. 75.

hanged, hung Though both are **past-tense forms**° of *hang, hanged* is used to refer to executions and *hung* is used for all

Words

other meanings: *Louis Riel was hanged* [not *hung*]. *I hung* [not *hanged*] *the picture you gave me.*

have, of   Use *have*, not *of*, after **helping verbs°** such as *could, should, would, may,* and *might: You should have* [not *should of*] *told me.*

he, she; he/she   Convention has allowed the use of *he* to mean "he or she," but most writers today consider this usage inaccurate and unfair because it excludes females. The construction *he/she*, one substitute for *he*, is awkward and objectionable to many readers. The better choice is to recast the sentence in the plural, to rephrase, or to use *he or she*. For instance: *After infants learn to creep, they progress to crawling. After learning to creep, the infant progresses to crawling. After the infant learns to creep, he or she progresses to crawling.* See also pp. 50 and 72.

herself, himself   See *myself*.

hisself   Nonstandard for *himself*.

hopefully   *Hopefully* means "with hope": *Freddy waited hopefully.* The use of *hopefully* to mean "it is to be hoped," "I hope," or "let's hope" is now very common; but try to avoid it in writing because many readers continue to object strongly to the usage.

idea, ideal   An *idea* is a thought or conception. An *ideal* (**noun°**) is a model of perfection or a goal. *Ideal* should not be used in place of *idea*: *The idea* [not *ideal*] *of the play is that our ideals often sustain us.*

if, whether   For clarity, use *whether* rather than *if* when you are expressing an alternative: *If I laugh hard, people can't tell whether I'm crying.*

illicit   See *elicit, illicit*.

illusion   See *allusion, illusion*.

immigrate   See *emigrate, immigrate*.

implicit   See *explicit, implicit*.

imply, infer   Writers or speakers *imply*, meaning "suggest": *Jim's letter implies he's having a good time.* Readers or listeners *infer*, meaning "conclude": *From Jim's letter I infer he's having a good time.*

irregardless   Nonstandard for *regardless*.

is, are   See *are, is*.

is when, is where   These are faulty constructions in sentences that define: *Adolescence is a stage* [not *is when a person is*] *between childhood and adulthood. Socialism is a system in which* [not *is where*] *government owns the means of production.*

its, it's   *Its* is the **pronoun°** *it* in the **possessive case:°** *That plant is losing its leaves. It's* is a contraction for *it is* or *it has: It's* [*It is*] *likely to die. It's* [*It has*] *got a fungus.* See also p. 98.

kind of, sort of, type of   In formal speech and writing, avoid using *kind of* or *sort of* to mean "somewhat": *He was rather* [not *kind of*] *tall.*

    Kind, sort, and *type* are singular: *This kind of dog is easily trained.* Errors often occur when these singular nouns are combined with the plural **adjectives**° *these* and *those*: *These kinds* [not *kind*] *of dogs are easily trained. Kind, sort,* and *type* should be followed by *of* but not by *a*: *I don't know what type of* [not *type* or *type of a*] *dog that is.*

    Don't use *kind of, sort of,* or *type of* unless the word *kind, sort,* or *type* is important: *That was a strange* [not *strange sort of*] *statement.*

lay, lie   *Lay* means "put" or "place" and takes a **direct object**:° *We could lay the tablecloth in the sun.* Its main forms are *lay, laid, laid. Lie* means "recline" or "be situated" and does not take an object: *I lie awake at night. The town lies east of the river.* Its main forms are *lie, lay, lain.*

less   See *fewer, less.*

lie, lay   See *lay, lie.*

like, as   In formal speech and writing, *like* should not introduce a **main clause**.° The preferred choice is *as* or *as if*: *The plan succeeded as* [not *like*] *we hoped.* Use *like* only before a word or phrase: *Other plans like it have failed.*

literally   This word means "actually" or "just as the words say," and it should not be used to intensify expressions whose words are not to be taken at face value. The sentence *He was literally climbing the walls* describes a person behaving like an insect, not a person who is restless or anxious. For the latter meaning, *literally* should be omitted.

lose, loose   *Lose* means "mislay": *Did you lose a brown glove? Loose* usually means "unrestrained" or "not tight": *Ann's canary got loose.*

may, can   See *can, may.*

may be, maybe   *May be* is a **verb**,° and *maybe* is an **adverb**° meaning "perhaps": *Tuesday may be a legal holiday. Maybe we won't have classes.*

may of   See *have, of.*

media   *Media* is the plural of *medium* and takes a plural **verb**.° *All the news media are increasingly visual.* The singular verb is common, even in the media, but many readers prefer the plural verb and it is always correct.

might of   See *have, of.*

must of   See *have, of.*

myself, herself, himself, yourself, ourselves, themselves, yourselves   Avoid using the *-self* **pronouns**° in place of **personal pronouns**:° *No one except me* [not *myself*] *saw the accident. Michiko and I* [not *myself*] *planned the ceremony.*

Words

The -*self* pronouns have two uses: they emphasize a noun or other pronoun (*Paul did the work himself. He himself said so.*), or they indicate that the sentence subject also receives the action of the verb: *I drove myself to the hospital.*

never, no one   See *all, always, never, no one.*

nowheres   Nonstandard for *nowhere.*

number   See *amount, number.*

of, have   See *have, of.*

OK, O.K., okay   All three spellings are acceptable, but avoid this colloquial term in formal speech and writing.

people, persons   Except when emphasizing individuals, prefer *people* to *persons: The people of the North . . .* ; *Will the person or persons who saw the accident please notify. . . .*

percent (per cent), percentage   Both these terms refer to fractions of one hundred. *Percent* always follows a number (*40 percent of the voters*), and the word should be used instead of the symbol (%) in nontechnical writing. *Percentage* usually follows an adjective (*a high percentage*).

persons   See *people, persons.*

phenomena   The plural of *phenomenon* (meaning "perceivable fact" or "unusual occurrence"): *Many phenomena are not recorded. One phenomenon is attracting attention.*

plus   *Plus* is standard as a **preposition**° meaning "in addition to": *His income plus mine is sufficient.* But *plus* is colloquial as a **conjunctive adverb**:° *Our organization is larger than theirs; moreover* [not *plus*], *we have more money.*

precede, proceed   *Precede* means "come before": *My name precedes yours in the alphabet. Proceed* means "move on": *We were told to proceed to the waiting room.*

prejudice, prejudiced   *Prejudice* is a **noun**;° *prejudiced* is an **adjective**.° Do not drop the -*d* from *prejudiced*: *I knew that my grandparents were prejudiced* [not *prejudice*].

principal, principle   *Principal* is an **adjective**° meaning "foremost" or "major," a noun° meaning "chief official," or, in finance, a noun meaning "capital sum." *Principle* is a noun only, meaning "rule" or "axiom." *Her principal reasons for confessing were her principles of right and wrong.*

proceed, precede   See *precede, proceed.*

raise, rise   *Raise* means "lift" or "bring up" and takes a **direct object**:° *The Kirks raise cattle.* Its main forms are *raise, raised, raised. Rise* means "get up" and does not take an object: *They must rise at dawn.* Its main forms are *rise, rose, risen.*

real, really   In formal speech and writing, *real* should not be used as an **adverb**;° *really* is the adverb and *real* an **adjective**.° *Popular reaction to the announcement was really* [not *real*] *enthusiastic.*

reason is because   Although colloquially common, this construction should be avoided in formal speech and writing. Use a *that* clause after *reason is*: *The reason he is absent is that* [not *is because*] *he is sick.* Or: *He is absent because he is sick.*

respectful, respective   *Respectful* means "full of (or showing) respect": *Be respectful of other people. Respective* means "separate": *The French and the Germans occupied their respective trenches.*

rise, raise   See *raise, rise.*

sensual, sensuous   *Sensual* suggests sexuality; *sensuous* means "pleasing to the senses." *Stirred by the sensuous scent of meadow grass and flowers, Cheryl and Paul found their thoughts turning sensual.*

set, sit   *Set* means "put" or "place" and takes a **direct object**:° *He sets the pitcher down.* Its main forms are *set, set, set. Sit* means "be seated" and does not take an object: *She sits on the sofa.* Its main forms are *sit, sat, sat.*

should of   See *have, of.*

since   *Since* mainly relates to time: *I've been waiting since noon.* But *since* can also mean "because": *Since you ask, I'll tell you.* Revise sentences in which the word could have either meaning, such as *Since you left, my life is empty.*

sit, set   See *set, sit.*

somebody, some body; someone, some one   *Somebody* and *someone* are **indefinite pronouns**;° *some body* is a **noun**° modified by *some*; and *some one* is a **pronoun**° or an **adjective**° modified by *some. Somebody ought to invent a shampoo that will give hair some body. Someone told James he should choose some one plan and stick with it.*

somewheres   Nonstandard for *somewhere.*

sort of, sort of a   See *kind of, sort of, type of.*

supposed to, used to   In both these expressions, the *-d* is essential: *I used to* [not *use to*] *think so. He's supposed to* [not *suppose to*] *meet us.*

sure and, sure to; try and, try to   *Sure to* and *try to* are the correct forms: *Be sure to* [not *sure and*] *buy milk. Try to* [not *Try and*] *find some decent tomatoes.*

take, bring   See *bring, take.*

than, then   *Than* is a **conjunction**° used in comparisons, *then* an **adverb**° indicating time: *Holmes knew then that Moriarty was wilier than he had thought.*

that, which   *That* always introduces **essential**° clauses: *Use the lettuce that Susan bought* (the clause limits *lettuce* to a particular lettuce). *Which* can introduce both essential and **nonessential**° clauses, but many writers reserve *which* only for nonessential clauses: *The leftover lettuce, which is in the*

°See "Grammar Terms," page 272.

refrigerator, would make a good salad (the clause simply provides more information about the lettuce we already know of). Essential clauses are not set off by commas; nonessential clauses are. See also pp. 90–91.

that, who, which Use *that* to refer to most animals and to things: *The animals that escaped included a zebra. The rocket that failed cost millions.* Use *who* to refer to people and to animals with names: *Dorothy is the girl who visits Oz. Her dog, Toto, who accompanies her, gives her courage.* Use *which* only to refer to animals and things: *The Zambezi River, which runs over two thousand kilometres, empties into the Indian Ocean.*

their, there, they're *Their* is the **possessive°** form of *they: Give them their money.* *There* indicates place (*I saw her standing there*) or functions as an **expletive°** (*There is a hole behind you*). *They're* is a **contraction°** for *they are: They're going fast.*

theirselves Nonstandard for *themselves.*

then, than See *than, then.*

these, this *These* is plural; *this* is singular. *This pear is ripe, but these pears are not.*

these kind, these sort, these type, those kind See *kind of, sort of, type of.*

thru A colloquial spelling of *through* that should be avoided in all academic and business writing.

to, too, two *To* is a **preposition;°** *too* is an **adverb°** meaning "also" or "excessively"; and *two* is a number. *I too have been to Europe two times.*

toward, towards Both are acceptable, though *toward* is preferred. Use one or the other consistently.

try and, try to See *sure and, sure to; try and, try to.*

type of See *kind of, sort of, type of.*

uninterested See *disinterested, uninterested.*

unique *Unique* means "the only one of its kind" and so cannot sensibly be modified with words such as *very* or *most: That was a unique* [not *a very unique* or *the most unique*] *movie.*

used to See *supposed to, used to.*

weather, whether The *weather* is the state of the atmosphere. *Whether* introduces alternatives. *The weather will determine whether we go or not.*

well See *good, well.*

whether, if See *if, whether.*

which, that See *that, which.*

who, which, that See *that, who, which.*

°See "Grammar Terms," page 272.

who, whom   *Who* is the subject of a sentence or **clause**:° *We know who will come. Whom* is the **object**° of a **verb**° or **preposition:**° *We know whom we invited.*

who's, whose   *Who's* is the **contraction**° of *who is* or *who has*: *Who's* [*Who is*] *at the door? Jim is the only one who's* [*who has*] *passed. Whose* is the possessive° form of *who*: *Whose book is that?*

would be   Often used instead of *is* or *are* to soften statements needlessly: *One example is* [not *would be*] *gun-control laws.*

would have   Avoid this construction in place of *had* in clauses that begin *if: If the tree had* [not *would have*] *withstood the fire, it would have been the oldest in town.*

would of   See *have, of.*

you   In all but very formal writing, *you* is generally appropriate as long as it means "you, the reader." In all writing, avoid indefinite uses of *you,* such as *In one ancient tribe your first loyalty was to your parents.*

your, you're   *Your* is the **possessive**° form of *you: Your dinner is ready. You're* is the **contraction**° of *you are: You're late.*

yourself   See *myself.*

Grammar Terms

This section defines the terms and concepts of basic English grammar, including every term marked ° in the text.

absolute phrase   A phrase that consists of a **noun**° or **pronoun**° plus the *-ing* or *-ed* form of a **verb**° (a **participle**°): *Our accommodations arranged*, we set out on our trip. *They will hire a local person, other things being equal*.

active voice   The **verb form**° used when the sentence **subject**° names the performer of the verb's action: *The drillers used a rotary blade*. For more, see *voice*.

adjective   A word used to modify a **noun**° or **pronoun**:° *beautiful* morning, *ordinary* one, *good* spelling. Contrast *adverb*. Nouns, word groups, and some **verb**° forms may also serve as adjectives: *book* sale; sale *of old books*; the sale, *which occurs annually; increasing* profits.

adverb   A word used to modify a **verb**,° an **adjective**,° another adverb, or a whole sentence: *warmly* greet (verb), *only* three people (adjective), *quite seriously* (adverb), *Fortunately*, she is employed (sentence). Word groups may also serve as adverbs: *drove by a farm*, plowed the field *when the earth thawed*.

agreement   The correspondence of one word to another in **person**,° **number**,° or **gender**.° Mainly, a **verb**° must agree with its **subject**° (*The chef orders eggs*), and a **pronoun**° must agree with its antecedent° (*The chef surveys her breakfast*). See also pp. 65–67 and 70–72.

antecedent   The word a **pronoun**° refers to: *Jonah, who is not yet ten, has already chosen the university he will attend* (*Jonah* is the antecedent of the pronouns *who* and *he*).

appositive   A word or word group appearing next to a **noun**° or **pronoun**° that renames or identifies it and is equivalent to it: *My brother Michael, the best horn player in town, won the competition* (*Michael* identifies which brother is being referred to; *the best horn player in town* renames *My brother Michael*).

article   The words *a, an,* and *the*. A kind of **determiner**,° an article always signals that a noun follows. See p. 261 for how to choose between *a* and *an*. See pp. 77–79 for the rules governing *a/an* and *the*.

auxiliary verb   See *helping verb*.

case   The form of a **pronoun**° or **noun**° that indicates its function in the sentence. Most pronouns have three cases. The **subjective case** is for **subjects**° and subject **complements**:° *I, you, he, she, it, we, they, who, whoever*. The **objective case** is for **objects**:° *me, you, him, her, it, us, them, whom, whomever*. The **possessive case** is for ownership:

°Defined in this section.

my/mine, your/yours, his, her/hers, its, our/ours, their/theirs, whose. Nouns use the subjective form (*dog, Newfoundland*) for all cases except the possessive (*dog's, Newfoundland's*).

clause A group of words containing a **subject**° and a **predicate**.° A **main clause** can stand alone as a sentence: <u>*We can go to the movies*</u>. A **subordinate clause** cannot stand alone as a sentence: *We can go <u>if Julie gets back on time</u>*. For more, see *subordinate clause*.

collective noun A word with singular form that names a group of individuals or things: for instance, *team, army, family, flock, group*. A collective noun generally takes a singular verb and a singular pronoun: *The <u>army is</u> prepared for <u>its</u> role*. See also pp. 66 and 72.

comma splice A sentence error in which two sentences (**main clauses**°) are separated by a comma without *and, but, or, nor,* or another **coordinating conjunction**.° Splice: *The book was long, it contained useful information*. Revised: *The book was long; it contained useful information*. Or: *The book was long, and it contained useful information*. See pp. 84–86.

comparison The form of an **adjective**° *or* **adverb**° that shows its degree of quality or amount. The **positive** is the simple, uncompared form: *gross, clumsily*. The **comparative** compares the thing modified to at least one other thing: *grosser, more clumsily*. The **superlative** indicates that the thing modified exceeds all other things to which it is being compared: *grossest, most clumsily*. The comparative and superlative are formed either with the endings *-er/-est* or with the words *more/most* or *less/least*.

complement See *subject complement*.

complex sentence See *sentence*.

compound-complex sentence See *sentence*.

compound construction Two or more words or word groups serving the same function, such as a compound **subject**° (<u>*Harriet and Peter*</u> *poled their barge down the river*), a compound **predicate**° (*The scout <u>watched and waited</u>*), or a **compound sentence**° (<u>*He smiled, and I laughed*</u>).

compound sentence See *sentence*.

conditional statement A statement expressing a condition contrary to fact and using the subjunctive mood° of the verb: *If she <u>were</u> mayor, the unions would cooperate*.

conjunction A word that links and relates parts of a sentence. See *coordinating conjunction* (*and, but,* etc.), *correlative conjunction* (*either . . . or, both . . . and,* etc.), and *subordinating conjunction* (*because, if,* etc.).

conjunctive adverb A type of **transitional expression**° that can relate two **main clauses**° in a single sentence: *We had hoped to own a house by now; <u>however</u>, prices are still too high*. The main clauses are separated by a semicolon or a period. Some common conjunctive adverbs: *accordingly,*

°Defined in this section.

also, anyway, besides, certainly, consequently, finally, further, furthermore, hence, however, in addition, incidentally, indeed, instead, likewise, meanwhile, moreover, namely, nevertheless, next, nonetheless, now, otherwise, rather, similarly, still, then, thereafter, therefore, thus, undoubtedly.

contraction   A condensed expression, with an apostrophe replacing the missing letters: for example, *doesn't* (*does not*), *we'll* (*we will*).

coordinating conjunction   A word linking words or word groups serving the same function: *The dog and cat sometimes fight, but they usually get along.* The coordinating conjunctions are *and, but, or, nor, for, so, yet.*

coordination   The linking of words or word groups that are of equal importance, usually with a **coordinating conjunction.**° *He and I laughed, but she was not amused.* Contrast *subordination.*

correlative conjunction   Two or more connecting words that work together to link words or word groups serving the same function: *Both Wanda and June signed up, but neither Stan nor Yann did.* The correlatives include *both . . . and, just as . . . so, not only . . . but also, not . . . but, either . . . or, neither . . . nor, whether . . . or, as . . . as.*

count noun   A word that names a person, place, or thing that can be counted (and so may appear in plural form): *camera/cameras, river/rivers, child/children.*

dangling modifier   A modifier that does not grammatically describe anything in its sentence. Dangling: *Having arrived late, the concert had already begun.* Revised: *Having arrived late, we found that the concert had already begun.* See p. 81.

determiner   A word such as *a, an, the, my,* and *your* that indicates that a noun follows. See also *article.*

direct address   A construction in which a word or phrase indicates the person or group spoken to: *Have you finished, John? Farmers, unite.*

direct object   A **noun**° or **pronoun**° that identifies who or what receives the action of a verb:° *Education opens doors.* For more, see *object* and *predicate.*

direct question   A sentence asking a question and concluding with a question mark: *Do they know we are watching?* Contrast *indirect question.*

direct quotation   Repetition of what someone has written or said, using the exact words of the original and enclosing them in quotation marks: *Feinberg writes, "The reasons are both obvious and sorry."*

double negative   A nonstandard form consisting of two negative words used in the same construction so that they effectively cancel each other: *I don't have no money.* Rephrase as *I have no money* or *I don't have any money.* See also p. 77.

°Defined in this section.

ellipsis   The omission of a word or words from a quotation, indicated by the three spaced periods of an ellipsis mark: "*all . . . are created equal.*" See also pp. 104–06.

essential element   A word or word group that is necessary to the meaning of the sentence because it limits the word it refers to: removing it would leave the meaning unclear or too general. Essential elements are *not* set off by commas: *Dorothy's companion the Scarecrow lacks a brain. The man who called about the apartment said he'd try again.* Contrast *nonessential element*. See also pp. 90–91.

expletive construction   A sentence that postpones the **subject**° by beginning with *there* or *it* and a form of *be: It is impossible to get a ticket. There are no more seats available.*

first person   See *person*.

fused sentence (run-on sentence)   A sentence error in which two complete sentences (**main clauses**°) are joined with no punctuation or connecting word between them. Fused: *I heard his lecture it was dull.* Revised: *I heard his lecture ; it was dull. I heard his lecture , but it was dull.* See pp. 84–86.

future perfect tense   The verb tense expressing an action that will be completed before another future action: *They will have heard by then.* For more, see *tense*.

future tense   The verb tense expressing action that will occur in the future: *They will hear soon.* For more, see *tense*.

gender   The classification of **nouns**° or **pronouns**° as masculine (*he, boy*), feminine (*she, woman*), or neuter (*it, computer*).

generic he   *He* used to mean *he or she*. Avoid *he* when you intend either or both genders. See pp. 50 and 72.

generic noun   A **noun**° that does not refer to a specific person or thing: *Any person may come. A student needs good work habits. A school with financial problems may shortchange its students.* A singular generic noun takes a singular **pronoun**° (*he, she,* or *it*). See also indefinite pronoun and pp. 71–72.

gerund   A verb form that ends in *-ing* and functions as a **noun**:° *Working is all right for killing time.* For more, see *verbals and verbal phrases*.

gerund phrase   See *verbals and verbal phrases*.

helping verb (auxiliary verb)   A **verb**° used with another verb to convey time, possibility, obligation, and other meanings: *You should write a letter. You have written other letters.* The **modals** are the following: *be able to, be supposed to, can, could, had better, had to, may, might, must, ought to, shall, should, used to, will, would.* The other helping verbs are forms of *be, have,* and *do.* See also pp. 56–58.

idiom   An expression that is peculiar to a language and that may not make sense if taken literally: for example, *bide your time, by and large,* and *put up with.*

°Defined in this section.

imperative See *mood.*

indefinite pronoun A word that stands for a **noun°** and does not refer to a specific person or thing. A few indefinite pronouns are plural (*both, few, many, several*) or may be singular or plural (*all, any, more, most, none, some*). But most are only singular: *anybody, anyone, anything, each, either, everybody, everyone, everything, neither, nobody, no one, nothing, one, somebody, someone, something.* The singular indefinite pronouns take singular verbs and are referred to by singular pronouns: *Something <u>makes its</u> presence felt.* See also *generic noun* and pp. 66 and 71–72.

indicative See *mood.*

indirect object A **noun°** or **pronoun°** that identifies to whom or what something is done: *Give <u>them</u> the award.* For more, see *object* and *predicate.*

indirect question A sentence reporting a question and ending with a period: *Writers wonder whether their work must always be lonely.* Contrast *direct question.*

indirect quotation A report of what someone has written or said, but not using the exact words of the original and not enclosing the words in quotation marks. Quotation: *"Just watch me."* Indirect quotation: *Pierre Trudeau said <u>to watch him</u>.*

infinitive A **verb form°** consisting of the verb's dictionary form plus *to: to swim, to write.* For more, see *verbals and verbal phrases.*

infinitive phrase See *verbals and verbal phrases.*

interjection A word standing by itself or inserted in a construction to exclaim: *<u>Hey</u>! What <u>the heck</u> did you do that for?*

interrogative pronoun A word that begins a question and serves as the **subject°** or **object°** of the sentence. The interrogative pronouns are *who, whom, whose, which,* and *what. <u>Who</u> received the flowers? <u>Whom</u> are they for?*

intransitive verb A **verb°** that does not require a following word (**direct object°**) to complete its meaning: *Mosquitoes <u>buzz</u>. The hospital <u>may close</u>.* For more, see *predicate.*

irregular verb See *verb forms.*

linking verb A verb that links, or connects, a **subject°** and a word that renames or describes the subject (a **subject complement°**): *They <u>are</u> golfers. You <u>seem</u> lucky.* The linking verbs are the forms of *be,* the verbs of the senses (*look, sound, smell, feel, taste*), and a few others (*appear, become, grow, prove, remain, seem, turn*). For more, see *predicate.*

main clause A word group that contains a **subject°** and a **predicate,°** does not begin with a subordinating word, and may stand alone as a sentence: *The boss was not overbearing.* For more, see *clause.*

°Defined in this section.

main verb   The part of a **verb phrase**° that carries the principal meaning: *had been walking, could happen, was chilled*. Contrast *helping verb*.

misplaced modifier   A modifier whose position makes unclear its relation to the rest of the sentence. Misplaced: *The children played with firecrackers that they bought illegally in the field*. Revised: *The children played in the field with firecrackers that they bought illegally*.

modal   See *helping verb*.

modifier   Any word or word group that limits or qualifies the meaning of another word or word group. Modifiers include **adjectives**° and **adverbs**° as well as words and word groups that act as adjectives and adverbs.

mood   The form of a **verb**° that shows how the speaker views the action. The **indicative mood**, the most common, is used to make statements or ask questions: *The play will be performed Saturday. Did you get tickets?* The **imperative mood** gives a command: *Please get good seats. Avoid the top balcony.* The **subjunctive mood** expresses a wish, a condition contrary to fact, a recommendation, or a request: *I wish George were coming with us. If he were here, he'd come. I suggested that he come. The host asked that he be here.*

noncount noun   A word that names a person, place, or thing and that is not considered countable in English (and so does not appear in plural form): *confidence, information, silver, work*. See pp. 78–79 for a longer list.

nonessential element   A word or word group that does not limit the word it refers to and that is not necessary to the meaning of the sentence. Nonessential elements are usually set off by commas: *Sleep, which we all need, occupies a third of our lives. His wife, Patricia, is a chemist.* Contrast *essential element*. See also pp. 90–91.

nonrestrictive element   See *nonessential element*.

noun   A word that names a person, place, thing, quality, or idea: *Maggie, Alberta, clarinet, satisfaction, socialism.* See also *collective noun, count noun, generic noun, noncount noun,* and *proper noun*.

noun clause   See *subordinate clause*.

number   The form of a word that indicates whether it is singular or plural. Singular: *I, he, this, child, runs, hides.* Plural: *we, they, these, children, run, hide.*

object   A **noun**° or **pronoun**° that receives the action of or is influenced by another word. A **direct object** receives the action of a **verb**° or **verbal**° and usually follows it: *We watched the stars.* An **indirect object** tells for or to whom something is done: *Reiner bought us drinks.* An **object of a preposition** usually follows a preposition:° *They went to Cape Breton.*

°Defined in this section.

Terms

objective case   The form of a **pronoun°** when it is the **object°** of a **verb°** (*call him*) or the object of a **preposition°** (*for us*). For more, see *case*.

object of preposition   See *object*.

parallelism   Similarity of form between two or more coordinated elements: *Rising prices and declining incomes left many people in bad debt and worse despair*. See also pp. 42–43.

parenthetical expression   A word or construction that interrupts a sentence and is not part of its main structure, called *parenthetical* because it could (or does) appear in parentheses: *Emily Carr (1871–1945) was a Canadian painter. Her work, incidentally, is in the museum.*

participial phrase   See *verbals and verbal phrases*.

participle   See *verbals and verbal phrases*.

particle   A **preposition°** or **adverb°** in a two-word verb: *catch on, look up*.

parts of speech   The classes of words based on their form, function, and meaning: nouns, pronouns, verbs, adjectives, adverbs, conjunctions, prepositions, and interjections. See separate entries for each part of speech.

passive voice   The **verb form°** used when the sentence **subject°** names the receiver of the verb's action: *The mixture was stirred*. For more, see *voice*.

past participle   The *-ed* form of most **verbs:°** *fished, hopped*. The past participle may be irregular: *begun, written*. For more, see *verbals and verbal phrases* and *verb forms*.

past perfect tense   The verb tense expressing an action that was completed before another past action: *No one had heard that before*. For more, see *tense*.

past tense   The verb tense expressing action that occurred in the past: *Everyone laughed*. For more, see *tense*.

past-tense form   The verb form used to indicate action that occurred in the past, usually created by adding *-d* or *-ed* to the verb's dictionary form (*smiled*) but created differently for most irregular verbs (*began, threw*). For more, see *verb forms*.

perfect tenses   The verb tenses indicating action completed before another specific time or action: *have walked, had walked, will have walked*. For more, see *tense*.

person   The form of a **verb°** or **pronoun°** that indicates whether the subject is speaking, spoken to, or spoken about. In the **first person** the subject is speaking: *I am, we are*. In the **second person** the subject is spoken to: *you are*. In the **third person** the subject is spoken about: *he/she/it is, they are*.

personal pronoun   *I, you, he, she, it, we,* or *they:* a word that substitutes for a specific **noun°** or other pronoun. For more, see *case*.

°Defined in this section.

phrase A group of related words that lacks a **subject°** or a **predicate°** or both: *She ran into the field. She tried to jump the fence.* See also *absolute phrase, prepositional phrase, verbals and verbal phrases.*

plain form The dictionary form of a verb: *buy, make, run, swivel.* For more, see *verb forms.*

plural More than one. See *number.*

positive form See *comparison.*

possessive case The form of a **noun°** or **pronoun°** that indicates its ownership of something else: *men's attire, your briefcase.* For more, see *case.*

possessive pronoun A word that replaces a **noun°** or other **pronoun°** and shows ownership: *The cat chased its tail.* The possessive pronouns are *my, our, your, his, her, its, their, whose.*

predicate The part of a sentence that makes an assertion about the **subject.°** The predicate may consist of an **intransitive verb°** (*The earth trembled*), a **transitive verb°** plus **direct object°** (*The earthquake shook buildings*), a **linking verb°** plus **subject complement°** (*The result was chaos*), a transitive verb plus **indirect object°** and direct object (*The government sent the city aid*), or a transitive verb plus direct object and object complement (*The citizens considered the earthquake a disaster*).

preposition A word that forms a **noun°** or **pronoun°** (plus any modifiers) into a **prepositional phrase**: *about love, down the steep stairs.* The common prepositions: *about, above, according to, across, after, against, along, along with, among, around, as, at, because of, before, behind, below, beneath, beside, between, beyond, by, concerning, despite, down, during, except, except for, excepting, for, from, in, in addition to, inside, in spite of, instead of, into, like, near, next to, of, off, on, onto, out, out of, outside, over, past, regarding, since, through, throughout, till, to, toward, under, underneath, unlike, until, up, upon, with, within, without.*

prepositional phrase A word group consisting of a **preposition°** and its **object.°** Prepositional phrases usually serve as **adjectives°** (*We saw a movie about sorrow*) or as **adverbs°** (*We went back for the second show*).

present participle The *-ing* form of a **verb**:° *swimming, flying.* For more, see *verbals and verbal phrases.*

present perfect tense The verb tense expressing action that began in the past and is linked to the present: *Dogs have buried bones here before.* For more, see *tense.*

present tense The verb tense expressing action that is occurring now, occurs habitually, or is generally true: *Dogs bury bones here often.* For more, see *tense.*

principal parts   The three forms of a verb from which its various tenses are created: the **plain form** (*stop, go*), the **past-tense form** (*stopped, went*), and the **past participle** (*stopped, gone*). For more, see *tense* and *verb forms*.

progressive tenses   The verb tenses that indicate continuing (progressive) action and use the *-ing* form of the verb: *A dog was barking here this morning.* For more, see *tense*.

pronoun   A word used in place of a **noun**,° such as *I, he, everyone, who,* and *herself.* See also *indefinite pronoun, interrogative pronoun, personal pronoun, possessive pronoun, relative pronoun*.

proper adjective   A word formed from a **proper noun**° and used to modify a **noun**° or **pronoun**:° *Manitoba winter.*

proper noun   A word naming a specific person, place, or thing and beginning with a capital letter: *Peter Mansbridge, Mount Robson, Ottawa, Canada Post.*

regular verb   See *verb forms*.

relative pronoun   A word that relates a group of words to a **noun**° or another **pronoun**.° The relative pronouns are *who, whom, whoever, whomever, which,* and *that. Ask the woman who knows all. This may be the question that stumps her.* For more, see *case*.

restrictive element   See *essential element*.

run-on sentence   See *fused sentence*.

-s form   See *verb forms*.

second person   See *person*.

sentence   A complete unit of thought, consisting of at least a **subject**° and a **predicate**° that are not introduced by a subordinating word. A **simple sentence** contains one main **clause**:° *I'm leaving.* A **compound sentence** contains at least two main clauses: *I'd like to stay, but I'm leaving.* A **complex sentence** contains one main clause and at least one **subordinate clause**:° *If you let me go now, you'll be sorry.* A **compound-complex sentence** contains at least two main clauses and at least one subordinate clause: *I'm leaving because you want me to, but I'd rather stay.*

sentence fragment   An error in which an incomplete sentence is set off as a complete sentence. Fragment: *She was not in shape for the race. Which she had hoped to win.* Revised: *She was not in shape for the race, which she had hoped to win.* See pp. 82–84.

series   Three or more items with the same function: *We gorged on ham, eggs, and potatoes.*

simple sentence   See *sentence*.

simple tenses   See *tense*.

singular   One. See *number*.

°Defined in this section.

split infinitive The usually awkward interruption of an **infinitive**° and its marker *to* by a modifier: *Management decided to not introduce the new product.* See p. 80.

squinting modifier A modifier that could modify the words on either side of it: *The plan we considered seriously worries me.*

subject In grammar, the part of a sentence that names something and about which an assertion is made in the **predicate**:° *The quick, brown fox jumped lazily* (simple subject); *The quick, brown fox jumped lazily* (complete subject).

subject complement A word that renames or describes the **subject**° of a sentence, after a **linking verb.**° *The stranger was a man* (**noun**°). *He seemed gigantic* (**adjective**°).

subjective case The form of a **pronoun**° when it is the **subject**° of a sentence (*I called*) or a **subject complement**° (*It was I*). For more, see *case.*

subjunctive See *mood.*

subordinate clause A word group that consists of a **subject**° and a **predicate,**° begins with a subordinating word such as *because* or *who,* and is not a question: *They voted for whoever cared the least because they mistrusted politicians.* Subordinate clauses may serve as **adjectives**° (*The car that hit Fred was blue*), as **adverbs**° (*The car hit Fred when it ran a red light*), or as **nouns**° (*Whoever was driving should be arrested*). Subordinate clauses are *not* complete sentences.

subordinating conjunction A word that turns a complete sentence into a word group (a **subordinate clause**°) that can serve as an **adverb**° or a **noun.**° *Everyone was relieved when the meeting ended.* Some common subordinating conjunctions: *after, although, as, as if, as long as, as though, because, before, even if, even though, if, if only, in order that, now that, once, rather than, since, so that, than, that, though, till, unless, until, when, whenever, where, whereas, wherever, while.*

subordination Deemphasizing one element in a sentence by making it dependent on, rather than equal to, another element. Through subordination, *I left six messages; the doctor failed to call* becomes *Although I left six messages, the doctor failed to call* or *After six messages, the doctor failed to call.*

superlative See *comparison.*

tense The verb form that expresses time, usually indicated by endings and by helping verbs. See also *verb forms.*

Present Action that is occurring now, occurs habitually, or is generally true

Simple present Plain form or *-s* form	Present progressive *Am, is,* or *are* plus *-ing form*
I *walk.*	I *am walking.*
You/we/they walk.	You/we/they *are walking.*
He/she/it *walks.*	He/she/it *is walking.*

°Defined in this section.

Past   Action that occurred before now

Simple past Past-tense form	**Past progressive** *Was* or *were* plus *-ing form*
I/he/she/it *walked*.	I/he/she/it *was walking*.
You/we/they *walked*.	You/we/they *were walking*.

Future   Action that will occur in the future

Simple future *Will* plus plain form	**Future progressive** *Will be* plus *-ing* form
I/you/he/she/it/we/they *will walk*.	I/you/he/she/it/we/they *will be walking*.

Present perfect   Action that began in the past and is linked to the present

Present perfect *Have* or *has* plus past participle	**Present perfect progressive** *Have been* or *has been* plus *-ing* form
I/you/we/they *have walked*.	I/you/we/they *have been walking*.
He/she/it *has walked*.	He/she/it *has been walking*.

Past perfect   Action that was completed before another past action

Past perfect *Had* plus past participle	**Past perfect progressive** *Had been* plus *-ing* form
I/you/he/she/it/we/they *had walked*.	I/you/he/she/it/we/they *had been walking*.

Future perfect   Action that will be completed before another future action

Future perfect *Will have* plus past participle	**Future perfect progressive** *Will have been* plus *-ing* form
I/you/he/she/it/we/they *will have walked*.	I/you/he/she/it/we/they *will have been walking*.

third person   See *person*.

transitional expression   A word or phrase that links sentences and shows the relations between them. Transitional expressions can signal various relationships (examples in parentheses): addition or sequence (*also, besides, finally, first, furthermore, in addition, last*); comparison (*also, similarly*); contrast (*even so, however, in contrast, still*); examples (*for example, for instance, that is*); intensification (*indeed, in fact, of course*); place (*below, elsewhere, here, nearby, to the east*); time (*afterward, at last, earlier, immediately, meanwhile, simultaneously*); repetition or summary (*in brief, in other words, in short, in summary, that is*); and cause and effect (*as a result, consequently, hence, therefore, thus*).

transitive verb   A **verb**° that requires a following word (a **direct object**°) to complete its meaning: *We raised the roof.* For more, see *predicate.*

verb   A word that expresses an action (*bring, change*), an occurrence (*happen, become*), or a state of being (*be, seem*). A verb is the essential word in a **predicate,**° the part of a sentence that makes an assertion about the **subject.**° With endings and **helping verbs,**° verbs can indicate **tense,**° **mood,**° **voice,**° **number,**° and **person.**° For more, see separate entries for each of these aspects as well as *verb forms.*

verbals and verbal phrases   Verbals are verb forms used as **adjectives,**° **adverbs,**° or **nouns.**° They form verbal phrases with **objects**° and **modifiers.**° A **present participle** adds *-ing* to the dictionary form of a verb (*living*). A **past participle** usually adds *-d* or *-ed* to the dictionary form (*lived*), although irregular verbs work differently (*begun, swept*). A participle or **participial phrase** usually serves as an adjective: <u>*Strolling*</u> *shoppers fill the malls.* A **gerund** is the *-ing* form of a verb used as a noun. Gerunds and **gerund phrases** can do whatever nouns can do: <u>*Shopping*</u> *satisfies needs.* An **infinitive** is the verb's dictionary form plus *to: to live.* Infinitives and **infinitive phrases** may serve as nouns (<u>*To design a mall*</u> *is a challenge*), as adverbs (*Malls are designed* <u>*to make shoppers feel safe*</u>), or as adjectives (*The mall supports the impulse* <u>*to shop*</u>).

 A verbal *cannot* serve as the only verb in a sentence. For that, it requires a **helping verb:**° *Shoppers* <u>*were strolling*</u>.

verb forms   Verbs have five distinctive forms. The **plain form** is the dictionary form: *A few artists* <u>*live*</u> *in town today.* The **-s form** adds *-s* or *-es* to the plain form: *The artist* <u>*lives*</u> *in town today.* The **past-tense form** usually adds *-d* or *-ed* to the plain form: *Many artists* <u>*lived*</u> *in town before this year.* Some verbs' past-tense forms are irregular, such as *began, fell, swam, threw, wrote.* The **past participle** is usually the same as the past-tense form, although, again, some verbs' past participles are irregular (*begun, fallen, swum, thrown, written*). The **present participle** adds *-ing* to the plain form: *A few artists are* <u>*living*</u> *in town today.*

 Regular verbs are those that add *-d* or *-ed* to the plain form for the past-tense form and past participle. **Irregular verbs** create these forms in irregular ways (see above).

verb phrase   A **verb**° of more than one word that serves as the **predicate**° of a sentence: *The movie* <u>*has started*</u>.

voice   The form of a **verb**° that tells whether the sentence **subject**° performs the action or is acted upon. In the **active voice** the subject acts: *The city* <u>*controls*</u> *rents.* In the **passive voice** the subject is acted upon: *Rents* <u>*are controlled*</u> *by the city.* See also pp. 63–64.

Credits

Page 18 Craig Holbrook (student), © Craig Holbrook.

Page 19 Laliberte, Richard W. "The Benefits of Laughter." *Shape*, Sept. 2003: 78–79. Published by American Media, Inc.

Page 19 Laliberte, Richard W. "The Benefits of Laughter." *Shape*, Sept. 2003: 78–79. Published by American Media, Inc.

Page 28 Statistics Canada. "Census Families in Private Households by Family Structure and Presence of Children, by Census Metropolitan Area (2011 Census) (St. John's, Halifax, Moncton, Saint John)." *2011 Census of Population and Statistics Canada*, Catalogue no. 98-312-XCB. 13 Feb. 2013, www.statcan.gc.ca /tables-tableaux/sum-som/l01/cst01/famil121a-eng.htm.

Page 29 Statistics Canada. "Estimates of Population, by Marital Status or Legal Marital Status, Age and Sex for July 1, Canada, Provinces and Territories, Annual (Persons)." CANSIM table 051-0042. 13 Nov. 2014, www5.statcan.gc.ca/cansim/a26?lang =eng&id=510042.

Page 30 Statistics Canada. "Use of Child Care Highest among Parents of Children between the Ages of 2 and 4." *Child Care in Canada*, Catalogue no. 89-652-X, Chart 1. 30 Oct. 2014, www.statcan.gc.ca/pub/89-652-x/89-652-x2014005-eng.htm.

Page 30 Statistics Canada. "Gasoline Prices Continue to Fall in December." *Consumer Price Index, December 2014*, CANSIM table 326-0020, Chart 2. 23 Jan. 2015, www.statcan.gc.ca/daily -quotidien/150123/cg-a002-eng.htm.

Page 93 McLuhan, Michael. From *Understanding Media: The Extensions of Man*, published by McGraw Hill.

Page 93 Excerpt from "Truth and Reconciliation: nearly 4 years of hearings wrap." Published by The Canadian Press, © 2014.

Page 99 Horney, Karen. *Our Inner Conflicts: A Constructive Theory of Neurosis*. W. W. Norton & Company, Inc., 1945.

Page 99 Parliament of Canada. Quote by Tommy Douglas. Debate in House of Commons, Ottawa, Ontario, 3 April 1939. Copyright © 1939 by Parliament of Canada. Used by permission of Parliament of Canada.

Page 100 Greene, Graham. *The Man Within*. Random House, Inc., 1929.

Page 104 Wilson, Edward O. From "Is Humanity Suicidal?" *In Search of Nature*, Island Press, 1996.

Page 135 Screenshot from "EBSCOhost Academic Search." Copyright © 2012 by EBSCO host. Used by Permission of EBSCO Host.

Page 143 Screenshot From Vegetarian Times by Alan Pell Crawford. Copyright © 2006 by Cruz Bay Publishing, Inc. Used by permission of Cruz Bay Publishing, Inc.

Page 143 Jackson, Tim. "Live Better by Consuming Less?" *Journal of Industrial Ecology*, 9.1-2 (2005): 19–36. Copyright © by John Wiley & Sons, Inc. Used by the permission of John Wiley & Sons, Inc via Copyright Clearance Center, Inc.

Page 147 "Canadian Environmental Sustainability Indicators (CESI): National Greenhouse Gas Emissions," www.ec.gc .ca/indicateurs-indicators/default.asp?lang=en&n=FBF8455E-1, Environment Canada, 2014. Copyright © Her Majesty The Queen in Right of Canada, Environment Canada, 2015. Reproduced with the permission of the Minister of Public Works and Government Services Canada.

Page 150 Dancocks, Daniel D. *Welcome to Flanders Fields: The First Canadian Battle of the Great War*. McClelland & Stewart, 1988, p. 40.

Page 161 Mitford, Jessica. *Kind and Usual Punishment: The Prison Business*. Knopf, 1973.

Page 166 Excerpt from *Three Day Road* by Joseph Boyden. Published by Viking Penguin.

Page 167 Copp, Tery, and Bill McAndrew. Excerpt from *Battle Exhaustion: Soldiers and Psychiatrists in the Canadian Army, 1939–1945*. Published by McGill-Queen's University Press.

Page 167 Cameron, Wilcox, Reber, and Shin. Excerpt From *Public Relations Today: Managing Competition and Conflict*. Allyn and Bacon. Published by Pearson Allyn and Bacon/Merrill Education, © 2007.

Page 168 Basler, Roy P. Quote by Abraham Lincoln from *Collected works of Abraham Lincoln*, Volume 5. Copyright © 1953 by Abraham Lincoln Association. Used by permission of Abraham Lincoln Association.

Page 169 Vance, Jonathan F. Excerpt from *Death So Noble: Memory, Meaning, and the First World War*. Published by University of British Columbia Press.

Page 177 From *Library Quarterly*, Vol. 78, No. 2, April 2008. Copyright © 2008. Reprinted by permission of University of Chicago Press.

Page 180 Shteir, Rachel. From *The Steal: A Cultural History of Shoplifting* by Rachel Shteir, copyright © 2011 by Rachel Shteir. Used by permission of The Penguin Press, a division of Penguin Group (USA) Inc. and the author.

Page 196 University of North Carolina Press. Abstract of "Missing Fathers: Twelfth Night and the Reformation of Mourning" by Suzanne Penuel. From *Studies in Philology*, Volume 107. Copyright © 2010 by the University of North Carolina Press. Used by permission of the publisher. www.uncpress.unc.edu. Copyright © by EBSCO Host. Used by permission of EBSCO Host.

Page 203 Purdy, Al. "Subject/Object," *Beyond Remembering: The Collected Poems of Al Purdy*, edited by Sam Solecki. Harbour Publishing, 2000, www.harbourpublishing.com. Reprinted by permission.

Page 203 Purdy, Al. "Separation." *Beyond Remembering: The Collected Poems of Al Purdy*, edited by Sam Solecki. Harbour Publishing, 2000, www.harbourpublishing.com. Reprinted by permission.

Page 204 Liebow, Elliot. *Tally's Corner: A Study of Negro Streetcorner Men*. Rowman & Littlefield Publishers, © 2003.

Page 213 The Centre for Literacy of Quebec. *HIPPY Montréal: Evaluation of Outcomes 2008–2009*. The Centre for Literacy of Quebec, 2009.

Page 234 Welch, Stuart Cary. Excerpt from *India: Art and Culture, 1300–1900*. Published by Metropolitan Museum of Art.

Page 235 Quote from *Young India 1919–1922* by Mahatma Gandhi. Published by B.W. Heubsch Inc.

Index

Index

Index

F

Index

Index

Index

S

Index

ESL Guide

Throughout this handbook the symbol ESL signals topics for students whose first language is not standard Canadian English. These topics can be tricky because they arise from rules in standard English that are quite different in other languages. Many of the topics involve significant cultural assumptions as well.

ESL

Whatever your language background, as a college or university student you are learning the culture of higher education and the language that is used and shaped by that culture. The process is challenging, even for native speakers of standard English. It requires not just writing clearly and correctly but also mastering conventions of developing, presenting, and supporting ideas. The challenge is greater if, in addition, you are trying to learn standard English and are accustomed to other conventions. Several habits can help you succeed:

- **Read**. Besides course assignments, read newspapers, magazines, and books in English. The more you read, the more fluently and accurately you'll write.
- **Write**. Keep a journal in which you practise writing in English every day.
- **Talk and listen**. Take advantage of opportunities to hear and use English.
- **Ask questions**. Your instructors, tutors in the writing centre, and fellow students can clarify assignments and help you identify and solve writing problems.
- **Don't try for perfection**. No one writes perfectly, and the effort to do so can prevent you from expressing yourself fluently. View mistakes not as failures but as opportunities to learn.
- **Revise first; then edit**. Focus on each essay's ideas, support, and organization before attending to grammar and vocabulary. See the checklist for revising academic writing on page 2.
- **Set editing priorities**. Check first for errors that interfere with clarity, such as problems with word order or subject-verb agreement. The following index can help you identify the topics you need to work on and can lead you to appropriate text discussions.

ESL

Detailed Contents